PSYCHODYNAMIC PSYCHOTHERAPY

PSYCHODYNAMIC PSYCHOTHERAPY

Learning to Listen from Multiple Perspectives

By

Jon Frederickson, M.S.W.

Chair, Advanced Psychotherapy Training Program
Washington School of Psychiatry

USA	Publishing Office:	BRUNNER/MAZEL 325 Chestnut Street Philadelphia, PA 19106 Tel: (215) 625-8900 Fax: (215) 625-2940
	Distribution Center:	BRUNNER/MAZEL 47 Runway Road, Suite G Levittown, PA 19057-4700 Tel: (215) 269-0400 Fax: (215) 269-0363
UK		BRUNNER/MAZEL 1 Gunpowder Square London EC4A 3DE Tel: 171 583 0490 Fax: 171 583 0581

PSYCHODYNAMIC PSYCHOTHERAPY: Learning to Listen from Multiple Perspectives

2 3 4 5 6 7 8 9 0

Printed by Braun-Brumfield, Ann Arbor, MI, 1998.

A CIP catalog record for this book is available from the British Library.
∞ The paper in this publication meets the requirements of the ANSI Standard Z39.48-1984 (Permanence of Paper)

Library of Congress Cataloging-in-Publication Data

Frederickson, Jon.
    Psychodynamic psychotherapy : learning to listen from multiple perspectives / Jon Frederickson.
        p. cm.
    Includes bibliographical references and index.

    1. Psychodynamic psychotherapy—Examinations, questions, etc.
I. Title.
RC489.P72 F74   1999
616.89'14'076—dc21   98-47697
                                                                      CIP

ISBN 0-87630-961-9 (CB : alk. paper)
ISBN 0-87630-962-7 (PB : alk. paper)

CONTENTS

ACKNOWLEDGMENTS

Any book of this sort synthesizes what one has learned from teachers, supervisors, colleagues, students, and, most importantly, one's patients. Pascal is reputed to have said "of those authors who always refer to their works as 'my book', 'my commentary', 'my history', etc., that they sound like solid citizens with a place of their own, always talking about 'my house'." They would do better, this excellent man added, to say "'Our book', 'our commentary', 'our history', etc., considering that there is usually more of other people's property in it than their own" (Pascal 1966:355).

Yet any acknowledgment would be inadequate if I did not highlight the role of the Washington School of Psychiatry in my training—a school dedicated to keeping the questions open. During my training, I was supervised by a former behaviorist, a Sullivanian, a Fairbairnian, and someone who was trained both by Anna Freud and Kleinians! Although my supervisors worked most of the time from a given theoretical perspective, each of them felt free to draw from anything that would help the patient. I entered training looking for answers, but they questioned every answer I had, insisting instead that I learn to think. One day a supervisor asked me what would be five different ways I could respond to a patient at a given moment! And there I had been wondering what might be the one, right, correct response! They were trying to teach me flexibility so I could use any approach rather than be the hostage of one approach, trapped without an alternative. I feel especially grateful to them for their help, their patience, and their insistence on flexibility of approach. I would like to thank Sarah Pillsbury, Michael McDermott, Mike Stadter, Harold Eist, Sue Roth, Louise DeLeeuw, Elizabeth Harper, Irv Scheider, Gerry Perman, Bernardo Hirschman, Elizabeth Buchanek, Damon Silver, Rosemary Segalla, Monroe Pray, Alberto Pieczanski, and Jack Love for their contributions to this book.

In addition, I would like to single out Nicole Lediard, Nancy Griscom, Maggie Silberstein, Terry DiNuzzo, Barton Evans, and Olga Meerson for their close reading of the manuscript and extremely helpful comments. I would also like to thank the students who read previous drafts, raised useful questions, and, most generously, shared case material from early stages of their work. Since some of their early sessions were used here, their names must remain anonymous, so to them I owe a special debt of gratitude.

PREFACE

"Crafty men condemn Studies, Simple men admire them, and wise
men use them: for they teach not their own use, but that there is
a Wisdom without them, and above them won by Observation."
Francis Bacon, "Of Studies," *Essays* (1625)

This book is designed to help you develop basic skills of psychodynamic
therapy: reflecting the patient's feelings, identifying conflict, hearing unconscious communication, and interpreting defenses. Without a solid understanding of basic principles, we cannot understand more complex theories
and approaches. Therapists often lack this understanding because our classes
emphasized the learning of theories rather than their application. Classes
often appear irrelevant because in practical terms they are. What good
does it do to be able to define transference if we can't hear or interpret
it? Or to be able to recite a list of defenses but be unable to identify them
in the session and interpret them? Knowing a theory without being able to
use it is like knowing how to identify a car but being unable to drive it. No
wonder much of psychodynamic theory as taught today *appears* to be
useless!

This book provides exercises that—if applied in the right way—will show
you how to translate four different theories into practice. Its theoretical
content has been set forth and explained countless times before. Unfortunately, however, most books present theory in a form accessible only to a
fairly advanced therapist already familiar with the theory and technique.
Such a therapist will find in them a remarkably good survey of the basic
material, but beginners (or experienced therapists new to psychodynamic
theory) are unable to digest the material, know what it looks like in practice, or select what is useful. Moreover, the examples given in such books
(when any are given) are insufficient.

There is a severe lack of specialized works, full of exercises, that would
develop the therapist's skills. These studies are designed to fill that lack.
Actual therapy sessions are analyzed with possible interpretations to illustrate the relationship of theory to practice.

Some may object that other listening approaches were not included. This is unavoidable in a single volume. Psychodynamic theory serves as an umbrella term covering many different listening strategies. I have chosen four listening approaches because the majority of psychodynamic approaches, whether self psychology, object relations, interpersonal, or relational, require the specific listening skills studied here. Learning these skills will provide you with the background necessary to acquire a deeper understanding of other approaches.

Others may object that this book places too great an emphasis upon technique, ignoring the artistic and intuitive aspects of psychotherapy. Yet this objection would be regarded as invalid to those trained in the fine arts, whether painting, sculpture, or music. Professional musicians, for instance, practice scales and arpeggios every day. They recognize that artistry is possible only when they have technical command of their instrument. They would agree that technique without intuition is not great art; but they would also insist that intuition without technical mastery is always arbitrary, incapable of accurately interpreting the composer's intentions. To give voice to the composer's intent, the musician must not only be able to hear his intent but convey it through his technical mastery. Every musician's artistry begins with a mastery of technique—it just doesn't end there. Think of this book as a set of musical etudes designed to enhance your artistry when interpreting the human dramas encountered in therapy. View it as merely a signpost, something that helps you get to your destination but is not the destination itself.

Others might object that the interpretations offered are too frequent, creating the image of a strange inhuman therapy. Of course they do. These examples are not provided with the purpose of suggesting that therapists should interpret this frequently or artificially. The examples are designed to provide the reader with as many opportunities as possible to formulate interpretations from within particular approaches. In other words, the aim of this book is *activity*. Readers can learn to hear transference, conflict, and defenses by actively listening, studying, and practicing. These exercises are designed to do just that. Scales and arpeggios are also artificial in a sense, yet their practice provides the mastery necessary to make beautiful music. Simone Weil (1952) once said, "Precepts are not given for the sake of being practiced, but practice is prescribed in order that precepts may be understood. They are scales. One does not play Bach without having done scales. But neither does one play a scale merely for the sake of the scale."

The reader should also keep in mind that no theory or approach should be believed. Theories are not beliefs but tools. This book will help you master four of the most common listening tools used today. Do not believe their utility until you can try them out and use them. Many therapists use these approaches as they are presented here, and others have adapted them in other ways. Only by learning these approaches will you be able to see where and how they are useful and where and how they are not. Even a carpenter does not always use sandpaper; but when he needs it, nothing else will do.

In addition, as you do the studies, notice how each psychodynamic listening approach tries to make sense "out of the flux of events and . . . give order and coherence. It is a latticework of evidence in which each strand supports the others and in which each piece of evidence *becomes* evidence only in the context of the other pieces. . . . To a very great degree, pieces of evidence gain meaning and evidential gravity *from each other*" (Wachtel 1987:115).

This does not mean that "anything goes" within a psychodynamic approach (Freud 1910a). Rather, each psychodynamic listening approach has rules of evidence, a discipline that is meant to be properly used. There are safeguards within each approach to show us when our interpretations are wrong. Each interpretation is a hypothesis that we must be prepared to discard if it is not confirmed. At the same time, there are guidelines for making interpretations that are based on the evidence of the hour and, hence, are more likely to be correct and empathic.

Most of these rules and guidelines have until now been passed down through oral tradition with little explicit written material on them. This lack has led some to write off psychodynamic approaches as simply arbitrary guesswork and others to believe in them without grasping their systematic approach to disciplined listening and responding. Each psychodynamic listening approach has rules for making inferences from the patient's associations, for interpreting, and for validating interpretations. I have included in the theoretical sections some brief guidelines regarding these rules.

A brief theoretical aside: since this book focuses on developing listening skills, it only briefly summarizes the theory of these approaches. For instance, transference analysis takes radically different forms today depending upon the theoretical perspective used. Yet learning to listen symbolically is a necessary precondition to understanding those perspectives. As a result, I focus on that listening skill and leave the theoretical issues for the reader to study elsewhere. Likewise, there are several models of defense analysis current today. Yet to understand the issues involved in any approach, one must be able to hear defenses in the process. Paul Gray's (1995) approach was chosen as the method best suited to train therapists to do that. If you succumb to the temptation to skip ahead and read the author's translation of examples and interpretations, you will sabotage your learning. These exercises are designed to exercise your mind, to develop your therapeutic intuition, acuteness, and creative ability to combine different elements into an interpretation. But this mastery can come only through doing the exercises yourself. What will you gain from a fruit if you don't eat it, but only hear my report of what it tasted like?

This book grew out of the demands of my students and supervisees and was written for their benefit. All the examples have been tested already by students and only those that were found useful were included. All identifying material has been cut out to ensure confidentiality. No histories have been provided to ensure that you focus your attention exclusively on what the patient says. By doing the exercises, you will learn to listen psychodynamically.

Introduction: What Do We Do When We Listen?

To be sure, not every ear does all this in the same way, nor does any individual ear do it in the same way at all times: still, the human ear itself does it in one way or another. Those who distrust the testimony of a highly developed and refined ear because they cannot keep up with it beyond a certain point by the same token demonstrate the reality of what prevents them from going beyond this point: the reality of a resistance which can be accounted for only by the fact that musical works differ in their structural complexity, and by a particular ear's ability or inability to keep pace with increasing complexity (Zuckerkandl 1973:195).

In my second week of graduate school, without any previous experience, I was supposed to be a therapist for schizophrenic patients just released from the hospital! Terrified, my classmates and I pulled our teacher aside and asked for advice. "Don't worry," she said, "whatever social skills you've acquired so far will pull you through." Unfortunately, that was not true. Social skills never prepared me for the patient who hallucinated the devil tempting him in my office.

Psychotherapy is a strange field. The musician practices in the privacy of a room at home, making all her mistakes outside the hearing of others. Years of lessons, rehearsals, and concerts take place before anyone actually pays to hear her. And all this time, the difficulty of the pieces she performs increases gradually according to her skills. In contrast, psychotherapy is a trial by fire. Without any experience, the therapist meets with a patient, all mistakes are made within hearing, and the patient is often paying. Not only that, but the therapist often sees the most difficult patients as a beginner. What student orchestra of beginners would ever be asked to perform Beethoven's Ninth Symphony for a paying audience?

☐ When We Listen, We Focus Our Attention

Obviously, we need more than social skills—but what skills do we need? Are psychotherapists really able to listen differently? Listening means different things to different therapists. A cognitive therapist listens for distorted cognitions in the patient's associations, while a Jungian therapist listens for archetypal patterns in the patient's associations and dreams. A self psychologist listens for fluctuations in the patient's self state that arise from the interaction between the patient and the therapist.

So what do we mean when we say we listen? Everyone claims to listen, but if five people listen to the same person, they would often come away with five different impressions. Why? Because we listen *for* different things. *What we hear when we listen depends on where we focus our attention.* For instance, imagine you are listening to your favorite singer at an orchestra concert. You might let the sounds wash over you and remember a general impression without many details. If you are poetically-minded, you might listen primarily to the words. If you are a singer, you might listen to her tone quality and phrasing. If you are a composer, you might focus on the relationship between the harmony and the emotional meanings of the words. If you are an arranger, you might listen for the sonorities created by the way the instruments are combined. Each of these qualities comprises parts of the whole: lyrics, singing, harmony, and orchestration. As a listener, you heard the part of the musical experience on which you focused your attention.

One might counter that these listeners were biased since they were focusing on only one thing instead of the whole. That's true because all listening is biased. Any listening experience, be it a concert or therapy session, is too complex to be grasped in all its detail at once. Out of an overwhelming amount of auditory information, we have to pick and choose. The question becomes whether we are aware of our bias and can shift from one focus to another.

The same is true of vision. What we see depends on where we look. To see a landscape we have to look around, taking several views in order to get a sense of the whole. In fact, our awe while gazing at a landscape is partly derived from knowing that we cannot grasp this view in a single glance. Simply staring in one direction won't be enough.

If we are curious about a bird we hear in the distance, we might exclude the entire landscape except for the minute area with the bird which we can see through a pair of binoculars. The use of the binoculars is a bias and a useful one as long as we are aware of the bias and can shift to other means of seeing when necessary. For example, we might use the extreme bias of a microscope to examine bacteria in the soil of that landscape but put on our glasses so we don't trip over a log.

It is impossible to see or hear everything at once. Each bias, *precisely because it excludes some things from our attention,* allows us to focus more easily on things that might otherwise escape our notice, like the bird and the bacteria. This seems obvious with vision, since we use glasses, binoculars, telescopes, x-rays, MRIs, and other visual aids to expand the range of what we can see. But what about listening?

Listening seems to occur naturally without any bias. People are usually unaware of their listening biases because *they do not take a physical form* as visual biases do. There is no physical corollary to the use of the microscope when we want to listen to something in detail. Hence, our listening biases are invisible although potentially perceptible.

How can people learn to observe their listening biases? To understand this question, it would be helpful to turn to the music profession, an occupation where listening skills must be highly trained. Music students take courses that train them to listen. In these courses, actually labeled "ear training," students learn to identify chords and intervals. Out of what initially sounds like a complex sound, students learn to pick out the notes that are being played. Having learned to distinguish one chord from another, students then learn to hear and write down a series of chords that are played. Finally, they learn to write down several lines of music being played simultaneously. It is one thing to hear notes, but quite another to be able to listen, identify them, and write them down. Musicians must train their attention to focus on and identify patterns in sound.

Applying this analogy to the field of psychotherapy shows that each theory implies a kind of listening. Each type of listening focuses one's attention on a pattern that can be interpreted. For instance, a rational-emotive therapist listens for irrational thoughts that are identified and challenged. A cognitive therapist listens for specific kinds of irrational thoughts and counters them with more rational alternatives. A Rogerian therapist listens for the patient's stated thoughts and feelings and reflects them back. Although all therapists listen, what each of them listens for depends upon their particular theory. Since therapists cannot hear everything, they have to decide what to listen for based on what they think would be the most helpful. Each theory posits a different focus as being most helpful—e.g., irrational thoughts, stated feelings, etc.

In addition to the foci proposed by different theories, we recognize another source of biases in our listening style. Each of us, due to personality and preference, has a customary or habitual listening style. We have our own personal, often unstated theories about why people are the way they are. And these personal theories about people dictate what we listen for. You may have noticed therapists who seem to say the same things about all their patients. This may not mean that their patients really are all the same. It may mean that that the therapists' listening focus allows them to see only one kind of thing over and over again. It's like wearing rose colored glasses or aggression colored glasses or separation colored glasses.

Another problem arises when we listen in the way we wish people would listen to us. This is fine, as long as the patient is you. Unfortunately, the patient isn't. What never ceases to amaze us as we gain experience is that patients require very different kinds of listening and responsiveness. What may be responsive for you may be overstimulating for one patient and depriving for another. We wish that we could find a "one size fits all" kind of listening that would be healing for all patients, but instead find that we need to become flexible in the way we listen and respond.

Hopefully, we learn in supervision what our innate listening style is, what it allows us to hear, and what it prevents us from hearing. Then we become free to shift our listening attention so we can hear other parts of the auditory "landscape." Remember that with two eyes, the slight difference in perspective gives us depth perception. The same is true in listening. Only by being able to listen in at least two different ways can we develop depth perception. The more ways we learn to be responsive, the more patients we will be able to help.

☐ What If I Don't Want To Change the Way I Listen?

Learning to be flexible in our listening focus can be frightening. We may equate who we are with how we listen. Changing listening styles can feel like an assault on our identity. This is partly because our listening biases are invisible. Let's imagine the same problem in visual terms. If you were looking at a landscape and someone said that you would need to use binoculars to see a bird, you would not say, "That's not how I look at things." If you were invited to look in all directions around you to get a feel for the landscape, you would not say, "Looking straight ahead is how I am." You would distinguish between who you are and where you focus your attention. Let's suppose you habitually focus your attention in only one direction. That habit is not you. A driver who goes only north or east is not the direction in which he is headed. There is a difference between the driver and the direction in which he drives his car.

"If I learn a new listening focus, I feel I have to give up the natural style of listening that feels right to me." If you learn a new listening style you can *add* it to your natural style of listening. Don't give up your habitual style of listening. Add listening styles to your repertoire. Then you can choose which approach would be most useful, rather than be the prisoner of the only approach you know. It is similar to having the option of using binoculars, telescopes, and MRIs to augment your eyesight. You still use your eyes, but they are enhanced by the tools you allow yourself to use.

In this sense, psychodynamic theories are aural aids. They are tools that direct our attention to certain patterns that we ordinarily wouldn't notice. Just think of when you first read about cognitive therapy and suddenly became so much more aware of irrational thought patterns and understood better than ever why they were irrational.

☐ Psychodynamic Listening

"Ok. I grant you that we use theories and that we should be aware of the assumptions that operate when we listen. But you still haven't told us what listening skills are. Are listening skills in psychodynamic psychotherapy so different from social skills? Maybe your teacher was right: do psychodynamic therapists really listen in ways that are different from the man on the street?"

In everyday speech, we don't think about how we will listen or even choose a particular mode of listening. We simply listen in the manner that seems natural to us. As a rule, we listen only to the content of what a friend says and our responses are based on what we are both aware of. Psychodynamic listening is different. When we listen psychodynamically, we are listening for what patients are aware of *and for what they are not aware of.* We are interested in both conscious and unconscious feelings and thoughts. Each psychodynamic listening approach focuses on feelings, thoughts, and processes that are outside the patient's awareness. In this book, you will learn four different psychodynamic listening approaches, each of which focusing on a different aspect of what the patient says in order to hear unconscious material.

Psychodynamic listening differs from "natural" listening in the following ways:

1. Psychodynamic listening focuses on both conscious and unconscious feelings and thoughts; "natural" listening focuses on only conscious thoughts and feelings. Ever since Freud's early writings, we have known that feelings and thoughts outside our awareness can influence our daily lives (Freud 1900, 1915a). As therapists, we need to be trained to hear them in the patient's associations. Each psychodynamic listening approach focuses on the patient's words in ways that help us hear unconscious feelings and thoughts at work (Freud 1912c). This is not to say that we are interested only in the unconscious feelings and thoughts; rather, we are very interested in the *interaction* between the patient's conscious and unconscious feelings and thoughts (Freud 1923, 1926).

2. Psychodynamic listening involves a conscious choice of how to listen; "natural" listening involves little or no awareness of how one is listening. Instead of just letting the patient's words wash over us and listening in our usual way, as psychodynamic therapists we add other listening approaches to our "natural" approach. And by choosing to listen in a particular way, we are aware of how we are listening and what we are focusing on. Since we are trying to infer feelings that are implicit and unstated, we follow guidelines for making those inferences (Freud 1912b, 1913; Gray 1995; Greenson 1967; Langs 1973a; Searl 1936). We consciously try to make sense of the patient's associations.

3. Psychodynamic listening involves attention to both the content of what patients say and the processes of how they say it; "natural" listening is unaware of process. In "natural" listening we simply listen to the content of what people say. Although we may be somewhat aware of the process (how they say it) we cannot be aware of process in the same depth and subtlety as in a psychodynamic approach. In a psychodynamic approach, one's attention may be completely focused on the process (Freud 1915b; Gray 1995), as demonstrated in the section on defense analysis.

4. Psychodynamic listening focuses both on what the patient has spoken and what is implicit, what the patient has not yet been able to say; "natural" listening focuses only on what the patient has said. In "natural" listening you easily hear your friend's conscious thoughts and feelings. In a psychodynamic approach, we add to that our perception and understanding of the patient's unconscious thoughts and feelings (Freud 1912c). Whenever the patient speaks, we try to discern what further meanings and subtleties are yet to be spoken.

In contrast to "natural" listening, psychodynamic listening hears every word of the patient as a vehicle of a dynamic quality, an intention, a direction, a feeling, an experience. Every sentence is heard as the living motion of spoken and unspoken meaning.

5. Psychodynamic listening understands the patient's motivations, both as the patient reports them and also as grounded in conflict (Brenner 1976, 1982; A. Freud 1926; Freud 1923); "natural" listening understands the patient's motivations only as the patient reports them. Psychodynamic listening focuses on the functions our feelings and thoughts can serve, functions of which the patient may be unaware.

6. Psychodynamic listening assumes that there is always more meaning than has been stated; "natural" listening assumes there is no more meaning than what has been stated. "Natural" listening assumes there is no such thing as emotions and thoughts outside our awareness. Psychodynamic listening assumes that our mind operates like an orchestra. We have many feelings and thoughts simultaneously, some in the foreground, some in the background, and some almost inaudible, but all sounding together to create a very complex sonority (Waelder 1936). We are a bundle of multiple experiences and feelings interpenetrating and influencing one another. We may have conscious feelings, preconscious feelings, and feelings that are unconscious, all at the same time, and all influencing us. Psychodynamic listening does not assume that any person can be summarized as a single musical note. In fact, psychodynamic listening assumes that no matter how much we understand a patient, there is still more to know that lies outside our awareness and that of the patient.

7. Psychodynamic listening focuses on movement from one state of experience to another; "natural" listening focuses on what is static. Henri Bergson (1946) once said that "our personality is precisely that: the continuous melody of our inner life." Psychodynamic listening is not dynamic in the sense of being dramatic or forceful. Rather, psychodynamic listening refers to our feelings and thoughts as psychic forces moving in a field both within the patient and therapist (Freud 1910b) and between them as well. To hear the patient's words is to hear directions and intentions (Nunberg 1925). The patient's words are only the material through which the forces reveal themselves. When we hear movement in a patient, or feel moved, this is not a movement from one place to another, but from one state to another. Movement in psychodynamic therapy refers to the change of state or experience.

Thoughts and feelings are heard as motion because they have different dynamic qualities. The dynamic quality of the patient's experience is a statement of its incompleteness, its will to completion (Brenner 1976, 1982; Freud 1923; Nunberg 1925). To hear the patient's experience as a dynamic quality, direction, or pointing *means hearing beyond it at the same time, beyond the direction of its will, and going toward the expected next state.* Listening psychodynamically means we are not simply describing one feeling of a patient, then the next, then another, as if the patient is in a series of static positions. Instead, we are always listening and interpreting movement. Our hearing and interpretations do not remain within one state but reach through a state and beyond it. We try to describe the movement at any given moment. Dynamic qualities of states "are not stationary, of the nature of fixed pillars, with no bridge between them until one is provided by the connecting transition of the step, they are themselves completely of the nature of a step, of a transition; they are, in other words, dynamic, not static, they are themselves the going on beyond . . . a passing over, a 'between'" (Zuckerkandl 1956:137).

Let us return to Bergson's image of the personality as "the continuous melody of our inner life" to see the implications for interpretation from a dynamic perspective. Imagine for a moment your favorite song or melody. Let yourself hear the entire song in your imagination. Now that you've finished, how would you answer if asked which note was the melody? You wouldn't be able to answer in those terms because no note could summarize the entire melody. Even if you listed all the notes, that would not summarize the melody because the melody involves the motion one experiences in the notes. Likewise, when we listen psychodynamically, if we simply summarize a feeling the patient has, we have only stated a note and have ignored the inner movement from one note to another. Instead, we listen for movement within patients, how their experiences move, flow, and interpenetrate.

8. Psychodynamic listening for unconscious feelings and thoughts is guided by rules of inference; "natural" listening usually does not involve inference, and when it does, there are no guidelines to justify, confirm, or disconfirm those inferences—they are simply guesses. Freud (1910a) referred to this as "wild analysis." Each psychodynamic approach to listening chooses a particular focus in the material. For instance, reflective listening focuses on the conscious and pre-conscious content of the patient's words. Listening for transference focuses on the unconscious symbolic meaning of the patient's words. Listening for defense analysis, as taught here, focuses exclusively on the process (how the words are said), not the content. Each of these approaches has rules for inferring unconscious feelings and thoughts, for creating interpretations, and for determining

if they are valid or not. In contrast to the guesses of the layman, the psychodynamic therapist makes inferences on the basis of rules and methods (Fenichel 1941; Freud 1910a, 1912b; Sterba 1941).

☐ Becoming a Flexible Listener

Each of the approaches mentioned here allows us to listen for and interpret unconscious material. Flexible psychodynamic therapists use whichever listening approach they think will be most helpful to the patient at the moment (Bollas 1989). But to be flexible, we must make an important distinction. Although psychodynamic theories share common assumptions, the techniques of listening vary. Psychodynamic theory might be best thought of as an umbrella term, under which are a variety of listening approaches that allow us to infer pre-conscious and unconscious feelings and thoughts. Although these listening techniques differ enormously, they share the assumptions described in the previous section.

In this book, we will study four types of psychodynamic listening: 1) listening for feelings just below the surface, 2) listening for conflict, 3) listening for unconscious communication: the transference, and 4) listening for defenses. Each of the focuses represents a different school of thought within the field of psychodynamic therapy. The chapters on reflective listening will help to say back to patients what they feel based on their conscious associations while bringing up material just outside their awareness. The surface focused on in reflective listening is the content of the patient's associations and the preconscious implications. The chapters on analysis of conflict will help to hear conflict, formulate interpretations, and inquire into aspects of conflict that are out of awareness. The chapters on analysis of transference will help to listen for the *latent, unconscious, symbolic meaning* of the patient's associations. And finally, the chapters on defense analysis will focus on the process, the shifts in the patients' ability to report their thoughts and feelings. In contrast to analysis of conflict and transference analysis, which focus on the manifest and latent content, defense analysis (as taught here) focuses on the process.

Each type of listening chooses a different focus in the material in order to find unconscious thoughts and feelings in action. Being able to hear from each of these perspectives will help the therapist to listen in a more complex way than the man on the street would. For example, if you listen to a string quartet, and someone asks you which instrument is the quartet, you would be at a loss to answer. The quartet by its very nature is not any one instrument but rather the combination of four players. If you were asked which musical line is most important, again it would be difficult to answer in those terms because sometimes the first violin has the most important line, and sometimes any one of the other players has that line. Sometimes two players have a duet with equally important lines. And, sometimes all four lines are equally important.

Imagine how impoverished our musical experience would be if we were able to hear only one voice in a choir or only one instrument in a string quartet. Yet that is how impoverished our psychotherapeutic listening is if we can focus our attention in only one direction. By learning to listen from multiple perspectives, we gain a more complex understanding of the forces that govern our lives.

CHAPTER

Theory of Reflection

When we are faced with a very great text, a very profound one, never can we maintain that the interpretation we give of it—even if it is very accurate, the most accurate, if need be, the only accurate one—coincides exactly with its author's thought.

The fact is, the text and the interpretation are not of the same order; they do not develop at the same level, and therefore they cannot overlay one another. The former expresses spontaneous, synthetic, 'prospective', in some fashion, creative knowledge. The latter, which is a commentary, is of the reflective and analytical order.

In a sense, the commentary, if it is at all penetrating, always goes farther than the text, since it makes what it finds there explicit; and if it does not in fact go farther, it is of no use, since no light would then be shed by it on the text. But in another and more important sense, the text, by its concrete richness, always overflows the commentary, and never does the commentary dispense us from going back to the text. There is virtually infinity in it.

Henri De Lubac (1958), *Further Paradoxes*

Whenever we listen to patients, we need to demonstrate that we have heard and understood them. As you will see in this book, understanding can take many forms and occur on many levels. For instance, we may show our understanding of conscious feelings, feelings slightly out of awareness, or feelings that are unconscious. When we use reflection, we try to establish a mutual understanding of feelings and thoughts in the patient's awareness and expand that awareness to what is implicit and thus far unspoken. Our ability to track the patient's

11

feelings and describe them accurately establishes rapport and demonstrates our ability to understand.

This demonstration of our empathy, our ability to feel with the patient, can take passive or active forms. We might simply repeat back or summarize what the patient has said. Rogerian therapy, for instance, involves echoing, supporting, and reflecting the patient's feelings. Or we might more actively feel into the patient's world and give voice to the patient's unspoken feelings. We can even test our empathy with the patient by seeing if we can complete the patient's sentences in our mind.

As a first step, we need to find patients through describing their states of mind in simple empathic statements. Our job is not to startle patients with our alleged mind reading abilities. Rather, we need to comfort them by our ability to find their feelings and state them in a way that reassures them that they can be known and understood.

Gendlin (1968) offers ten rules to follow when using a reflective approach:

1. Respond to the felt meaning.
2. Explicate the felt meaning so that new facets emerge concretely from it. Point to feelings that are implicit though not directly stated with the hope that the client can explore and elaborate more deeply on her experience.
3. Help the patient by tentatively trying out various directions until the client experiences new facets or a clearer feeling.
4. Our sensitivity consists in carefully noting the client's response to what we say.
5. Aim at the patient's own directly felt sense of what s/he is talking about.
6. Focus less on finding out the facts than on clarifying what the patient feels and experiences.
7. Follow what the patient experiences.
8. Only the emergence of new experience is progress.
9. Use only words that point to felt experience.
10. Try to facilitate a greater depth of experience.

By "respond to the felt meaning," we don't mean simply saying to someone, "You were angry." Anger is, of course, a feeling, but in real life our feelings and thoughts are the result of a complex web of desires and motivations (Waelder 1936). Rarely can our experience be summarized in a word. Further, our feeling is not a thing within us but a response to a situation. For instance, suppose a patient is telling us about her experience on Saturday night when her boyfriend showed up an hour late and made a half-hearted apology. We could intuit that she was angry, but with a little empathic imagination we realize she probably had a number of feelings at the same time. She may have been angry that he didn't apologize, disappointed that he turned out to be so much less than she had hoped for, hurt that he could dismiss her feelings and treat her so shabbily—revealing a lack of interest in her, and perhaps helpless in the face of this insensitivity. In other words, we need to tease out the web of feelings, the experience of being in that situation. Further, her feelings are the result not only of the situation, but of the way she perceives and interprets it. Thus, her feelings can not be summarized in one simple emotion but must be understood as a movement of combined feelings, thoughts, and perceptions within a situation.

☐ Focus on Implicit or Pre-Conscious Feelings

Although the patient may have a variety of feelings in a situation, many of them may only be implicit, not explicitly articulated or recognized yet (Freud 1912c, 1915a). We can almost always assume that the patient's experience is more complicated than she has described, that the described feeling also implies much more that has not been put into words. Hence, we try to respond in ways that invite the patient to become aware of these implicit feelings. For example, suppose that the patient reported her anger at the boyfriend who showed up late for the date but alluded to no other feelings. One might say, *"Perhaps you were furious with him not only for being late, but for being such a disappointment, for being so much less than you hoped he would be."* Here one articulates feelings that were possibly true for her, but not yet put into words. The response is intended to help broaden and deepen her awareness of her experience.

This focus on implicit feelings is known as focusing on preconscious feelings and thoughts that the patient is unaware of but are in principle accessible to consciousness. The preconscious is "descriptively" unconscious, i.e., for all practical purposes, the patient is unaware of preconscious feelings and thoughts. But the patient can become aware of them if they are pointed out by the therapist (Freud 1915a; Laplanche and Pontalis 1973). When we bring up feelings that are implicit in the patient's statements, she may be reticent but able to speak about them (Laplanche and Pontalis 1973). This is not necessarily true with unconscious experience. In contrast, if we try to bring up material that is dynamically unconscious, the patient will resist it strongly (Freud 1915a, 1923). So when listening for preconscious material, our inferences must stay very close to what the patient has stated, clearly following from her words.

By offering possible implicit feelings, the therapist directs the patient's attention to more complex experience. We operate on the assumption that the patient has a directly felt sense of the complexity of the problem, even if she cannot articulate it, and we must always be pointing towards that complexity. We offer various tentative possibilities until we find one that enables the patient to feel more intensely, or to be able to describe more fully what she feels.

Understandably, these tentative offerings often will be mistaken. What is crucial is not to avoid mistakes but to be sensitive to them when they occur. We should always monitor the impact our comments have. By following what furthers the patient's experience, we can avoid getting in the way too often.

Focus your comments on the patient's directly felt experience of the problem. No matter how detailed her description is of herself, we assume that this description is only a partial understanding. By clarifying what the patient explains, we help her feel more, become more aware of what she feels, and become more able to put her experience into words.

Our purpose is to deepen the patient's experience of herself. What we pursue depends on what deepens her experience. Only her experience can guide us. The deepening or furthering of her experience will be seen when a problem resolves itself, a feeling becomes clearer, a new understanding emerges, or different facets assume importance and others fade away.

However, this movement occurs not as the result of a single explanation or concept, but through an experience of increasing awareness. We use our ideas and concepts not so much to explain as to explore the patient's experience. We reflect not to summarize and bring thought to a stop, but to notice and promote movement. Reflections should not close a chapter but open a new one. Our ideas can be used to point towards experience rather than explain it away. This occurs not through logical steps of explanation but unpredictable steps of experience. What we think is the case at one moment will often turn out to be entirely wrong five minutes later. When you follow the patient's experience, prepared to be surprised.

Reflection is a process that is used differently by Rogerian, Sullivanian, and self psychological therapists. But the following studies will help you acquire skill in making simple empathic statements that reflect conscious and preconscious feelings of the patient. As a preparation for those studies, we will review the three kinds of reflection you will be asked to do. The first kind of reflection simply summarizes what the patient has said. It goes no further than the conscious feelings and thoughts of the patient, and does not explore any possible preconscious feelings or thoughts. It has what we call a closed form.

Example

Patient: *I've been thinking about our last session. And especially this week, how one of my students actually came up to ask questions after class. That felt really good. But overall some good and some bad things happened this week. And I've been struggling about my religious beliefs. I guess things happen for a reason—but here I go again, talking in a tirade.*
Therapist: *You feel you're talking in a tirade.*

The response summarizes what the patient has just said without exploring any further feelings. It has a closed form: it does not open up further thoughts or feelings. This kind of response is helpful with paranoid patients who fear therapist intrusion and experience questions as invasive. It is also useful with some patients who are learning disabled or who have problems with symbolic thinking. These patients can become extremely anxious if we allude to implicit feelings. However, this kind of reflection is usually not particularly helpful with other patients because it closes off exploration. Ironically, with more disturbed patients, this kind of reflection provides a defense for the patient by closing off inquiry, and it makes it safer for the patient to explore (Havens 1986; Spotnitz 1976, 1985). With other patients, however, this kind of reflection blocks the patient. Its summarizing quality gives a static definition to the patient, which in turn can lead to stasis in treatment. Reflections with more paranoid patients will simply describe a state. With other patients, it is better to not simply describe a state, but a movement from one state to another, a shift or flow in the patient's experience.

When we reflect only a single feeling or thought, we state only one quality without giving any sense of its dynamic meaning, structure, or order. Only through talking about how other feelings and thoughts coexist with that feeling, superimposed and interpenetrating, does the first feeling or thought exhibit its diversity and structure as part of a dynamic field (Freud 1896, 1910b, 1917). Static observations like the one above impede the search for new meaning and ignore the movement that occurs in the patient.

It is important to note that different kinds of reflections are used with different patients precisely because what will help one patient will block another (Havens 1976, 1986). This is why it is important to note how the patient responds to your reflections. The patient's response will guide your choice. For example, here is a vignette from work with a paranoid patient:

Patient: *I'm just so tired. Did poorly on my test and I was supposed to talk to the professor. Really didn't want to. And I slept through the class.*
Therapist: *I wonder if sleeping in was a way for you to avoid talking to the professor.*
Patient: *No. I was tired.* [Becomes anxious and falls silent.]

The therapist makes a reasonable inference clearly related to the material, but the patient denies its relevance and is unable to elaborate. He cannot tolerate inferences. In contrast, note how he responded to a different kind of reflection later in the same hour:

Patient: *I feel like I've got so much to do and just don't have the time to do it.* [Relates different responsibilities he has.]
Therapist: *Just not enough time.*
Patient: *Yeah. You know I have trouble organizing myself. I do one thing and get involved and have trouble going on to the next thing and then the first thing I know it's the middle of the night and I need to go to bed to get up in the morning.*

This patient at this moment is helped more by a reflection that does not allude to implicit feelings. Alluding to them shuts him down, whereas not alluding to them allows him very gradually to elaborate them. In the studies in the following chapter, you will be asked to make this form of reflection precisely so that you can more clearly see the difference between static and dynamic reflections.

The second kind of reflection you will be asked to make is a dynamic reflection in which you address the patient's conscious feelings and also infer possible preconscious feelings and thoughts of the patient. Your reflection will infer the inner movement within the patient based on what the patient has said.

Example

Patient: *I was kind of disappointed Saturday night. I don't know. I guess I figured that when Roy said he would pick me up at eight for the dance that he'd be there at 8. But then it got to be eight thirty, nine, then nine thirty he shows up. No call. And says, "Hey, let's go." And when I asked why he was so late he said, "Oh, don't spoil things, honey." So I shut up and went.*

Therapist: *"And just when you were feeling hurt and disappointed. So you were teetering between whether to keep quiet or to tell him more of what you thought."*

This reflection addresses the patient's conscious thoughts and then inquires into implicit feelings and thoughts. Further, rather than describing this patient as in a single state, the reflection depicts her feelings in tension with one another, tempted to move in different directions at the same moment. The therapist tries to expand the possible range of meanings and understandings she can experience. The reflection has an open form that invites the patient to talk about something more, something that so far has been unsaid. In addition, the reflection is noting the movement from one feeling to another. The therapist is not describing her as someone who is unable to challenge her boyfriend. He is describing the changes in her ability to do so, the movement of feelings and desires within her (A. Freud 1936).

This example also illustrates what we mean by the term "psychodynamic." Feelings and thoughts can be interpreted as events occurring in a field. We can clearly hear the pressing ahead, the direction, or intention when she describes her disappointment, when she asks him why he is late, when she shut up. We can hear a desire to speak about her feelings and movement away from that urge. Even in this brief passage, we witness states of mind in motion, affecting one another. Hearing psychodynamically involves the immediate perception of experiences, feelings, and thoughts as forces in action occurring at the same time (Freud 1912c). This tuning in to a variety of feelings acting simultaneously is referred to by Havens (1986) as "complex empathy," in contrast to the simple empathy of static reflections that address only one feeling.

A third kind of reflection will be asked for as well in the next chapter. This kind of reflection is one made from within the perspective of the patient (Havens 1976, 1986; Spotnitz 1976, 1985).

Example

Therapist: *"I just wish he could have said he was sorry,"* or *"Should I tell him what I think and get him ticked off, or should I forget it and go out."*

This kind of reflection addresses the patient's conscious feelings and thoughts and infers preconscious feelings and thoughts as well. But in contrast, the therapist states them as if he were the patient. This is particularly useful with some patients, and it is always useful to be able to think this way even if you don't use this intervention, because it helps you feel your way into the patient's experience and articulate what has not yet been said. In this kind of reflection, you are speaking as if you are standing next to the patient looking at things from the same perspective, but with the ability to articulate more of her experience.

☐ Validation of Reflections

Having formulated a reflection, we need to listen to the patient's response for validation. A reflection is validated if the patient is able to elaborate on the previous feelings she was describing, if her affect deepens, if her understanding becomes more complex, and if new thoughts, feelings, and memories emerge—in other words, if the reflection results in movement. In the next chapter you will be asked to analyze responses to reflections to see if they are validated. Let's look at an example from Rogers (1961:121–122):

Patient: *Really, I don't think I've had that feeling before. I've—uh, well, this really feels like I'm saying something that, uh, is a part of me really.* [Pause] *Or, uh* [quite perplexed] *it feels like I sort of have, uh, I don't know. I have a feeling of* strength, *and yet, I have a feeling of—realizing it's so sort of fearful, of fright.*

Therapist: *That is, do you mean that saying something of that sort gives you at the same time a feeling of strength in saying it, and yet at the same time a frightened feeling of what you have said, is that it?*

Patient: *M-hm. I am feeling that. For instance, I'm feeling it internally now— a sort of surging up, or force or outlet. As if that's something really big and strong. And yet, uh, well, at first it was almost a physical feeling of just being out alone, and sort of cut off from a—a support I had been carrying around.*

Therapist: *You feel that it's something deep and strong, and surging forth, and at the same time, you just feel as though you'd cut yourself loose from any support when you say it.*

Patient: *M-hm. Maybe that's—I don't know—it's a disturbance of a kind of pattern I've been carrying around, I think.*

[Notice the therapist's reflection now and the patient's response to it.]

Therapist: *It sort of shakes a rather significant pattern, jars it loose.*

Patient: *M-hm.* [Pause, then cautiously, but with conviction.] *I, I think— I don't know, but I have the feeling that then I am going to begin to do more things that I know I should do. . . . There are so many things that I need to do. It seems in so many avenues of my living I have to work out new ways of behavior, but—maybe—I can see myself doing a little better in some things.*

Notice how the therapist picks up the patient's reference to a disturbed pattern, but then takes it a little farther: "jars it loose." The patient, though initially hesitant, validates the reflection by expanding on a new sense of himself, becoming loose from patterns of the past, developing new behaviors in the future. There is a deepening sense of conviction, a sense of movement towards the future, an elaboration of the reflection. All these things indicate validation.

Now let's look at an example of a reflection that is not validated from Shave (1968:106):

Patient: *I feel as though God has forsaken me, and I'm a burden to everyone.* [She breaks down and cries for several minutes.]

Therapist: *God won't let you down.*

Patient: *You don't understand. I feel as though I've let him down.*

Therapist: *He knows you haven't let Him down and He understands.*

Patient: *It's so inconvenient for my husband to bring me here. He doesn't know what he's getting into at all. He has a very busy schedule and I can't be expecting him to be waiting on me hand and foot.*

The therapist's first reflection is not based on the patient's feelings at all; in fact, it contradicts her feelings. The patient corrects him in response, invalidating his reflection. The therapist's next reflection once again contradicts her feelings rather than explore them. This time the patient does not even respond to the reflection. She gives up trying to explore the topic of her relationship to God and begins to talk about her husband. There is no elaboration of the reflection, there is a failure to expand on her feelings and thoughts about her relationship with God, there is no further complexity to her understanding of herself, and there is no deepening of affect. Both reflections are shown to be invalid by the patient's response.

In conclusion, psychodynamic reflections are always based on what the patient has most recently said. They are intended to expand the patient's awareness, not by focusing on unconscious material but on pre-conscious thoughts and feelings that are implicit in the patient's associations. Inferences are not situations for wild guessing (Freud 1904, 1910a) but for making reasonable judgements based on what the patient has said. By imagining yourself in the patient's situation, you will be able to feel your way into her world and find the words to describe it. The resulting reflection should describe the patient not as having one feeling, but as having a variety of feelings within a situation, feelings that are in a dynamic, moving relation.

Once you offer the reflection, disconfirmation will be obvious if the patient is unable to elaborate her experience, if it becomes less rich, more constricted, or if the patient becomes confused or derailed (Kohut 1959, 1971). Confirmation will be seen if the patient is able to experience herself more deeply, describe herself in more complex terms, and through this experience gain increased freedom of talking and eventual relief of her symptoms. Even if the patient agrees with your reflection, listen further. Does her subsequent talking indicate a deeper, richer, more complex experience of herself? Her experience as demonstrated in the hour must be your guide, not her simple agreement or disagreement.

☐ Further Readings

Gendlin, E. (1968). In his unique blending of Rogerian and existentialist approaches, Gendlin offers a concise presentation of the principles of reflective listening.

Havens, L. (1986). By far the best book ever written on the development of empathic responses to patients. It goes beyond simple reflective statements to ones that are far more complex and subtle. This books rewards many readings.

Rogers, C. (1961).

Wachtel, P. (1993). Wachtel's work is extremely important and merits close study. Chapters seven and eight of his book use a different rationale and language, but they offer many useful suggestions for making comments that pick up on the dynamic quality of the patient's conflicts.

3
CHAPTER

Reflection Studies

As you read through the following sessions, write down reflections that infer what the patient feels. After you have written your reflections, compare them with the suggested reflections at the end of each section. Each section for reflections will be divided into three parts:

> *Reflection A* should state conscious feelings without inferring implicit, preconscious feelings.
>
> *Reflection B* should try to open up implicit feelings not yet stated. It should ideally take an open form that reveals the movement of the patient's feelings as discussed in the previous chapter.
>
> *Reflection C* should be stated from within the patient's perspective, as if giving voice to her silent thoughts.

☐ Case #1: A Patient in the Sixth Month of Therapy

Patient: *I don't know if this is good or not. Well . . . L . . . Friday night . . . we all went to a party, and then all went to a bar, and I didn't go, and L came back and came into my room. My roommate and I were in bed, he just came into my room. I kept hinting for him to leave but he wouldn't. Then a few more guys came in and they were drunk and he comes up my ladder and talking to me and touching my leg. I was just "no": giving him big signals. When they came in he said, "what's my odds." For him to do that in front of me. They said five to one against you. I just jumped down and went out of my* *room and went to talk to his roommate. When L came in, he said "stay" and it was . . . I said "no" and it was great, like I had no feelings, like I didn't even really want to be with him at all. I was so excited. I never said "no" to him before.*

Write down 3 reflections to this passage now.

Suggested Reflections

Reflection #1A: *"It was exciting to be able to say no to him."*

Reflection #1B: *"It was exciting to discover a new way of being, of asserting yourself."* This reflection picks up on her forward movement. The next one goes even further, intuiting what it is like for her to be changing and reframes and highlights this change as "the new you. *"And it raises the whole question of what it will be like for you as this new you emerges."*

Reflection #1C: *"I couldn't believe I'd actually said it!"*

The hour continues:

Therapist: *What was it like this time to be different?*

Patient: *It was nice but I kind of felt bad for him. Like there are certain people you can always talk into doing things, like you make nice. But I just said goodnight. The next day he wouldn't talk to me, like he got the hint. Then on Valentine's day, they're laughing at him and saying he wants to ask me out. Well I was sitting with K, watching him play Nintendo. Well last semester K and I had a bet that if I didn't have a date all semester he'd have to take me to [a restaurant]. Well I didn't, and he had to take me. Everyone knew about it and it was funny. Well on Valentine's day, L said to me, "why don't you go to the party with me and let K get his free meal at [the restaurant]" and I said no. And he said, "Don't you want to let K get his free meal?" and I said, "No, I don't want to go out with you."*

Therapist: *That sounds like a real different place for you.*

Author's Commentary

In the previous chapter, you read that we listen to the material after a reflection to hear if it has been validated or not. In this case, I will analyze the therapist's reflections for you, then in the later cases, you will analyze them to develop the skill of listening for validation.

The reflection above, "That sounds like a real different place for you," is excellent. Notice how it points to change and movement within the patient. The reflection encourages her to describe more fully this new sense of herself implicit in her action of saying no. It is clearly based on the material. The patient's response, which follows, confirms this reflection. The patient articulates more bluntly and powerfully her desire not to see this boy and her conflict about doing so. Thus, we see her feelings and experience deepen within a more complex understanding of herself.

The hour continues:

Patient: *Yeah, it was weird. He walked out and he was mad and I followed him out because it was mean to say in front of others and I said, "Look. I really don't want to go out with you." He said, "Why?" I said, "This may sound really mean but you're probably one of the last people I'd want to spend Valentine's day with." It was nice but I felt bad because I'm not a person who would want to hurt him in any way.*

Write down 3 reflections to this passage now.

Suggested Reflections

Reflection #2A: *"Sounds like it felt so nice to be able to say no to him, but then you worried that saying no might hurt him."* Notice that although this is a partially accurate reflection, it empathically abandons her at the very moment she became stuck—when she worried that saying no might hurt him. Notice the more dynamic quality in the following reflections.

Reflection #2B: *"Maybe you wish that he had paid more attention to your feelings already so that you wouldn't have been in the position of having to tell him you didn't want to go out."* This reflection points more towards her desire for a different response and relationship. The next reflection alludes to the internal movement within her as she evolved to a more assertive stance. *"I wonder if it was really frustrating to have him ignore all your subtle hints when you were trying to assert yourself without hurting his feelings."*

Reflection #2C: *"How to say no when I know he'll feel hurt?" "If he'd only listened to me already I wouldn't have had to do this." "In fact, I tried to say no to him every subtle way I could think of so I wouldn't hurt his feelings."* Notice how the third reflection in this group is the most dynamic.

The hour continues:

Therapist: *What kind of person is that?*

Patient: *When you say no. I don't know.* [laughed] *I usually just go with the flow.*

Therapist: *When you think of someone "like that" who doesn't go with the flow, what is that person like?*

Patient: *I don't know. Not that it's bad.*

Therapist: *Maybe part of you does think it's bad.*

Author's Commentary

This reflection is less successful because the therapist is addressing unconscious rather than preconscious material. The patient by saying, "not that it's bad," may be defending against the idea that she might think she is bad for saying no. At any rate, she is saying in effect that "this is what I do not think." The therapist contradicts her stated feeling rather than explore it. In her response to the reflection, the patient clarifies what she means, but we see no elaboration or deepening of feeling. So we end up with a mixed validation: in thoughts but not feelings. A better reflection might have been: "That somehow it's more complex." This reflection would have helped her amplify her wish to describe someone who doesn't go with the flow in a way that is broader than simply summarizing such a person as "bad." And it would also have addressed another kind of movement implicit in her statements: a movement toward a more complex, nuanced understanding of herself. What might be misunderstood as simply a resistance on her part, may also be understood as her attempt to reach for a less simplistic understanding.

The hour continues:

Patient: *Yeah. Well yes I do. I know what you're getting at. It's not that it's bad but I'm not a person who causes problems. Any added tension I avoid. It's my personality.*

Write down 3 reflections to this passage now.

Suggested Reflections

Reflection #3A: *"It's your personality to go with the flow."*
Reflection #3B: *"Wanting something different from someone else is a*

problem that you try to solve by appearing to want the same thing— going along. But then you probably wish they could tolerate your difference so you wouldn't always have to do that."

Reflection #3C: *"If only I could find another way to deal with the tension."*

The hour continues:

Therapist: *Has it always been that way for you?*

Patient: *Yeah, definitely. I'd know that someone would want to do something and I wouldn't but I'd do it for that person. But finally I was saying, "NO, I DON'T WANT TO!"*

Write down 3 reflections to this passage now.

Suggested Reflections

Reflection #4A: *"You really didn't want to!"*

Reflection #4B: *"And this was something new—realizing that just because he wanted it didn't mean you had to want it too."* Notice how this reflection underscores the forward movement in the patient, a bit of progress that might otherwise escape her attention.

Reflection #4C: *"I won't give up what I want just because you want me to."* This reflection gives voice to the implicit feelings and thoughts that may have allowed the patient finally to stand her ground.

The hour continues:

Therapist: *Where do you think that you learned to go along?*

Patient: *I guess, I don't know. My mom's totally not like that. She's a real dominating person. She's a real control freak.*

Therapist: *You were in reaction to her.*

Author's Commentary

Another excellent reflection. Notice that the therapist infers that the patient was reacting to her mother's domineering behavior. This inference helps the patient distance herself from this behavior. Instead of feeling "it's my personality," she is able to view this as a behavior, a choice that can be changed. Often we must help patients disidentify with a behavior before they can analyze it. The patient confirms this in the comments below. She begins to describe her mother more vividly and emotionally than ever before.

The hour continues:

Patient: *I guess my dad is accommodating. I have a car. My dad really wanted a truck and it was his turn (they take turns), but she was really complaining so they bought what she wanted. She doesn't threaten, but you get that sense you do whatever she wants. She's not horrible or anything.*

Write down 3 reflections to this passage now.

Suggested Reflections

Reflection #5A: *"It's just that she'll keep saying what she wants until she gets it."*

Reflection #5B: *"It's just really hard for her to accept that people have desires different from hers."* This reflection infers feelings of the mother in order to help the patient adopt a more observant stance while reframing the problem in terms of separation. *"She keeps saying what she wants until he gives in. But I bet he still wants something different."* This reflection infers the father's feelings as a way to invite the patient to understand her own feelings when in conflict with her mother.

Reflection #5C: *"It's just that I wish she could give in and let him have what he wanted more of the time."*

The hour continues:

Therapist: *What was it like growing up with that kind of person as your mother?*

Patient: *I was terrified. A lot of other things. She's a lot better than when I was young. She's great with my sister.*

Therapist: *What was she like for you when you were young?*

Patient: *She was very tough. She hit maybe too much. Her parents were really bad. She doesn't even speak to them. I would never hit a kid because of how my mom was.*

Therapist: *How badly did she hit you?*

Patient: *Not like I did things to warrant being hit but she didn't know when to stop. My father had to intervene and tell her to stop.*

Therapist: *Did she ever beat you up pretty badly?*

Patient: *Not that I ever had scars. It was more like yelling would have been enough. She's not evil but she didn't realize that just talking to me or hitting me once was enough but she didn't realize it. I don't know if I'm making sense. She wanted to make sure I got the point; but I did the first time. She* *couldn't differentiate how much was required. She had her own problems. She was abused. Not that it gives her the right.*

Therapist: *It made it feel normal to her.*

Author's Commentary

A very sensitive reflection. Notice how she reaches for the patient's implicit understanding of her mother. She amplifies the meaning of the patient's understanding of her mother rather than pursue the anger which the patient is not describing at this moment. Her statement also alludes to the movement in the patient, her yearning to understand her mother. In the comments below, we see a dramatic validation of this reflection: two vivid and powerful memories come up that elaborate her understanding of her mother and how it changed over time.

The hour continues:

Patient: *Yes, and she finally realized. When I was twelve, she hit me really hard and I never said anything. Then one day she hit my sister and I thought she was hitting her too much that if she didn't stop, I'd call my father. And that was the last time she ever hit anyone. I think she realized then it was wrong. We've never talked about it, but my dad and I talked. She's so much more calm. She's a different person.*

Write down 3 reflections to this passage now.

Suggested Reflections

Reflection #6A: *"She's different from the way she was when she used to hit you."* This reflection picks up on where she left off: that her mother is different now. Adding "when she used to hit you" invites her to elaborate on that experience since you have protected her defense by noticing that the mother is different now.

Reflection #6B: *"She realized she couldn't hit you anymore. And you began to realize you wouldn't be hit; things would never be the same."* This reflection infers what must have taken place within her when she realized she would not be hit again. This reflection is focused on the past, but highlights the dynamic, changing experience she had in the past.

Reflection #6C: *"The relationship is not just different; it is changing."*

The hour continues:

Therapist: *Did she seem out of control?*

Patient: *Yes, definitely. Sometimes when she hit me I don't think she even knew she was.*

Therapist: *That must have been so frightening for you.*

Author's Commentary

Another good reflection inferring the patient's feelings. Notice as confirmation that the patient for the first time describes feeling terrified— a deepening of affect.

The hour continues:

Patient: *I was terrified of my mother. I'd drop a book and my papers would fall out and I'd look to see if she'd get mad.*

Therapist: *You'd always have to watch her.*

Author's Commentary

This reflection is less successful; it fails to explore the patient's experience. In response, the patient moves away from the past to the present, from her mother to her father. The reflection addressed the patient's action, watching, but not what she thought or felt as she watched to see if her mother was angry.

   Alternative reflection: *"Wondering, 'Uh oh. What will she do now.'"* This reflection would have more actively entered into the patient's experience, addressing her feelings and thoughts as well as the movement where things were going to lead when she dropped something. This reflection would try to infer the patient's experience at the moment she feared another beating.

The hour continues:

Patient: *Now. Recently my dad and I were talking about how much better she is.*

Therapist: *What was it like for you to share that with your dad?*

Patient: *It was good. When she'd hit me, she'd say bad things and it would hurt and I'd go into my room and my dad would come in and make it better and convince me to go out and make up.*

Therapist: *It's tough when parents are like that because they're the most important people in the world when you're little.*

Author's Commentary

This reflection is only moderately helpful. When the patient responds, she shifts from describing her experience to her father's experience. The reflection does not amplify what it was like to have to go out and make up when she had not been at fault. Rather than say "it's tough", the therapist should have described the toughness, the feelings and thoughts the patient had as she walked out of her room to apologize to her mother.

Alternative reflection: *"When a moment before you probably wished he would take your side."*

The hour continues:

Patient: *My father was hit too but he completely turned the other way. She didn't. She never realized until I confronted her.*

Therapist: *How was that for you to confront her like that?*

Patient: *After I ran into my bedroom crying, I thought she wouldn't speak to me. She was the total authority figure.*

Write down 3 reflections to this passage now.

Suggested Reflections

Reflection #7A: *"She was the one in control."*
Reflection #7B: *"And might not ever speak to you again after what you had said."* This reflection would attempt to infer what was going on inside her when she was crying in her room, wondering what would happen next.
Reflection #7C: Static: *"I thought it was the end."* Or dynamic: *"Even though I knew she was in control, I still felt I should have the right to speak up."*

The hour continues:

Therapist: *I wonder if at that moment, you were afraid it would be a permanent rupture.*

Author's Commentary

This reflection looks great at first since it flows right out of the material, but the patient moves away as soon as she addresses the theme of abandonment. This suggests that unconscious material is being resisted.

The hour continues:

Patient: *I thought she'd never speak to me again. But since I was thirteen, we've gotten along great. I have a new mom. I didn't want you to think she hit me all the time, just every four months.*

Therapist: *What would it mean if I pictured her worse?*

Patient: *I say those things and I don't want you to think they are horrible people.*

Write down 3 reflections to this passage now.

Suggested Reflections

Reflection #8A: *"You don't want me to think they are horrible."*

Reflection #8B: *"That there's more to them than just the fact that they sometimes hit you. That's not the only thing that's true about them."* You may have been tempted to write, *"Horrible people?"* This would follow from the material, but since this is not a possibility she wants the therapist to consider, she is unlikely to want to explore it herself either. This kind of reflection often elicits flat, unproductive responses from the patient. It's a lazy kind of stereotyped reflection which avoids the more difficult work of inferring implicit feelings. For instance, an alternative reflection might be: *"It sounds like that when a mother loves you sometimes and hits you sometimes, that words like good, bad, and horrible just don't do justice to all the feelings we have."* This infers a movement on her part towards a more complex understanding of her mother. Or the therapist might say something which doesn't allude directly to the patient at all: *"It sounds like you're hoping I don't lose sight of how complex a person your mother is; that although she hit you, she also loved you, even if we're only beginning to understand what that means."* This reflection addresses her implicit striving for a more nuanced understanding of her mother at the same time that it implies that there is more to be known. It leaves space open for her to address further meanings.

Reflection #8C: *"Just because my mother hit me doesn't mean she didn't love me."*

The hour continues:

Therapist: *What if they are or were?*

Patient: *It would change my image of them. If you could tell that someone's bad, what does that say about you?*

Therapist: *I think you can tell. I think sometimes it's hard to just say it out loud.*

Patient: *Yeah. I don't know.*

Therapist: *Do you feel like you're being disloyal?*

Patient: *Yes. I don't want to say bad things about her. She's incredible now. I'm not afraid anymore.*

Write down 3 reflections to this passage now.

Suggested Reflections

Reflection #9A: *"Then you felt afraid, but now you don't."*

Reflection #9B: *"Sounds like you are trying to figure out how to talk about the hitting mom of the past while remembering the incredible mom of the present."*

Reflection #9C: *"Now I can be close to her and not worry about what might happen next."*

The hour continues:

Therapist: *How long did it take for that to disappear?*

Patient: *Through high school. We talk now. It's really nice. It's great to see her.* [Described an incident where mother did not get angry at her sister.] *And I thought, 'aren't you supposed to get angry, aren't you supposed to hit her?" I was happy.*

Therapist: *Part of you felt glad for your sister but part of you felt that you had to get through it when she didn't.*

Author's Commentary

This is an excellent reflection, inferring implicit feelings. It appears to be validated except that the therapist intervenes before giving the patient a chance to elaborate on her experience of this conflict. This prevents the patient from deepening her experience of herself, and it blocks the therapist from discovering the next implicit feelings which need to be inferred.

The hour continues:

Patient: *Yes and I felt really bad for feeling that.*

Write down 3 reflections to this passage now.

Suggested Reflections

Ordinarily, one would not offer a reflection yet, but would allow the patient to elaborate more.

> Reflection #10A: *"You felt bad for resenting her."*
> Reflection #10B: *"It's as if when you saw her have the relationship you always wanted, you realized what you lost."*
> Reflection #10C: *"If she only knew what I had to go through."*

The hour continues:

Therapist: *It's pretty natural what you thought. You don't have to beat yourself up for it.*

Author's Commentary

The therapist reassures the patient rather than explore her feelings of guilt and badness. The patient's response does not develop the previous feeling and thought. The therapist is correct in one sense that the patient does not have to beat herself up. But in a more profound sense, the therapist is wrong: the patient believes she must do that. The therapist's job is to figure out why it makes sense to the patient to beat herself.

The hour continues:

Patient: *That's when I realized she really changed.*
Therapist: *It sounds like you had a lot of really tough years.*

Author's Commentary

In contrast, this excellent inference leads to a beautiful deepening of feeling in the patient's response along with a new memory which elaborates on this feeling.

The hour continues:

Patient: *Oh I don't know. She had her good days too. She was great at other times. And I learned to stay out of her way.* [Describes telling her father for the first time of the beatings and realizing how much it affected him because she never said anything to him before.]
Therapist: *Why do you think you never talked to your dad about it?*

Patient: *I don't know. Mom never dealt with her parents. Cut off all contact with them. She didn't deal with them. Wouldn't feel comfortable talking about things. She deals with the feelings by pushing them away.*

Therapist: *Which is exactly what you tried to do.*

Author's Commentary

This reflection fails to address implicit feelings. While it may be correct that the patient pushes feelings away, the therapist does not infer the thoughts and feelings that make the patient do that. In other words, this is a static reflection: the patient is portrayed only as someone who pushes feelings away.

   Alternative reflection: *"The fact you're here shows that you want to deal with your feelings. Only when you think you won't be able to deal with them do you push them away. Yet the fact they still bother you suggests you are trying to find another way to deal with them."*

   Notice that this dynamic reflection addresses a variety of feelings that are in tension with one another. And perhaps most importantly, a dynamic reflection notes movement, or in its absence, the desire for movement. In response to the therapist's static reflection, the patient agrees, but there is no deepening of material and she describes herself in the same static terms.

The hour continues:

Patient: *Which is exactly what I tried to do. Yeah, you're right. Maybe it works for her. I don't know her family at all. When my sister asks about them, I tell her to stop.*

Therapist: *What do you think would happen if you didn't stop her?*

Patient: *I think my mom would walk out of the room. She didn't even tell me her father died. In her family, no one talks about the past. They say this is us now. I can't imagine not speaking to them for years. I could never do that. It's not that I'm angry with her. It's that I feel I lost something because I don't have all that extra family. My sister is more like my mom. I'm more like my father. I hate to start fighting and disappear with people.*

Therapist: *So what was it like to stand up to L that way?*

Patient: *Well, I felt good. Well, I didn't feel bad. Well, I don't like anyone to feel bad but I knew I had to do it. My dad says I think of others too much.*

Therapist: *It sounds like it feels like there are two choices, bad like your mother or an accommodation like your dad.*

Patient: *I don't want to hurt people.*

Author's Commentary

This reflection elicits the patient's fear of hurting people if she says what she thinks. Unfortunately, the session ended at this point so we don't have a chance to see if there was further validation.

   Alternative reflection: *"Sounds like you are trying to find a way to think of others' feelings without denying your own."*

☐ Case #2: A Patient in the Tenth Month of Treatment

Patient: *I'm doing a lot better but I'm trying not to think about anything much. Trying not to obsess. I don't know how I'm supposed to feel about my dad. I think when your father is sick you're supposed to feel depressed, that's what I should be feeling.*

Therapist: *It feels like there's only one right way to be.*

Patient: *Yes. I should be somber, depressed. I almost don't want to deal.*

Reader's Commentary

Judging from the patient's response, did the above reflection address implicit feelings based on the material? Was it validated?

Author's Commentary

This reflection is based on the material and the sense that there is only one right way to be is implied in what the patient says. The patient's response validates the reflection: "somber, depressed", deepening and elaborating the feelings implied in her previous statement.

The hour continues:

Therapist: *What are you feeling?*

Patient: *Guilty, as usual. On Sunday I went out. My parents usually call from five to six and I was out, but I had talked to them earlier in the week so it was ok, but when I got back, my uncle said they called and my dad was back in the hospital, so he must be sicker because he went back before four weeks or maybe it was four weeks.*

Therapist: *So what are you feeling towards your dad if not depressed?*

Patient: *Not feeling very much.*

Therapist: *That's not acceptable to you.*

Patient: *I tried to think about him in the hospital or dying and I said so. I'm not really concerned. If it had been my mother, I'd be there. This bothers me that I won't with him.*

Reader's Commentary

Does the reflection above address feelings implied in the material? Is it validated? Is this a static or dynamic reflection? Would you offer a different reflection?

Write down 3 reflections to this passage now.

Author's Commentary

Yes, this reflection is implied in the material and it is validated. However, it is a rather static reflection to which the patient responds in static terms, "I'm not really concerned." Notice how the following suggested reflections try to capture the dynamic quality of her conflict.

> Reflection #1A: *"It bothers you that you don't want to visit him."*
> Reflection #1B: *"It bothers you that you aren't more concerned, that where you would expect to find feelings for him, you wish you found more."* Notice how this reflection goes beyond the static quality of not having feelings for her father by addressing her implicit wish that she did have those feelings.
> Reflection #1C: *"I wish I could feel differently about him."* This reflection too has a dynamic quality in that it implies her wish to have more feelings for him.

The hour continues:

Therapist: *Where do you think that comes from?—that you can let him go so much more easily.*

Patient: *Because he left me. It was easier to say goodbye to him than mother, even though I might never see him again. I should be having equivalent feelings. I need him to stay alive to support our family.*

Write down 3 reflections to this passage now.

Suggested Reflections

Reflection #2A: *"You think you should feel the same way about him as you do about your mother."*

Reflection #2B: *"And yet you wish you wanted him to stay alive for other reasons than just that."* This invites her to expand on the implicit wish.

Reflection #2C: *"I wish I could feel as much for him as for my mother."*

The hour continues:

Therapist: *I'm struck by how you're now seeing him through your mother's eyes. That's how she sees him.*

Patient: *Yeah. I'm definitely turning into her. My best friend said the older I get, the more I get like her. I even started smoking again after two months.*

Reader's Commentary

Does the above reflection address implicit feelings based on the material? Is it validated? What might have been a better reflection more related to her previous statement?

Author's Commentary

Although the patient agrees with the therapist, the reflection is not implicit in the patient's previous statement. Furthermore, the material the patient discusses is not related to the previous material. In fact, the static quality of the reflection is mirrored in the patient's static description of herself as a copy of her mother.

   Alternative reflection: *"And yet you wish you needed him to stay alive for other reasons too."*

The hour continues:

Therapist: *What made you start?*

Patient: *It think it's so I'm stressing about something. There's something wrong inside. There should be, or is. I can't have feelings for the man. Something is shut out, I don't know why.*

Therapist: *So you punished yourself by starting smoking again.*

Patient: *Is that it or did I need a cigarette? It started Friday, had a lot to do with N too. Maybe it is punishment. It also reminds me a lot of my mother too. I feel stressed and I need one. People say I look like her when I smoke.*

Reader's Commentary

Does the above statement by the therapist address feelings implied in the material? Is it validated? Would you offer an alternative reflection?

Author's Commentary

This statement is not clearly implied in the material. The patient gives only a weak validation: "Maybe it is punishment." If the patient is punishing herself, she is unaware of it and thus unable to think about it except in an intellectualized manner. There is no deepening of experience. Her response seems to be confusion rather than increased understanding or clarity of feeling.

Alternative reflection: *"I wonder if you're stressing because feelings for your father have been shut out and now you wish they could be opened up again."*

The hour continues:

Therapist: *How do you feel when they say that?*

Patient: *I used to hate it, but now I like it. It makes me feel more connected to her. The fourth of July was really hard with my best friend. Went to a place I used to go with my mother. One year I wouldn't, can't remember why I wouldn't. Think it was the year my dad left. Anyway it felt funny to be back there. They played her favorite song and I started crying. I felt like I can't make it up to her. This is what I do when things go wrong. It's the only way I can tell that something has gone wrong—by me getting closer to her, feeling guilty over things I did to her.*

Write down 3 reflections to this passage now.

Suggested Reflections

> Reflection #3A: *"You feel guilty over what you did to her."*
>
> Reflection #3B: *"Feeling guilty about things you did to her in the past helps you feel more connected to her now. Yet it also sounds like you want to find another way to feel close to her."*
>
> Reflection #3C: *"I wish I could feel close to her without feeling guilty."*

The hour continues:

Therapist: *It sounds like you're able to label and understand the process.*

Patient: *I've been trying to be in a good mood and people say I'm acting better. But I can tell I'm not, that I want to go home to be with her.*

Reader's Commentary

Does the above reflection address feelings implicit in the material? Is it validated?

Author's Commentary

This reflection has an intellectualized, experience-distant quality and does not elaborate on the patient's experience. The patient's response is intellectualized in turn. The patient's response seems to correct the therapist: ". . . people say I'm acting better. But I can tell I'm not. . . ." The patient did not want simply to be told she had a good understanding of her process. She wanted to know what understanding the therapist had that might take her further. Notice how the previous reflections are much closer to her feelings.

The hour continues:

Therapist: *What's happening in your life that's pushing you back to that place to be so connected with her?*

Patient: *I'm failing with N. Not in life. Made reconnections with old friends and it feels good to get this out in the air. It should reassure me that I can talk with N and we'll still be friends but I can't do it. I'm very rude to him now. No matter how hard I try not to think about him, I think about him all the time. I can't let it go, it's in my face every day. I try to let it go but I just can't do it.*

Write down 3 reflections to this passage now.

Suggested Reflections

Reflection #4A: *"You wish you could let go of thinking about N."*
Reflection #4B: *"It's hard to let go when you want to hold on."*
Reflection #4C: *"It's too hard."* This reflection might be too static, leaving her in her despair. The next reflection might be more dynamic: *"I don't want to let him go. I still want him."* This captures more of her sense of agency: it's not that she can't let go of him. She doesn't want to.

The hour continues:

Therapist: *Can you be more gentle with yourself for not being able to let it go?*

Patient: *I can't let him go. It's not possible. I don't want to, won't do it. Some part of me likes feeling bad. I feel like it's payback time for all the things I've done to people. It's not real. I feel like I'm having a relationship with myself. It's all in my mind. When I talk about him to people who know him they tell me he isn't like that. That he wouldn't do that, that he's much more gentle. So I know I'm misinterpreting something. I take everything for the worst. I stopped seeing a girlfriend two years ago because I thought she was stabbing me in the back with this man I liked. But it was all in my imagination. Completely. Realizing it and having to speak to her I was glad she took the first step.*

Write down 3 reflections to this passage now.

Suggested Reflections

> Reflection #5A: *"You were glad she let you know it had just been in your imagination."*
>
> Reflection #5B: *"You suddenly realized it had all been in your imagination, then you probably wondered, 'why did I believe a woman would steal a man from me?'"* Notice how this imputes a question that she has not stated but that is implicit. It also distances her from the fantasy so that she can begin to analyze it.
>
> Reflection #5C: *"But then I began to wonder, why did I have this fantasy, that a woman would steal a man from me?"*

The hour continues:

Therapist: *What is it like hearing people say you're doing the same thing with N? Misinterpreting.*

Patient: *I used to be shocked by it but I'm not anymore. Maybe I still am. Not a lot of people notice. Yesterday a friend said, 'why don't you tell him the truth?' How many people have said that! But she was the one from two years ago and she made me realize I'm back where I was two years ago. I feel like I've grown a lot in those two years and I'm handling things differently, but I'm not. I'm still doing the same thing.*

Therapist: *What's the same thing?*

Patient: *Not telling him. Not telling him. Although two years ago I didn't have a relationship like I do with N. It was a real fantasy crush. When I think of him now, I don't even like him. It makes me laugh now that I know him better. I want a different person in my life now. He was quick in and out. Now I want someone more stable. That changed but not my reaction to it.*

Write down 3 reflections to this passage now.

Suggested Reflections

Reflection #6A: *"So that even though you want a more stable relationship now, you're unable to say certain things to N."*

Reflection #6B: *"Maybe it's because you want a more stable relationship now that you are trying to figure out how to be honest and still keep him with you."* This reflection tries to capture the tension between her desire to speak and her fear of losing N. Another reflection might be: *"What has changed is your desire for a more stable man. What you are struggling with now is the fear of being left if you tell the truth. You feel so anxious now because your wish to tell the truth has become stronger."* This captures a key point: if we had no urge towards growth and change, we would feel no anxiety. By pointing out the conflict and anxiety she feels, we help her see the dynamic forces towards growth within her (Nunberg 1925) striving for expression. Although she is using the same defense as in the past, it is in response to a freer expression of her wish. This is progress she needs to see.

Reflection 6C: *"Even though my reaction is the same, my desire has changed. I want someone better for me, someone more stable."* Notice how the reversal of her last statement changes the meaning from a static to a dynamic quality and directs her attention to that which has changed.

The hour continues:

Therapist: *I feel like you're beating yourself up because you're not handling it as well as you could. It feels the same as when you came in the room angry at yourself for not being a good daughter, not feeling sad enough.*

Patient: *I'm seeing myself get into habits that I don't want again. I'm afraid I'm getting into the wrong thing. One thing is central in my life now and it's the wrong thing.*

Reader's Commentary

Does the above reflection address feelings implied in the material? Is it validated? Are there any problems with the reflection?

Author's Commentary

This reflection is problematic because it is not based on the material and it describes the patient in static terms: "you're beating yourself up." There is no sense of what combination of feelings, thoughts, and desires might be in tension with one another. As a result, the patient's comments reveal only a static sense of herself that appears to validate the reflection. However, the reflection is not validated on another dimension: there is no deepening of her understanding, feeling, or curiosity. If anything, she seems even more stuck.

The hour continues:

Therapist: *One thing?*
Patient: *N, and it should be my father.*
Therapist: *We're back to 'I should be.' It's hard to accept yourself where you are.*
Patient: *I try to be, 'it's ok,' but not people with a father dying in the hospital. I exaggerate it. They assure me he's not really dying but I exaggerate it. If the chance is there, I exaggerate it.*

Reader's Commentary

Does the above reflection address feelings implied in the material? Is it validated? Are there problems with this reflection? If so what are they? What might be a better reflection?

Author's Commentary

The difficulty with self-acceptance is implicit in the material and it is validated. But again the static reflection leads to a static response from the patient. The reflection does not address why she can't accept herself, what she can't accept, what it is like to live in her skin being unable to accept herself.

    Alternative reflection: *"You know you're able to feel a lot for N. So you wonder what prevents you from being able to feel that way about your father too since you wish you did."* This reflection is more dynamic since it acknowledges her capacity to feel for others and her wish to feel for her father.

The hour continues:

Therapist: *What would it mean if he is dying and you weren't feeling that bad?*
Patient: *I couldn't live with myself. How could I be any kind of daughter and not care that my father was dying?*

Therapist: *What kind of daughter might not care?*

Patient: *The kind of daughter whose father left her when she was 11 years old. I feel like I should just be able to deal with it and get over it and get on with things and accept him but I can't. I don't want him in my life but that's not acceptable to me, so I just beat myself over the head and the more I think about N, the worse I feel. "All energy is being taken up by a stranger" but then I think who's the stranger, N or my father?*

Therapist: *N and your father become one person.*

Patient: *I need to feel loyal to my father but that loyalty is going to someone else, and he's the stranger. But my father should be close and N should be the stranger because he's not blood, not a part of me.*

Reader's Commentary

Does the above reflection address feelings implied in the material? Is it validated? Could it be improved?

Author's Commentary

This reflection misses the point. The patient is not saying that her father and N become one person. She is saying she has feelings for N that she should have for her father. The patient corrects the therapist by clarifying this conflict. But the fact that she feels for N the way she thinks she should feel for her father is implicit in the therapist's statement, so the patient is able to use it. It's not a bad reflection, but it could have been improved.

  Alternative reflection: *"You're able to care and feel loyal to N so you know you can care. But ever since your father left you, your hurt feelings have prevented you from feeling the same for him, even though you wish you did."*

The hour continues:

Therapist: *Who makes those rules about should/shouldn't?*

Patient: *Maybe I make them. In my homeland, my mother said my brother was so wonderful because he stayed near my father. That used to be my role. But now I don't feel loyal and devoted.*

Therapist: *What was it like coming in here and telling me you're not feeling those feelings?*

Patient: *I felt like I was in confession: forgive me, Father, for I have sinned.*

Therapist: *How do you see my reaction?*

Patient: *You seem ok, that who I am doesn't change your feelings. But you don't have to live in here.*

Therapist: *It's very painful for you to feel cut off from your father.*

Patient: *No, it feels painful to be near him.*

Reader's Commentary

Does the above reflection address feelings implied in the material? Is it validated? What is the problem with this reflection?

Author's Commentary

This reflection is not validated and is not based on the patient's last statement. Yet one could see that the reflection was implicit in the previous material. The problem is that the therapist failed to note the complex of feelings which together create the patient's difficulty.

    Alternative reflection: *"I don't have to live with the feeling of having left someone, needing to be forgiven, and not knowing if I will be, yet wanting forgiveness so much."* Notice how different the patient's response was to the next reflection. Also notice how the patient is identified at this moment with her father.

The hour continues:

Therapist: *What I'm hearing is that it's painful to be near him but painful to be cut off because then you feel guilty. You ricochet between the two and both feel bad.*

Patient: *I can't feel good. I try not to think about it but it doesn't always work. I try to ice them off but then I feel guilty. That's where I am with N now. There are two feelings confusing me.*

Reader's Commentary

Does the above reflection address feelings implied in the material? Is it validated? Would you offer a different reflection?

Author's Commentary

This is a better reflection that notes her movement back and forth between several feelings. This helps the patient describe herself in more complex terms with deeper understanding. Clear validation.

The hour continues:

Therapist: *I wonder how that could be ok. I think that when you distance, like with your father, you feel guilty, so you don't allow yourself to stay distanced.*
Patient: *Once you're a bad person, it's over. Once I feel like a bad person, I dissociate myself from them.*

Reader's Commentary

Does the above reflection address feelings implied in the material? Is it validated?

Author's Commentary

There are several problems with this reflection. "I wonder how that could be ok," attempts to reassure the patient but it ignores the fact that the patient does not experience her confusion as ok; it troubles her very much to be confused and in conflict regarding her father. The second sentence, "I think that when you distance . . .," is problematic on a more subtle level. Clearly the patient feels guilt and she distances herself; both the patient and therapist said this already. As a result, this statement is static—it misses the movement implied in the patient's last statement, "there are two feelings confusing me." A dynamic reflection would pick up on the patient's new insight and try to infer what these two feelings were, the feelings that drive her approach and withdrawal pattern.

Alternative reflection: *"A desire to love and be loved, and a fear that if you open yourself to them they will leave you again."*

The hour continues:

Therapist: *Is that what you've been feeling this past week?*
Patient: *I've been feeling that N doesn't deserve someone like me. Although I haven't felt strongly for a long time. I want to tell him. He doesn't deserve someone like me. Everyone has baggage but not like me.*

Write down 3 reflections to this passage now.

Suggested Reflections

Reflection #7A: *"You feel that since you have all this baggage you don't deserve to have someone like N."*

Reflection #7B: *"Sounds like you're afraid you're so bad that it's only a matter of time before he finds out and rejects you. So you'd almost prefer he reject you now and get it over with. Yet the fact that you've waited suggests that you hope there may be another way out of this."*

Reflection #7C: *"I don't know why, but I feel I don't deserve to be loved."* This reflection includes an implicit question to herself that adds the dynamic element.

The hour continues:

Therapist: *You're really starting to beat yourself up. You must be feeling horrible inside to want to verbalize that.*

Patient: *I do. I feel terrible, nervous.*

Therapist: *You sound very alone right now.*

Patient: *I've cut myself off from my father. I have no friends. I know I'm not all alone but it's terrible because the loneliness is all my own doing.*

Therapist: *How did you get there?*

Patient: *I take every comment the wrong way. Usually I take things lightly. I'm sarcastic and sometimes I take others' sarcasm lightly, other times not. I play it over in my head to make it bad for me.*

Therapist: *I'm struck by how different you feel today than last week. Last week you were feeling good about yourself. Wanting to talk to N, see where he stood. Today you hate yourself. What happened in the middle to change that?*

Patient: *Friday N said he'd be in the neighborhood. Didn't say anything about going out and talked on the phone to another woman and made plans to see her. Made me so angry when he was gone and it's been building, things not resolved and he won't talk to me. I'm angry.*

Write down 3 reflections to this passage now.

Suggested Reflections

Reflection #8A: *"You've been angry since he left."*

Reflection #8B: *"He made plans to be with her, not you—and right in front of you to boot!"* This reflection tries to expand her awareness of her anger and the reasons for it.

Reflection #8C: *"How dare he treat me as if I'm his second choice!"*

The hour continues:

Therapist: *Where in the process did you start smoking?*

Patient: *That night at dinner with a friend. I was so maxed out, left without saying goodbye. He's a friend and I was so angry, I didn't say goodbye.*

Therapist: *When did the anger at him Friday turn to self hatred that I see today?*

Patient: *I felt like I hurt him.*

Therapist: *So the anger turned in when you started feeling guilty. Feeling angry at someone you care about is real tough for you.*

Patient: *When I try to resolve it and can't, I can't recuperate. No talking takes place. I called him Friday; he never called back all weekend. I came in today and he ran up to me saying, "I called you last night and there was no answer. Let's get together tonight." I said I'd gone to bed but I was so angry I wanted to punch him. What! He has no idea what I'm going through. I'm hurting myself. He doesn't know. Can't I just tell him telepathically? I can't explain what I've been going through. Then I start feeling good again. But I called Friday and he didn't call back til Sunday. He used to call back in ten seconds. I'm sure he's still pissed. I just want to take a hatchet to his head. . . . The truth of what he feels scares the shit out of me. He used to care but something happened this past month. Now I know he would laugh.*

Reader's Commentary

Does the above reflection address feelings implied in the material? Is it validated?

Author's Commentary

An excellent inference based on the material which is validated by her elaboration of her experience, vividness of language, and deepness of affect.

Write down 3 reflections to this passage now.

Suggested Reflections

> Reflection #9A: *"If you told him how hurt you were when he didn't call back, he would laugh at you."*
>
> Reflection #9B: *"So you're wondering how to tell him what you feel when he doesn't get back to you, especially when these feelings are so powerful."*
>
> Reflection #9C: *"Yet I wish he cared."*

The hour continues:

Therapist: *It sounds like you've become so paralyzed in relation to him, you can't take care of yourself at all.*

Patient: *I'm more worried about how he would feel and having to deal with him. I feel sick that I have those feelings that he'd have to deal with me. My friends are all on me for putting myself down.*

Reader's Commentary

Does the above reflection address feelings implied in the material? Is it validated? What is the problem with this reflection?

Author's Commentary

This reflection is off target, not based on the material. It is also static. The patient corrects her immediately by stating what feelings she is struggling with as if she is inviting the therapist to get back on track. And by alluding to people who "are all on me for putting myself down," she may be saying that she experienced the therapist's reflection as a criticism.

Write down 3 reflections to this passage now.

Suggested Reflections

Reflection #10A: *"You're worried about how he would handle your feelings."*

Reflection #10B: *"It sounds like your fear of how he would respond to your feelings is so strong precisely because you are feeling so tempted to tell him."* This reflection tries to balance her awareness of her fear and her defense of holding back with an awareness of what is implicit, her wish to speak to him.

Reflection #10C: *"If only I didn't fear that my feelings would make him abandon me like my father did."* Or less inferential, *"They just don't understand that I'm afraid he wouldn't be able to handle my feelings about being left behind."*

The hour continues:

Therapist: *What's so comfortable about being in that place that you fall into that place so easily?*

Patient: *I'm all alone. I'm a control freak and that way I can control every-thing because it's in my mind. I've made the night I told N into a fantasy. It didn't happen.*

Write down 3 reflections to this passage now.

Suggested Reflections

Reflection #11A: *"If you can make something into a fantasy, you can control it."*

Reflection #11B: *"If it's a fantasy, his feelings and your feelings go away, but you're left alone."* This reflects her understanding of the defense but shows the price she pays for it.

Reflection #11C: *"I wish."* This underscores the emotional yearning implicit in her wish.

The hour continues:

Therapist: *I think the new place is very frightening.*

Patient: *I'm afraid if it does come out I'll be in the old place but feeling worse.*

Reader's Commentary

Does the above reflection address feelings implied in the material? Is it validated?

Author's Commentary

The reflection is based on the material and appears to be confirmed, but the therapist interrupts her before it is possible to see how much the patient's experience was deepened.

The hour continues:

Therapist: *I don't think so. I think the old place represented your inability to trust what was inside you. There you feel alone, contempt, separated.*

Patient: *I downgrade myself so others don't feel self conscious. I don't see it anymore. I doubt it. I doubt everything.*

Reader's Commentary

Does the above reflection address feelings implied in the material? Is it validated? Would you offer an alternative reflection?

Author's Commentary

This reflection is problematic. The inferences are not all implicit in the material. Furthermore, the therapist makes a static reflection: *"There you feel alone, contempt, separated."* There is no sense of the tension between various feelings.

Write down 3 reflections to this passage now.

Suggested Reflections

Reflection #12A: *"You doubt all your feelings."*

Reflection #12B: *"Maybe doubting your feelings helps you hold back from telling them to N. Yet I sense you wonder sometimes if he could handle more than you've told him."* Notice how pointing out the function of self-doubt gives her a more dynamic view of herself and it also reminds her of her wish to tell him.

Reflection #12C: *"I have to because if I told him one feeling, I'd tell him everything."* This infers the function of self-doubt and her fear of what would happen if she spoke. Adding the possibility of saying only one thing instead of everything may also make if easier for her to break down this problem to a more manageable size.

CHAPTER

Theory of the Analysis of Conflict

What do we mean when we say someone is in conflict? In everyday speech, we'll often refer to someone who is doing something he shouldn't and say, "Well, on the one hand, he wants to quit drugs," for example, "but, on the other hand, he doesn't." We imagine that he has a conflict between doing what he knows he should do and not wanting to do it. Or we imagine that there is no conflict. For instance, "He really doesn't want to stop taking drugs. He just wants to use." When a borderline woman in a drug rehabilitation center punched one of the staff, other staff members concluded that she was simply a nasty, aggressive person who felt no conflict. "What conflict?" they asked. So, in common parlance, laymen think of conflict in terms of a wish to do something and a wish not to do something, or they imagine a person has only a wish to do something without any other conflicting feelings.

When we analyze conflict from a psychodynamic perspective, however, we assume that three groups of feelings are in tension with one another: a wish, a fear, and a defense (Freud 1923; A. Freud 1936). For instance, the patient mentioned above may wish to stop doing drugs, but he may also fear what would happen if he did, so he uses drugs to ward off that fear. We would understand his use of drugs not as his wish but a defense against his wish. His defense was obvious, but not his fear. Hence, our work would focus on trying to understand his fear. If we can understand the fear and analyze it, the need for the defense would decrease. So when we analyze a conflict from a psychodynamic perspective, we are trying to discover what makes a defense necessary. If we analyze the fear properly, the defenses will lessen and the repressed wishes will emerge more strongly, arousing new anxieties for us to interpret.

When analyzing conflict, we try to understand all three aspects of conflict: wish, fear, and defense (Brenner 1976, 1982). If we pay attention only to the defense, we will ignore the patient's wish to stop taking drugs and the anxiety that prevents him from fulfilling that wish (A. Freud 1936; Searl 1936). For example, let's go back to the vignette of the borderline patient. When we look at the entire context of her hitting one of the staff, another view of conflict emerges. The patient, though obstreperous, was beginning to settle in at the rehabilitation center but was terrified of being abandoned again as she had been throughout her life. Interestingly, she wanted to stay at the center but feared she would be told to leave; she hit the staff member to stop her from telling her to leave, but also to provoke the leaving so that it would be under her control.

These vignettes illustrate how understanding conflict allows us to focus our inquiry. For example, the drug abusing patient's defense, drug use, was obvious, but his anxiety wasn't. Hence, the therapist would pursue that in order to understand why the defense was necessary (Freud 1926). With the borderline patient, a clear focus on her fear of being rejected would have lessened her anxiety and brought the defense under her control. Thinking in terms of a wish, fear, and defense allows us to explore the patient's experience by knowing what to look for.

What do we mean by a wish, fear, and defense? A wish refers to anything the patient wants to say, do, or think. This expression of a desire can take many forms (Freud 1900). A patient may describe her mother's domineering behavior during a visit the previous weekend and then mention how she (the patient) is too critical. Her wish is to describe her mother; her defense to criticize herself. Wishes in therapy often take subtle forms such as a wish to say something, describe someone, or think out loud. Sometimes we don't know if something is a wish until we see how that feeling or thought is related to other feelings and thoughts. Sometimes the pattern only becomes clear as the material unfolds. But when a wish is clear to us, we listen, waiting to see what its fate will be.

When the patient shifts away from her wish (such as the patient describing her mother), we infer that a fear is active even if it is unstated. Fear is unfortunatly a vague term, but it is one that is so commonly used that we will use it here too. Fear, in analysis of conflict, refers to any unpleasant thought, feeling, or experience that is aversive (Freud 1923,1926). So the term "fear," as we use it here, can refer to experiences as varied as anxiety, guilt, shame, and disgust. Although we might infer that a patient is experiencing fear, often the patient is not aware of it. We need to pay attention then to any aversive experience the patient reports. To summarize, a wish becomes risky enough that the patient begins to experience a fear that, in turn, causes the patient to engage in a defense.

A defense is not a thing in a patient, but an action, something the patient does (Gray 1995; Schafer 1976). A defense involves a group of feelings, thoughts, or actions that function as a barrier to other feelings, thoughts, or actions (Freud 1915a, 1923, 1926). Remember the patient who was describing her mother as domineering? When she criticizes herself, that thought and feeling about herself has the function of blocking her from describing another group of thoughts and feelings—those she has about her mother (Freud 1917). This defense, like all defenses, is partly conscious and partly unconscious. She is aware of the content of her defense: "I am too critical." She is unaware, however, of the *function* that thought serves: to block her from describing her mother's behavior.

This helps us understand a crucial concept in the analysis of conflict: the difference between content and process. When listening for content, we want to know what a feeling, thought, or experience *is*. When listening for process, we want to know what a feeling, thought, or experience *does*. What is its function? We are aware of our feelings, but we are not usually aware that our feelings are not only how we feel but what we do. A girl whose date shows up late feels angry at him but starts to criticize herself for being impatient. At that moment she feels she really *is* impatient. That is the feeling she is aware of, not her anger at her date. As outsiders, we can see how feeling she is impatient has a defensive function, but she can't. She is only aware of "having a feeling"; we are aware that her feeling is an activity, something her mind does to avoid being aware of other feelings.

☐ Listening for Conflict

So how does one listen from a conflict oriented perspective? There are several ways, but the one we will learn here involves listening to the patient's associations, just as you do when you are reflecting the patient's comments. With a reflective approach you simply summarize what the patient has reported, focusing only on what is in the patient's awareness, or you reflect back implicit feelings. With a focus on analysis of conflict, however, we listen for conflicts that are portrayed in the content of her associations. In reflection, we infer preconscious feelings. When we listen for conflict, we try to infer preconscious and unconscious feelings. In reflection, our inferences are based on whatever we intuit. In analysis of conflict, our inferences are guided and informed in several ways. First of all, we attempt to infer not just one feeling, but three groups of feelings that are active at any time within the patient: the wish, fear, and defense. Further, we try to infer how these three groups of feelings relate to one another. Which one functions as a wish, which one as a fear, and which one as a defense? Now we will study several vignettes to illustrate how to listen for conflict.

Vignette #1

We'll analyze this vignette in order to infer the patient's wish, fear and defense.

Therapist: *It's real hard to see yourself trusting a guy.*

[She distrusts men. Is that a wish, fear, or defense? Probably a wish or a defense. Let's listen further for evidence to refine our understanding.]

Patient: *If a guy really felt that way. L was my first love and I really made him up to be more than he was and that was really bad.*

[If she loves and trusts a man, she fears she could make him up to be more than he is. We can infer that her wish is to trust a man, her fear is that she will make him more than he is, and her defense is to distrust men.]

Therapist: *Why do you think that you made him up to be more than he was, so wonderful, ideal?*

Patient: *I don't know. It was my own fault. My friend K said a lot of things in the beginning like the first time we were together freshman year and he comes to my room and he pours his heart out to me and it's hard to trust him.*

[Now our understanding of her conflict is deepened: she wants to trust but fears she will fall for K as she did for L and something bad will happen as it did before, so she distrusts him to keep that from happening.]

Therapist: *It sounds like it's hard to know what's real and what's not.*

Patient: *I mean I don't know. I've been raised to be a very trusting person* [Wish: I want to trust], *but every time I do it I get stabbed in the back* [Fear]. *It's like a joke, but it really hurts. It makes me want to never trust a guy again* [Defense]. *It's ok for a friendship but not if it's more than that.*

Conflict: a wish to trust K, a fear she will be stabbed in the back, and a defense of not trusting him.

Vignette #2

Therapist: *Does your family not talk about things when things are going wrong?*

Patient: *No, I think that it's completely me. I just didn't want them to know* [Defense]. *I don't know why I didn't.* [I don't know what fear leads me to use this defense.] *I think if I would have told them* [Wish], *it would have made it worse* [Fear]. *Without telling, I thought I could make it go away* [Defense]. *It took coming here to make me realize that that wasn't true. It's not them but me not wanting to deal with it at all.*

You may wonder how I decided that not telling her family was a defense. It is hard to tell initially because our understanding emerges only as a result of understanding the other feelings that are active. Putting those understandings together helps us infer how the different feelings relate to one another. Let's go through the passage again and track the thinking that goes on.

Therapist: *Does your family not talk about things when things are going wrong?*

Patient: *No, I think that it's completely me. I just didn't.want them to know* [Is this a wish ("I don't want them to know") or a defense? Let's see what other feelings emerge and then we'll be in a better position to infer.] *I don't know why I didn't.* [I don't know what anxiety leads me to use that defense.] *I think if I would have told them , it would have made it worse.* [Having asked herself what anxiety leads to defend herself, she then says that she fears things would get worse if she told them. In other words, telling them arouses anxiety. Therefore, telling them is the wish, the fear is of things getting worse, and the defense is not telling them.] *Without telling, I thought I could make it go away* [This statement confirms our inference, since she is describing the defensive functions of not telling: she could make something "go away."] *It took coming here to make me realize that that wasn't true. It's not them but me not wanting to deal with it at all.*

Conflict: a wish to tell her family something, a fear it would make things worse, a defense of not telling them.

Vignette #3

Patient: *I'm jittery as usual today.* [Fear: but what are the wish and defense related to this fear? Let's listen and find out.] *I get that way every time I drive down that road that leads to the main gate.*

Therapist: *I know you are frightened.*

Patient: *But I shouldn't be. I see my neighbor regularly now. She helps my loneliness. I think she helps me most with her understanding. She's very patient with me and she told me it will take time. I do get to feeling lonely and blue, though, in spite of her.*

Therapist: *She'll always be around for you.*

Patient: *Her hours of work change around now and then so I'm not quite sure of her work schedule. I didn't see her for two weeks last month and I missed her, but I didn't tell her* [Defense] *as I felt angry at her* [Fear]. [Her defense is not telling her friend. Her fear is of her anger coming out apparently. From these two parts of the conflict we can infer that the wish is to tell her friend she missed her.]

Each of these conflicts probably seems straightforward now, but simply stating them as we have here might not help the patient. Instead, once we hear a conflict we have to go further. We have to explore parts of that conflict that are unclear (Brenner 1976, 1982). For instance, in the first vignette, how does she idealize men? What is the betrayal she fears? How is it related to her idealization? In the second vignette, how would telling her family make it worse? What is she afraid would happen? What would she want to tell her friend if she felt free to do so? In the third vignette, what feelings did she have about missing her friend? What is she afraid will happen if the friend finds out about her disappointment? Having defined a conflict, we need to go further and explore it to discover why it is so powerful. That is the function of an interpretation.

☐ Interpreting Conflict

How does an interpretation of conflict differ from a reflection?

Example

Patient: *My father told me that daughters only come to their fathers for money. He made me so angry. I really blew up when he said that. But there are all kinds of things you can't talk about in my family. So when you get angry, you get angry about something else that you can talk about. That's the way I am with everyone. I'll be angry about something someone did, but I won't be able to tell them. So later I'll blow up at something else they did.*

Reflection: "*So when you get angry at one person, you blow up at something else instead.*"

Interpretation of Conflict: *"It sounds like when you are angry at someone* [wish] *that you are afraid of what would happen if you let them know* [fear], *so you turn it towards someone or something else instead* [defense]. *What is it you are afraid would happen if you expressed your feelings towards the person who has upset you?"*

In the reflective approach you reflect back to the patient what she has said: her wish (to express anger) and her defense (to blow up at someone else). In the conflict approach you also reflect back her wish and defense (what she has said), but *you would also inquire into what she has not said*: the fear that was motivating the defense. In other words, an interpretation from this model always functions as a focused inquiry into missing pieces of conflict. Our inferences are guided by a search for three types of feelings and their relationships to one another.

As we shift from the reflective approach to the analysis of conflict, our stance shifts. We no longer simply reflect what the patient says, we interpret things that the patient has not said or we make a focused inquiry into something that has not been said. We are paying greater attention to hidden feelings of which the patient is not yet aware.

Focus of the Interpretation

It is never enough to ask the patient what she feels. First of all, if patients knew what their feelings were, they wouldn't need to be in therapy. Secondly, the role of feelings is much more complex than it might seem at first glance. For instance, in the above vignette we have the following conflict:

- wish: to express anger at a father
- fear: some unspecified anxiety over what would happen
- defense: she expresses anger at other people or things

Notice how each aspect of conflict involves feelings! The wish involves expressing anger, as does the defense, and of course anxiety is obvious. So when we focus on the patient's conflicts, we need to think about each of these feelings and the patient's awareness of them. In this example, the patient knows that she was angry at her father and that she expresses it towards others. She knows those feelings and can express them to the therapist relatively well. What stands out by its omission is her anxiety over expressing her anger at her father. So we would explore that. When we analyze conflict, we look for the missing feelings and their function.

However, anxiety is not the only group of feelings we interpret when analyzing conflict. We focus on aspects of conflict that are out of the patient's awareness. Interpretations of conflict can be focused on the wish, the fear, and the defense.

A wish-focused interpretation of conflict:

"It sounds like you were afraid of what would happen [fear] *if you told your father how angry you were* [wish], *so you got angry at someone else* [defense]. *What did you want to tell him* [wish]?" This kind of interpretation encourages the patient to talk about the consciously expressed wish.

An anxiety-focused interpretation of conflict:

"It's clear how angry you were with your father [wish] *and that you turned it onto other people and things* [defense]. *What were you afraid would happen* [fear] *if you expressed your anger to him?"* [wish] Or a different question at the end of the interpretation might be: *"I wonder what you were afraid of* [fear] *that led you to turn your anger away from him and onto others* [defense]?" This interpretation of conflict concludes with a question to the patient to explore the anxiety that is driving the defense.

A defense-focused interpretation of conflict:

"I wonder if blowing up at others [defense] *allows you to express your anger* [wish] *without having to feel the anxiety* [fear] *of telling your father how you feel* [wish]." Or *"Maybe you are so afraid of what would happen* [fear] *if you expressed yourself to your father* [wish], *that you turn your anger onto others instead* [defense]." She knows she blows up. The content of the defense is conscious. That is why the therapist interprets the function of the defense, its purpose, which is unconscious.

These focused interpretations help the patient untangle her web of feelings by focusing her attention on the group of feelings that needs the most attention. Conflict is not simply a defense against feeling. In fact, a defense always involves a group of feelings that wards off another group of feelings. Conflict always involves awareness of some feelings but not others. We need to help the patient find out where to look for her missing feelings. Analysis of conflict helps us figure out where to look.

The Equidistant Stance

You will notice that although we may focus on a single aspect of conflict, we try to keep our interpretations balanced. Anna Freud (1936) first noted the problem of emphasis in interpretations. To illustrate this problem let's go back to the patient who was angry at her tardy boyfriend and began to criticize herself as impatient.

Conflict
- wish: to express anger at boyfriend
- fear: unclear
- defense: of criticizing herself

Her wish to criticize him frightens her and leads her to use a defense. If we interpret only her anger at him *["Sounds like you were angry with him"]*, she will experience us as pushing her to do or feel something dangerous. In response, she will become more anxious and her defenses will become more rigid and primitive. In this case, she would probably become even more self critical.

If we focus only on her fear *["Perhaps you were afraid of what you felt about his lateness"]*, she will feel relief insofar as we aren't stimulating her to feel her anger. But she may also feel stuck and become hopeless as a result. She will agree that she is anxious, bu,t unaware of other feelings she has, she will be left with a static image of herself as simply stuck in her anxiety.

If we focus only on her defense *["You criticized yourself instead of him"]*, she will experience us as criticizing her as if she is a bad patient to criticize herself. This leads to more self criticism such as, "Yes. I know I shouldn't do it. I just can't help it." In other words, a focus on a single group of feelings yields a predictable set of static responses from the patient. For these reasons, complete interpretations of conflict try to address all three groups of feelings and the relationships between them to reflect the dynamic movement of feelings within the patient. We don't try to be the advocate of her desires, her fears, or her defenses. Instead, we adopt a stance that is equally responsive to her desires, fears, and defenses (A. Freud 1936). Each feeling receives equal emphasis. An equidistant interpretation might be, *"It sounds like you were upset with him and wanted to say something, but were afraid of what would happen so you began to criticize yourself instead of him. And although criticizing yourself helped you not criticize him, it still left you feeling upset with his lateness."*

Triangles of Conflict

The triangle of conflict (Malan 1976) involves a wish, fear, and defense. Since conflict occurs in all areas of our lives, we often need to link a conflict in one part of life to conflict in another to see a pattern in the way we struggle with our desires. To do this we interpret the triangle of conflict as it occurs in the patient's relationships: the triangle of person (Malan 1976). By the triangle of person, we refer to relationships in the past, in the present, and with the therapist.

These interpretations fall into three categories: 1) those that link past and present relationships, 2) those that link past relationships with the therapy, and 3) those that link present relationships with the therapy.

> **Interpretation linking conflicts in past and present relationships:**
> *"You mention that you were angry with your father* [wish] *but feared what would happen* [fear] *if you told him* [wish], *so you took it out on someone else* [defense]. *I wonder if that's what happened when you yelled at your roommate just after your boyfriend had cancelled your date."*
>
> **Interpretation linking a conflict in a past relationship with the therapy relationship:**
> *"You mention that you were angry with your father* [wish] *but feared what would happen* [fear] *if you told him* [wish], *so you took it out on someone else* [defense]. *I wonder if that's what happened when you yelled at your roommate just after I told you I would be going on vacation."*
>
> **Interpretation linking a conflict in a present relationship with the therapy relationship:**
> *"It sounds like you were upset when your boyfriend cancelled the date* [wish], *but you were afraid* [fear] *if you told him* [wish] *that he might dump you* [fear], *so you held it back then blew up at your roommate later* [defense]. *I wonder if something similar happened here. Maybe you were also upset when I cancelled our "dates" by announcing my vacation, but didn't want to risk saying so, so you ended up expressing your frustrations to your roommate right after our session."*

Validation of Interpretations

Up to this point, we have studied how to listen to the content of the patient's associations to see how conflict is depicted. Having sorted out feelings and thoughts into the three groups of wish, fear, and defense, we made an interpretation which includes those three elements. Having made our interpretation, we listen to the following associations to find out if it will be confirmed or not. Regardless of how the patient answers your interpretations (Freud 1925), their validity will be proven or disproved by the following comments (Brenner 1976, 1982). We listen for elaboration of the interpretation, greater freedom in describing previously difficult material, greater rapport with the therapist (Greenson 1967), and positive images of people symbolizing your helpfulness (Langs 1973a, 1973b).

Example of a Confirmed Interpretation

Interpretation: *"It's clear how angry you were with your father and that you turned it onto other people and things. What were you afraid would happen if you expressed your anger to him?"*

Patient: *"I guess I was afraid he would use it as evidence that I really didn't like him and that all I really did want was money. Because I really was angry with him and feel I just can't tell him everything I would like to. I tell my uncle and he seems to be able to listen without having to defend my dad and I really appreciate that."*

In this example, the patient elaborates on the anxiety about her anger and is able to talk more freely about it. And she concludes with an image of someone who is able to listen non-defensively. We would regard this image as an unconscious reference to the way she appreciates the therapist's non-judgmental listening style.

Example of a Disconfirmed Interpretation Followed by a Correction

Interpretation: *"It's clear how angry you were with your father and that you turned it onto other people and things. What were you afraid would happen if you expressed your anger to him?"*

Patient: *I wasn't afraid. I just knew it wouldn't do any good. I've confronted him before and it gets nowhere.* [Patient invalidates the therapist's interpretation.]

Therapist: *So actually you stopped yourself because if you went further, you knew you'd reach the limit of what is possible between the two of you.* [Therapist picks up the actual danger.]

Patient: *Yes. It is limited. There's so much he can't talk about.*

Therapist: *And I suppose if you tried to push the limit you'd be reminded of the sadness of what isn't possible with him.* [He infers the fear.]

Patient: *Yes. (tearful) It was so unfair of him to say that all I wanted was his money.* [Patient confirms his inference.]

Therapist: *It hurt. Maybe one reason you stopped yourself from expressing your anger at him wasn't fear of your anger, but fear of the sadness you feel when confronted by his limitations.* [Therapist elaborates his inference of her fear.]

Patient: *That feels right. I could always blow up at him. But I've never let myself cry in front of him.* [Patient confirms the interpretation.]

This vignette illustrates how our attention to the following associations can guide us so that we can become more in tune with the patient.

Example of a Confirmed Interpretation

We noticed above that we must pay attention to the following associations, not just to the initial remarks. Pay close attention to the following interpretation and the patient's response to see how an apparent rejection of an interpretation may in fact turn out to be a confirmation.

Interpretation: *"It's clear how angry you were with your father and that you turned it onto other people and things. What were you afraid would happen if you expressed your anger to him?"*

Patient: *"How many times do I have to tell you I didn't feel anxious. I was angry. God! I feel like you never listen to anything I say! I was angry with him. Angry. Got it? And you can never say anything to him because if you do he'll just blow his cork and let loose. I mean he's even hit me in the past. I remember when I was twelve and I came into the living room with my new dress and he just yelled at me for no reason, hit me, and told me to get the hell out. Nobody tells him nothin'."*

Here we can see that despite her initial disclaimer, she really is terrified of speaking back to her father for fear he may become violent as he has in the past. So the interpretation was correct, but her response indicates that the therapist needs to be careful when addressing her anxiety because it is so powerful and linked to painful memories. She was rejecting not so much the interpretation as the anxiety it reminds her of.

Non-Validated Interpretation

Interpretation: *"It's clear how angry you were with your father and that you turned it onto other people and things. What were you afraid would happen if you expressed your anger to him?"*

Patient: *Hm. I'm not sure where you got that. I mean, yeah, I was angry at my dad but I told him. I don't see where you got that I was afraid to say it to him. Are you saying I should have been more angry? I suppose I could have but, I don't know, it seemed to fit to me at the time. I don't know where to go with that. (Silence.) I was late coming today. I'm sorry. I had to go over an assignment with my professor. He had told us what to do in class, but he was so confusing nobody could understand him. And so I went up to him afterwards to try to clarify just what I was supposed to do. It was weird. I don't think he really understood what I was trying to ask him."*

Her response shows several indications of non-validation: there is no elaboration of any aspect of conflict; there is no deepening of affect; no new insight. Instead of increased clarity of understanding, we see increased confusion. She finally is unable to continue and falls silent. When she resumes she describes an image symbolic of the therapist: someone who is unclear and who does not understand what she is trying to say.

Validation or non-validation of interpretations is always important because the patient's following associations to an interpretation guide our inferences. This principle will become even clearer in later chapters.

Layering of Defenses

We have discussed so far conflicts involving conscious wishes that are depicted in the content of the patient's associations. However, one can also infer unconscious conflicts as well. To illustrate the layering of conflicts, we will return to the wish-focused interpretation we studied earlier.

Interpretation of conflict involving the conscious wish: *"It sounds like you were afraid of what would happen* [fear] *if you told your father how angry you were* [wish], *so you got angry at someone else* [defense]. *What did you want to tell him* [wish]?" This kind of interpretation encourages the patient to talk about the consciously expressed wish. Based on the other material, however, we could infer that her anger at her father, which is her wish at this moment, also functions as a defense against longings for him.

Unconscious conflict
- wish: to express her longing for love
- fear: of his rejection
- defense: anger at father

Pre-Conscious conflict
- wish: to express anger
- fear: of consequences
- defense: express anger at others

Interpretation of conflict involving the unconscious wish: *"I wonder if you were angry with him* [defense] *for not realizing that you come to him not for money but for love, but were afraid* [fear] *to let him know that* [wish], *so you got angry instead* [defense]." This kind of interpretation views the wish to express anger at the father as simultaneously functioning as a defense against a deeper wish.

Psychotherapists have debated the relative merits of these two approaches to conflict analysis. One approach focuses on conflict regarding conscious wishes as it is expressed in the associations and infers relatively little. In contrast, the focus on unconscious conflict relies more on inference and intuition (Reich 1928). However, one way around this apparent conflict is to approach the unconscious conflict by way of the conscious conflict; go from surface to depth (Fenichel 1941; Sterba 1940, 1941, 1953). Interpret the pre-conscious conflict first. Once the patient has understood her anxiety over expressing her anger at her father and can tolerate that wish, then you could shift the focus and interpret how that anger also functions as a defense against her loving wishes towards her father.

Illustration of Layered Defenses

First layer to be analyzed
- defense: expressing anger at others
- fear: of consequences
- conscious wish: to express anger at father

Next layer to be analyzed
- defense: to express anger at father
- fear: he will reject (accept?) her
- unconscious wish: to express longing for father

Notice how the wish on one level of conflict functions as the defense on the next level down. When interpreting conflict sequentially, one might first interpret the first layer as follows: *"It sounds like you wanted to express your anger at your father but were afraid of what would happen so you turned it onto others. What were you afraid would happen?"* As she describes her fear and better tolerates her angry impulses at her father, then it would be more possible for her to tolerate and use an interpretation of more unconscious material. For example, you might proceed to the next level of conflict by saying: *"You mentioned you became angry when he said all you do is come to him for money. I wonder if you wanted to tell him that you come to him for more than that, that you wish he would love you too. But maybe it felt too risky to say that, so you became angry instead to hide your longings."*

A focus on unconscious anxiety might be: *"I wonder if you were afraid that he might find out that you not only were angry with him, but that you also long for his love."*

Now we can look back at the vignette and realize that if we asked the patient to describe her feelings, she could report to us any of the following: a wish to express anger, a wish to tell of her longing for love, a fear of being rejected, anger towards her father, and anger towards others. All those feelings exist at the same time in this patient. That is why we try to analyze conflict so that we can figure out what feelings are the ones with which the patient needs the most help.

It should be clear now that analysis of conflict operates with a model of complex empathy where the therapist empathizes with the patient, not in a global sense, but in a highly focused manner. Through trial identifications with the patient's wish, fear, and defense, the therapist enters into the patient's emotional world. Empathy from this perspective always involves a kind of vicarious introspection into the three groups of feelings (wish, fear, and defense) at both conscious and unconscious levels. Although the therapist tries to interpret conflicts that are near to the patient's conscious experience, the purpose of interpretation is to move towards conflicts which are not yet conscious.

☐ Conclusion

Listening for conflict involves focusing on the content of the patient's associations and sorting out three groups of feelings: wish, fear, and defense. Interpretations focus on implicit feelings that are defended against and the defensive functions of feelings that are unconscious. Through these interpretations, the anxiety is reduced, defenses weaken and the patient's desires enter the room in a less disguised fashion, causing a new round of conflicts. Following the interpretation, we listen for validation based on the subsequent associations that guide us for our next intervention.

Since the purpose of this book is skill building through learning how to listen, the theory section on conflict is kept intentionally brief. To understand better the theory of interpretation of conflict consult the following readings.

☐ Further Readings

In keeping with the emphasis upon practice and the application of theory, the following readings provide examples of analyzing conflict or guidelines for doing so.

Malan, D. (1979). One of the clearest writings in the literature on analysis of conflict. He takes the reader through a sample therapy case illustrating how he would intervene.

Pottash, R. (1957). A classically oriented psychoanalyst provides a transcript of an hour to show how he interprets unconscious conflict. In contrast to the approach used in this book, the author uses a great deal of inference.

Searl, M. (1936). One of the gems of the literature. In plain English, she describes the basic principles for the analysis of conflict and defense.

Strean, H. (1990). An outstanding book that analyzes resistances from the point of view of conflict, providing many examples of an equi-distant approach.

5

CHAPTER

Conflict Studies

"There are many ways and means of practicing psychotherapy. *All that lead to recovery are good.* Our usual word of comfort, which we dispense very liberally to our patients—'Never fear, you will soon be all right again'—corresponds to one of these psychotherapeutic methods; only, now that deeper insight has been won into the neuroses, we are no longer forced to confine ourselves to the word of comfort. We have developed the technique of hypnotic suggestion, and psychotherapy by diversion of attention, by exercise, and by eliciting suitable affects. *I despise none of these methods and would use them all under proper conditions."*
Freud (1904), italics added.

A series of therapy sessions will be presented here. Each is divided into sections where the reader will be asked to identify what conflict is active in that section and to propose possible interpretations. When the phrase [wish, fear, or defense?] appears after a sentence, label the wish, fear or defense depicted in the previous sentence or sentences. When it appears after a therapist's statement, try to figure out what aspect or aspects of conflict the therapist is addressing.

A reminder may be in order here. Remember that these studies are designed to develop your interpretive skills. You will be asked to create many more interpretations in a session than you would ever offer. Numerous examples simply give you more opportunities to learn listening and intervention skills.

Also keep in mind that there are many acceptable ways to phrase your interpretations. Don't worry if your phrasing differs from that used here in the commentary. Just notice whether you are picking up the elements of conflict depicted in the material.

☐ Case #1: Male Patient in the Seventh Month of Treatment

In this portion of a session, we will listen for the parts of conflict as they are depicted in the associations. After outlining the parts of conflict, we will develop an interpretation. In later studies, you will do this yourself.

Patient: *I'm tempted to say, 'how are you* [Wish]?' *But that's not the way we do it in here* [Defense]. *It's kind of like how I am with my students.*

Author's Commentary

The wish is to greet the therapist by saying, "how are you?," and his defense is to refrain from doing so. But his fear is unclear. Although the interaction in psychotherapy and the classroom are different, we still might wonder what inhibits him from greeting the therapist anyway. After all, greeting the therapist would be a way to say what comes to mind. Instead, he blocks himself from doing so.

The hour continues:

Patient: *I've had an interesting week, because I've been reading a novel,* Dr. Jekyll and Mr. Hyde, *and it really resonated with me. It's very psychological.* [Psychological? Is this a hint of conflict between two parts of himself?]

Therapist: *Sounds like it really had an impact on you.*

Patient: *Yeah, and I've been thinking about our last session. And especially this week, how one of my students actually came up to ask questions after class. That felt really good. But overall, some good and some bad things happened this week. And I've been struggling about my religious beliefs. I guess things happen for a reason,* [Wish to express his thoughts about why things happen.] *but here I go again, talking in a tirade.* [Defense. He is criticizing himself for going into a tirade when just a moment before he was talking freely. We continue to wonder what the anxiety is that motivates this defense. We can see that he wants to talk [wish] but apparently there is something he is afraid of [fear] that leads him to hold himself back [defense].]

Therapist: *You're also not looking at me.* [We feel much more in control of our words than our facial habits and pointing them out will make the patient self-conscious and embarrassed rather than self-reflective and curious. If the therapist had to say anything at this moment, it might have been more helpful to say, "Tirade?"]

Patient: *Yeah, I've noticed that. I don't look at you a lot.* [In response to the therapist pointing out only his defense, the patient is unable to elaborate or explore its meanings. This often happens when we focus only on the defense. The patient feels pinned down and criticized, as if he is bad for having defenses. In fact, we always have defenses and always will, long after psychotherapy is completed.]

Therapist: *Yes. I've noticed it periodically.*

Patient: *It makes me uncomfortable and I don't know why. I wasn't uncomfortable with the therapist last year. But I don't really feel comfortable talking to you. Or talking at you, in reality. I know most of the books on your bookshelf by now.* [The patient is describing some discomfort about being with the therapist. We might wonder if this is related to his anxiety about talking freely.]

Therapist: *Yeah, I've noticed that. What makes it uncomfortable for you?* [Therapist inquires into the patient's fear.]

Patient: *I don't know. I guess I look at the person when I feel an emotional connection. When I'm walking around, I'll generally look down. But I don't feel an emotional connection.* [As soon as he says this, notice how quickly he wards it off.] *Look, this is making me uncomfortable* [This is his fear.], *how we talk about our relationship* [This apparently is what stimulates the fear, so we would infer that it is the wish: the wish to describe how he feels about the therapist—"I don't feel an emotional connection."]. *I have trouble with that. I want to treat you well. I don't want to be rude.* [Now the conflict is becoming clearer. He wants to say what he feels, but fears he will be thought of as rude for what he says.] *It's good manners and polite to look at people. I don't know what it is about you. It's probably not something wrong with you.* [Now he downplays the therapist's lack of emotional connection, what he has been trying to say. This suggests that he is engaging in a defense. The conflict now looks like: wish—"I want to say I have no emotional connection with you"; fear—"You will think I am rude"; defense—"So I deny that there is anything wrong with you."] *You look at me and I'm the patient. But it's like you're trying to figure me out. You're very attentive. But I'm always aware of you looking at me.* [Now he seems to be elaborating on his fear: a sense of the therapist as perhaps too attentive, always staring at him.]

Therapist: *You're aware that I'm looking at you. What's that feel like for you?* [The therapist inquires into the patient's fear.]

Patient: *At times, somewhat uncomfortable. It would bother me more if you were looking out the window.* [Notice how this inquiry into the patient's fear does not facilitate the patient but leads him to shut down. Simply telling a patient he is anxious when he already knows this is not helpful. He just becomes more anxious. He needs to know what makes him anxious [wish] and how he handles his anxiety [defense].]

Therapist: *What's it like for you in other relationships? Do you seldom have eye contact?* [The therapist redirects the patient away from his anxiety in the therapy to anxiety in other relationships. The therapist, by doing this, inadvertently provides the patient with a defense of displacement that allows him to describe his anxiety more safely.]

Patient: *Well, it depends on who it is. I'm more uncomfortable talking to women. The setting has something to do with it. With my male friends, I have some eye contact, but not a lot.*

Therapist: *I'm wondering how you consider our relationship in here.*

Patient: *Well, it's not really a friendship. It really allows me a lot of liberties. To be selfish, really. I can talk here about anything I want, and that allows me to be selfish. I never hear what bothers you.* [He fears that if he gives in to his wish to say what comes to mind, he might be considered selfish. This elaborates his anxiety of being thought of as rude.]

Therapist: *So it's slated in your mind as a time for you. A time for you to be selfish.* [Therapist underlines the patient's anxiety.]

Patient: *Yeah. I don't need to be thinking about anybody else in here. Don't have to give any attention if I don't want to. And nothing will be said. Until today, I guess.* [The reference "until today" suggests that the therapist's comment about his not looking at the therapist may have felt like criticism, an instance of not giving attention to the therapist, of his selfishness. This would illustrate how the patient experienced a comment that only addressed the defense as a criticism.] *Ideally, you come up with ideas, and suggestions. If you're just here to listen, then I could be talking to a wall. As your patient, you offer me ideas and suggestions. Is that a relationship? Yes, it is, but. . .*

The wish remains the same: to say what comes to mind. The fear, though, is getting elaborated. At first he says he feels uncomfortable; then, that he fears being rude; then, that the therapist is scrutinizing him; and now, he fears being considered selfish. As we listen, let's see what more we can learn about his anxiety so we will understand what motivates his defenses.

The hour continues:

Therapist: *Yeah, we began to talk about some of this last semester, how in some respects the work we do isn't really about giving suggestions, or advice.*

Patient: *Well, I just assumed that in the rule book of psychotherapy, that's what you do. I guess that's a stereotype, but I know you just can't tell me what to do. I need to figure out things for myself. But sometimes, I wish for concrete suggestions! I suppose I could ask you. Do you have any ideas about something? For example, we know I have problems with my self-esteem. I could ask you, 'what can I do to change that?'* [Notice how he returns to the first conflict of the session: "Is it acceptable for me to say something to you, like greet you?" He seems to wonder if he is selfish if he asks such questions here, as if he is breaking rules in the rule book of psychotherapy.] *It gets back to what we were talking about last week. Is this about understanding things, or about doing something?*

Therapist: *I think we talked some about part of therapy being about the relationship between us. I know that really made an impact on you when we spoke about it last semester, but we really haven't revisited it since.*

Patient: *I don't know. I'm just uncomfortable with you* [Fear]. *I wish you could just say what I think* [defense] *. . . so I don't have to worry about if you're offended* [Fear]. *You're a human being, but somehow you're an exception* [After having raised the possibility that the therapist could be offended, he instead defends against this by suggesting the therapist might be an exception, someone who would not feel offended]. *I'm more or less rude to you. But maybe it's just when we talk about our relationship. Maybe you're just a man, an authority figure, or something. But you're unemotional* [Defense]. *I don't know really what I want. The other side of it is that you can't be my friend because we only see each other once a week* [Perhaps there is a wish that he could say whatever came to mind and the therapist could be a friend, or at least friendly.] *That's not enough time. And it's horrifying, all you know about me is bad stuff. All you're seeing is my Mr. Hyde* [Fear].

Now his fear emerges more clearly. If he speaks freely, the therapist will see only his rude, selfish Mr. Hyde. No wonder he didn't feel free to greet the therapist at the beginning of the session. To greet the therapist would reveal his selfish Mr. Hyde. Hence, he has to soften his statements so they don't seem rude and he has to deny that there is anything wrong with the therapist since this would also be revealing the rude part of him. And if these defenses fail, he can imagine that there is no emotional connection because then his Mr. Hyde cannot hurt or offend the therapist.

Let's review how the patient's preconscious feelings of anxiety emerged so we can recognize when they can be interpreted:

Emergence of His Anxiety Out of Repression

1. "Look this is making me *uncomfortable,* how we talk about our relationship."
2. "I don't want to be *rude.*"
3. "It's like you're trying to figure me out."
4. "It really allows me . . . to be *selfish.*"
5. ". . . what *bothers you.*"
6. ". . . *if you're offended.*"
7. "*all you know about me is bad stuff.*"
8. ". . . *all you're seeing is my Mr. Hyde.*"

The previous statements illustrate the increasing strength of his anxiety as his fantasy about the therapist becomes increasingly specific. His fear of the therapist figuring him out becomes his fear that the therapist will see his Mr. Hyde. His fear of appearing rude or selfish evolves into a fear of offending the therapist. The fear becomes specific and his fantasy about the therapist becomes explicit so they can be interpreted. The therapist tries to discern this specific anxiety so it can be interpreted. When it does not come out spontaneously, the therapist makes comments that help the patient observe and describe his anxiety.

Formulating the Interpretation

Throughout this session, we were listening to find out what anxiety was preventing this patient from speaking more freely. Simply pointing out that he was anxious would not have helped. We had to understand why he was anxious: he was afraid of how the therapist would react if he spoke freely. With the emergence of this fantasy we can now interpret.

Up to this point there have been no interpretations. We knew he wanted to express himself and that he held himself back, but we didn't know why he was anxious. So we waited for it to get elaborated so we could interpret the entire conflict of wish, fear, and defense. In terms of timing, we might interpret now because his anxiety has been elaborated and because he is blocked.

Possible interpretation of conflict: *"Perhaps that's what makes it uncomfortable to talk here. You're afraid if you speak freely* [wish] *that all I will see is the selfish, rude Mr. Hyde part of you and I won't see the Dr. Jekyll part of you* [Fear]. *And maybe that fear leads you to hold yourself back when you're tempted to be more assertive* [Defense]."

Interpretations of conflict do not have to include all three parts of conflict. Often therapists will break down an interpretation into parts and offer it bit by bit. For instance, the therapist might offer the first two sentences of the interpretation above to address the wish and fear. Then, if the patient confirms that part, interpret the defense with the third sentence. Notice that the interpretation begins with what is in the patient's awareness: the wish to speak and the anxiety which he just described. The interpretation moves from there to infer something that is implicit, the defense. This is an example of interpreting from surface to depth: starting with what the patient is aware of and then inferring something that is just beneath the surface.

Another principle of analysis of conflict is to address conflict regarding what is stated. This patient is in conflict over something as minimally assertive as greeting the therapist. We could infer that the patient has aggressive, critical, hostile feelings about the therapist and that he wants to reveal his Mr. Hyde. This may be true. However, even if it is true, he is not aware of wanting to be Mr. Hyde. He is afraid he will appear to be a Mr. Hyde. That is where we start. As we interpret his conflicts over expressing his thoughts in this session, he will become freer to express other thoughts. And eventually there may be quite aggressive thoughts that emerge in the session when the wish to be Mr. Hyde will be apparent to him. Then we can begin to interpret that conflict.

☐ Case #2: A Female Patient at Her Tenth Session

The following is the tenth session of a depressed female patient (Shave 1968:126–133). The therapist missed the session two weeks previously.

Patient: *I'm jittery as usual today* [Wish, fear or defense?]. *I get that way every time I drive down that road that leads to the main gate.*

Therapist: *I know you are frightened.* [Wish, fear or defense?]

Patient: *But I shouldn't be. I see my neighbor regularly now. She helps my loneliness. I think she helps me most with her understanding. She's very patient with me and she told me it will take time. I do get to feeling lonely and blue, though, in spite of her.*

Therapist: *She'll always be around for you.*

Patient: *Her hours of work change around now and then so I'm not quite sure of her work schedule. I didn't see her for two weeks last month and I missed her, but I didn't tell her* [Wish, fear or defense?] *as I felt angry at her* [Wish, fear, or defense?].

Write down the wish, fear, and defense.

Author's Commentary

The wish is to tell her friend that she missed her, her fear appears to be that her anger might come out, and her defense was not to tell her friend that she was lonely. No interpretation would be necessary because she is describing her conflict clearly. Since she has mentioned her anger, we would wait to see what she does. Will she continue to describe her anger or will she become anxious and begin to defend against it in the session? Unfortunately, the therapist intervenes before we could learn from the patient what it is like for her to feel anger.

You may have written down that expressing her anger was the patient's wish. This may well be true on an unconscious level, but we don't have any evidence that this was a conscious wish for her. Since she was aware that she was unable to tell her friend that she missed her, we would focus on this conflict first. If she is afraid her anger would come out, she will become anxious if we tell her she wants it to come out because she will feel we are trying to make her do something she is afraid of. We need to help her with conflicts over expressing mild thoughts (such as missing her friend) before she will be able to tolerate and explore more dangerous feelings.

The hour continues:

Therapist: *We'll go on very regularly.*
Patient: *I sure would hate to feel like I used to. It's that awful fear of being alone* [Wish, fear, or defense?]. *That's why I go and visit this neighbor so much.*
Patient: *It keeps my mind off my loneliness when Bill is away. I don't know why I have this loneliness—other housewives don't have it. And Bill is the best husband a woman could hope for. He never seems nervous or afraid. That fear shouldn't be with me if I only knew of a way to get it out. I wish I could get those feelings out* [Wish, fear, or defense?]. *Dr. H told me once that I was hostile deep down within me* [Wish, fear, or defense?], *but I don't think I'm hostile at all* [Wish, fear, or defense?]. *I'm not hostile when I talk to you.*

What was her conflict with Dr. H? Write down the patient's wish, fear, and defense, and give your interpretation.

Author's Commentary

Therapist: *We'll go on very regularly.*
Patient: *I sure would hate to feel like I used to. It's that awful fear of being alone* [fear]. *That's why I go and visit this neighbor so much.*

Patient: *It keeps my mind off my loneliness when Bill is away. I don't know why I have this loneliness—other housewives don't have it. And Bill is the best husband a woman could hope for. He never seems nervous or afraid. That fear shouldn't be with me if I only knew of a way to get it out. I wish I could get those feelings out* [wish]. *Dr. H told me once that I was hostile deep down within me* [fear: perhaps that this doctor will judge her as hostile too if she lets out her feelings.], *but I don't think I'm hostile at all* [defense]. *I'm not hostile when I talk to you.*

Her conflict in the past was a wish to get her feelings out, a fear that Dr. H would criticize her (which he did) as hostile, and a defense of denying that she could have hostile feelings.

Possible interpretation that links her conflict with her friend to the one with Dr. H: *"Maybe with Dr. H and your friend you just wanted to get your feelings out* [wish], *but were afraid they would judge you* [fear] *rather than understand your anxiety and loneliness. I wonder if you held back those feelings with your friend* [defense] *so she wouldn't judge you too."*

Possible interpretation that focuses on her anxiety: *"No. But it sounds like you might be afraid I would think so, like Dr. H did."*

The hour continues:

Therapist: *We can handle it.* (There is knocking at the door.)

Patient: *Is there someone at the door?*

Therapist: *It's okay. You're more important.*

Patient: *Tuesday evening Bill has to bowl, and last time I asked to go along with him* [Wish, fear, or defense?] *as I didn't want to stay home but I think I hurt him* [Wish, fear, or defense?]—*that's his night out. His chance to get away from me for a while. It hurts me* [Wish, fear, or defense?] *to know I wouldn't let him go alone. I think of things that might happen to him when he's away from home. I worry that he might be hurt in some way or that some thing could happen to him because of me* [Wish, fear, or defense?].

What are the wish, fear, and defense in the conflict which she expresses in this passage?

Author's Commentary

Therapist: *We can handle it.* (There is knocking at the door.)

Patient: *Is there someone at the door?*

Therapist: *It's okay. You're more important.*

Patient: *Tuesday evening Bill has to bowl, and last time I asked to go along with him* [wish] *as I didn't want to stay home but I think I hurt him* [fear]—

that's his night out. His chance to get away from me for a while. It hurts me [defense] *to know I wouldn't let him go alone. I think of things that might happen to him when he's away from home. I worry that he might be hurt in some way or that some thing could happen to him because of me.*

She asked her husband to take her along but fears by doing so she has hurt him, so she turns that experience on herself and feels hurt. That is, she identifies with the person she feels she has hurt. Her wish and fear is conscious, but her defense is not. She is aware of the content of the defense, that she feels hurt, but she is not conscious of its function. Although we know what her fear is, we don't know what her fantasy is of how she would be hurting him by wanting to be with him. No interpretation would be offered yet. You may have written that her wish was to hurt her husband since he did not take her out. This would be related to anger at her friend who also left her. If true, however, it is unconscious. Hence, the unconscious wish would be to hurt him, the fear is of being judged and perhaps abandoned, and the defenses are denial of her hostility and turning of anger on herself [feeling hurt] to control her angry impulses. This conflict, though plausible, is still unconscious and not yet interpretable. Yet it helps us understand why she has trouble saying what she feels to her friend, Dr. H., and to the therapist.

Conflict #1: wish to get feelings out [conscious], fear of being judged as hostile [preconscious], defense of keeping silent [conscious], denying anger, and feeling hurt [content conscious; function unconscious]

Conflict #2: wish to hurt others out of anger [unconscious], fear of being judged [conscious], defenses of turning anger on self and denial of hostility [content conscious; function unconscious]

The hour continues:

Patient: *Some people think that I am looking better. Maybe I do on the outside, but it's on the inside that really hurts. I think a lot about religion; it seems all mixed up to me. God gave me a mind and a body for good things, yet I think such awful thoughts.* [She grimaces, breaks down, and then cries for several minutes.]

Therapist: *I understand.*

Patient: *It says in the Bible, "Fear not for God is with you," but I can't "fear not." Therefore, He's not with me* [Wish, fear, or defense?].

Therapist: *You aren't alone now.*

Patient: *They say the Devil tempts a person. I wonder if that's what is happening now. God doesn't help a person—he has to be able to help himself. God helps those that help themselves and I just can't seem to do it.* [She cries.] *I don't have normal fear. It used to be unbearable but it doesn't seem to bother me so much now. It's still there, though—I fear its being there. I fear fear itself and what it can do to me. It is like I told Sandra, I don't feel I'm a good Christian. I don't feel good in God's sight. It's as if I've committed some unforgivable sin.* [Wish, fear, or defense?]

If the fear outlined here is linked to her previous conflicts with her friend, Dr. H, and her husband, how might we understand her conflict about telling them what she feels?

Write down the patient's wish, fear, and defense, and give your interpretation.

Author's Commentary

Patient: *Some people think that I am looking better. Maybe I do on the outside, but it's on the inside that really hurts. I think a lot about religion; it seems all mixed up to me. God gave me a mind and a body for good things, yet I think such awful thoughts.* [She grimaces, breaks down, and then cries for several minutes.]

Therapist: *I understand.*

Patient: *It says in the Bible, "Fear not for God is with you," but I can't "fear not." Therefore, He's not with me* [fear].

Therapist: *You aren't alone now.*

Patient: *They say the Devil tempts a person. I wonder if that's what is happening now.* [Perhaps a reference to the therapist who is tempting her to say terrible things.] *God doesn't help a person—he has to be able to help himself. God helps those that help themselves and I just can't seem to do it.* [She cries.] *I don't have normal fear. It used to be unbearable but it doesn't seem to bother me so much now. It's still there, though—I fear its being there. I fear fear itself and what it can do to me. It is like I told Sandra, I don't feel I'm a good Christian. I don't feel good in God's sight. It's as if I've committed some unforgivable sin.* [fear]

She wants to say what comes to mind [wish], but fears she will reveal awful thoughts, thereby committing an unforgivable sin [fear]. Fearing she has already committed this sin, and fearing God's judgement, she judges herself first [defense] in order to keep herself from saying more.

Interpretation of conflict with friend and husband: "*Maybe that's why* *it was so hard to say what you felt to your friend and your husband. Maybe you're afraid that in saying what you want [wish], these awful thoughts will come out. And fearing that they would not be able to forgive you [fear], you judge yourself to help keep those thoughts inside you, unspoken [defense]."*

Interpretation of conflict in the therapy: *"Maybe you're even afraid of that here. You're trying so hard to say what comes to mind [wish], but it sounds like you're afraid that by talking freely you will be giving in to temptation and committing a sin that even God could not forgive [fear]. So maybe you're feeling torn here between your wish to speak up and your temptation to be silent [defense]."*

The hour continues:

Therapist: *God can accept you just the way you are.*

Patient: *Yes, but people don't go around thinking they might hurt someone or even kill them. It seems as though I'm fighting the feeling of hurting someone; that I might lose control and hurt someone I love and need* [Wish, fear, or defense?]. *Does that make sense? Do you know what I mean?* [In other words, do you understand how anxious I am about what I might say and do?]

Write down the patient's wish, fear, and defense, and give your interpretation.

Author's Commentary

The wish is to speak, the fear is if she voices her wishes she might act on them and hurt someone, and the defense is to criticize herself and keep silent.

Possible interpretation of conflict: *"You wonder if I realize how scared you are that if you say what you feel [wish] that you might lose control and hurt someone [fear]. Maybe that's why you fight your thoughts [defense]; you're not sure what else to do to keep them from becoming actions."*

The hour continues:

Therapist: *I understand.*

Patient: *It frightens me. Sitting here, I get very anxious that the fear will come back to me* [Wish, fear, or defense?].

Therapist: *I can accept your feelings.*

Patient: *I can't accept them.* [Wish, fear, or defense?]

Therapist: *We'll go on together.*

Patient: *Sometimes I think I don't want to go on* [Wish, fear, or defense?].

Yet I don't know why. I have everything a woman could want. I pray every day I won't be afraid. I pray that nothing can take me from Bill and the children [Wish, fear, or defense?]. [Here she breaks down and cries for several minutes. She then blows her nose, recovers, and smiles warmly.] *I feel as though I could throw things at times. That I could smash up things if I let myself go* [Wish, fear, or defense?]. *I rebel against these feelings and have to fight myself to keep control* [Wish, fear, or defense?].

Outline the conflict in terms of a wish, fear, and defense.

Author's Commentary

Therapist: *I understand.*

Patient: *It frightens me. Sitting here, I get very anxious that the fear will come back to me* [fear].

Therapist: *I can accept your feelings.*

Patient: *I can't accept them* [defense].

Therapist: *We'll go on together.*

Patient: *Sometimes I think I don't want to go on* [defense]. *Yet I don't know why. I have everything a woman could want. I pray every day I won't be afraid. I pray that nothing can take me from Bill and the children* [fear]. [Here she breaks down and cries for several minutes. She then blows her nose, recovers, and smiles warmly.] *I feel as though I could throw things at times. That I could smash up things if I let myself go* [wish]. *I rebel against these feelings and have to fight myself to keep control* [defense].

Her wish is to describe her feelings, her fear is that she would act on them, and her defense is to fight to keep control over talking about her feelings.

The hour continues:

Therapist: *It's okay to have feelings.*

Patient: *I pray that if I ever do anything like that I do it here and not at home.*

Therapist: *We can handle it.*

Patient: *I don't know why I have to be so afraid* [Wish, fear, or defense?]. *I feel as though I have to punish myself* [Wish, fear, or defense?].

Author's Commentary

Her wish is to talk about her feelings, her fear is that she might act on them, so her defense is to punish herself for even having the feelings so that she won't act on them.

The hour continues:

Therapist: *You don't seem bad.*

Patient: *Then why do I feel the way I do?*

Therapist: [Gestures.]

Patient: *I don't want my life to end.*

Therapist: *We have a way to go together.*

Patient: *I know, but I don't want to keep coming back here to this place all my life.* [Wish, fear, or defense?]

Therapist: *You're stuck with me.*

[The patient laughs and then smiles warmly.]

Patient: *It's like when I was working here as a patient, I wanted to work* [Wish, fear, or defense?] *but it frightened me* [Wish, fear, or defense?] *and didn't want to work at the same time* [Wish, fear, or defense?].

Write down the patient's wish, fear, and defense when she worked as a patient and offer an interpretation. How do these relate to the therapy in the present?

Author's Commentary

Therapist: *You don't seem bad.* [The therapist denies her feelings rather than explore them.]

Patient: *Then why do I feel the way I do?* [The patient invites the therapist to interpret her conflict.]

Therapist: [Gestures.]

Patient: *I don't want my life to end.* ["I need to find a way to express myself without feeling I have to punish myself."]

Therapist: *We have a way to go together.*

Patient: *I know, but I don't want to keep coming back here to this place all my life.* [I am stuck with this defense and fear and I want to be able to move beyond them.]

Therapist: *You're stuck with me.*

[The patient laughs and then smiles warmly.]

Patient: *It's like when I was working here as a patient, I wanted to work* [wish] *but it frightened me* [fear] *and didn't want to work at the same time* [defense].

She wanted to work [wish], but some [fear] made her not want to work [defense].

Interpretation of conflict in the past: "*You wanted to work* [wish] *but there was something you were afraid of* [fear] *that made you hold back from working* [defense]."

If we translate that conflict from the past into the present, she wants to work in therapy. We would infer that she fears once her feelings come out she will act on them. Although she is afraid to come to the same place and be stuck again, being stuck also prevents her thoughts from turning into actions. So her defense is not to work on revealing her feelings.

Interpretation of conflict in the present: "*Maybe this is like when you worked here as a patient. Here you want to work and talk about your feelings* [wish] *but it sounds like you are afraid we might get stuck* [fear] *so you feel hesitant to say those feelings* [defense]."

The complexity that analysis of conflict provides can add to our understanding of the patient's feelings.

Conflict #1: wish to speak, fear of getting stuck [conscious], defense of holding back thoughts

Conflict #2: wish to speak, fear of feelings coming out, defense of being stuck [preconscious],

Conflict #3: wish to be stuck [unconscious], fear of being judged, defense of judging herself as bad

Notice how feeling stuck has at least three possible meanings, all true, and all existing at the same time. This is what is meant by multi-determination: a symptom or feeling may have several meanings and functions simultaneously. These meanings can be categorized according to the degree of her awareness of them. She is conscious of her fear of being stuck. She is conscious that she is afraid of her feelings coming out. Thus, she might be able to entertain the idea that being stuck functions as a defense. That may be pre-conscious. Having interpreted the first conflict, we might be able to interpret how getting stuck helps her restrain dangerous feelings. And finally, her wish to be stuck is completely out of her awareness because it is presented as something she is afraid of, not as something she desires. But given the conflicts as they are presented, we could infer that this is a possible unconscious wish. We would not interpret it, however, until we had first interpreted the conscious and preconscious meanings of being stuck. Then, what is currently unconscious would come to the surface on its own, we would see if our inference was correct, and we would interpret the conflicts it evokes.

You may have observed that the patient is also stuck because the therapist is unable to explore her feelings. Although true, I will defer discussion of these implications to later chapters.

The hour continues:

Therapist: *I understand*

Patient: *I rebel against my own mind* [Wish, fear, or defense?]—*against breaking things, or hurting people, and against harsh feelings* [Wish, fear, or defense?]. *Does that mean I feel that way deep down? Am I really that way* [Wish, fear, or defense?]? *Am I actually hostile?*

Write down the patient's wish, fear, and defense. Would you interpret now? If so, what would you say? If not, why not?

Author's Commentary

She wants to understand why she wants to break things and hurt people but fears that this would mean that she is hostile, so she asks the therapist questions, asking, in effect, for help to ward off the dangerous implications of her thoughts.

It may be best to be silent at this point in order to see what she does with these frightening thoughts she is entertaining. Can she tolerate the possibility that she may have hostile thoughts and explore it, or will she move away? If she moves away, we can describe her conflict about thinking and talking.

You may have decided to interpret anyway. Let's look at a couple of possible interventions and reflect on their strengths and weaknesses.

Interpretation of conflict focusing on the fear: *"As soon as you talk about these feelings of wanting to break things and hurt people* [wish] *you become afraid* [fear]. *So you find yourself wondering whether it means you're hostile* [defense] *or if there's more to it than just that. You wonder where this might lead."*

This interpretation focuses on her fear of what meaning will emerge and does not infer any preconscious feelings. The problem is that it forecloses the opportunity to learn from the patient what her conflict might be at this moment; that is, where will she go now having raised the issue of hostility?

Interpretation of conflict focusing on the defense: *"If I did think you were hostile, perhaps my judgment would help you rebel against these thoughts and keep them from turning into actions."*

This interpretation aims at the function of her defense. It is unlikely, however, that she would be able to use this interpretation. Although she knows she is afraid of being judged, she is unaware that her fear might function as a defense. This interpretation focuses on something out of her awareness which she could agree to only on blind faith, not on the basis of her own observation.

These two interpretations illustrate different focuses of surface and depth. The first interpretation infers no preconscious feelings, but through an open statement invites the patient to describe her fear. The second interpretation infers an unconscious wish to be judged.

Conflict: wish to speak about hostility [conscious], fear of being judged [preconscious], defense of inviting therapist to judge her [unconscious]

Dosage in Interpretation

Interpretations raise the issue of dosage. How much of the wish do we bring up for the patient? The language we use and the balance of defense, fear, and wish in the interpretation allow us to titrate the dosage of uncomfortable feelings and thoughts. Although it would be best not to interpret at this point in the hour, let's look at possible interpretations of the wish to illustrate the concept of dosage.

The patient described some violent fantasies she had and concluded by asking the therapist, "Am I actually hostile?" The following interpretations of her hostility are listed in order of increasing dosage.

1. *"Or am I someone who* struggles [defense] *with hostile feelings* [wish] *that* frighten [fear] *me?"* These words distance the patient from the hostility, perhaps making it more possible to tolerate looking at it. In addition, by portraying her as struggling with hostile feelings rather than being hostile, the therapist is countering the patient's possible assumption that he thinks she is hostile (Havens 1986).
2. *"Sounds like you're afraid* [fear] *you* could be [wish] *if you didn't rebel against your mind* [defense]." The patient is still described as rebeling against her hostility, but posing the possibility of being hostile could increase the dosage.
3. *"Or am I someone who* struggles with a wish *to be hostile that frightens me?"* She is portrayed as struggling but with her wish to be hostile, not something alien to her.
4. *"Sounds like you're afraid* [fear] *that you* are (hostile) [wish]. And to show your love you rebel against your mind* [defense] *so nobody gets hurt* [fear]." Here she is hostile; hostility is not simply an abstract wish she struggles with. To increase the dosage, we shift the emphasis from the defense and fear to the wish. We also reduce the distance between the patient and her wish. We can judge what dosage is useful for the patient by using the language she uses. Since her word choice reflects the compromise between her wish to reveal dangerous feelings and the fear of doing so, her words show what dosage she can tolerate.

For instance, she becomes anxious when she uses the word "hostility." Although we can infer from her fantasies that she has violent urges, we would not refer to them yet but instead focus on her conflict over simply entertaining the possibility that she is hostile. Further, her question suggests that she is afraid of the answer. A reflective question may meet her best since she is not ready for an answer but seems to be teetering between wanting to know and being afraid of knowing. Hence, if we were to interpret, we might consider the first interpretation which is in question form, reflecting her state of struggle.

Beginning therapists often make the mistake of using the word that made the patient shut down. For example, "It sounds like you're afraid you might be hostile." The word, feeling, and idea of hostility is the dangerous wish that stimulates her anxiety and defense. If we use the words that made her resort to a defense, we will stimulate more anxiety and another defense. The patient will be unable to elaborate or will fall silent. We run the risk of becoming Mr. Id, someone who is pushing the patient to say dangerous things. Instead, refer to all the parts of the conflict if you can. And rather than repeat the dangerous idea, understate it in abstract terms (Gray 1995), thereby creating the space for her to think about it. Rather than use the word "hostility," you might say, "It sounds like you're afraid of what it means when your imagination goes off in these directions." This might seem hopelessly limp in contrast to the "real" interpretations listed above. However, patients' capacity for tolerating their wishes and fantasies and their capacities for self regulation vary enormously. As a result, tremendous flexibility and creativity may be required when we interpret. We need to pay close attention to what dosage works at this moment for this patient.

Let the patient's words guide your dosage. If you overstate what the patient said, you may get a lot of affect but you will bypass her defenses and leave her anxiety unaddressed—for instance, "In fact you know you feel hostile and want revenge; that's what frightens you." You may get a response of denial, of intense anxiety, or even a tentative acknowledgment of her hostility (perhaps submitting to the therapist). But she won't gain any insight into what is so dangerous about her hostility, nor into her defenses against it.

The hour continues:

Therapist: *I find you're quite acceptable.*
Patient: *But I can't. I never could watch mysteries on TV before, but you know, this past week I actually watched a couple. I wasn't completely relaxed. It takes time, Bill says.*

Empathy from the Perspective of Analysis of Conflict

The therapist's attempt to reassure the patient is an empathic error. The patient does not find herself acceptable. The fact that the therapist finds her acceptable is fine. We hope he does! But he is distancing himself from her. He is refusing to enter into her experience of herself. When we listen for conflict empathically we identify with the patient's wish, fear, and defense (Racker 1968). By saying that he finds her acceptable, the therapist fails to identify with someone who does not find herself acceptable. Even though not accepting herself is a defense, he must try to identify with that aspect of her. This doesn't mean that he should not accept her either. It means he needs to feel his way into her feelings, to imagine why it makes sense for her not to accept herself, what it is like for her to inhabit such a world. Ironically, we demonstrate our acceptance of a patient, by our ability to identify with and embrace all the seemingly unacceptable parts of the patient even when that takes the form of identifying with someone who cannot accept herself!

This passage illustrates the complexity of empathy from the perspective of analysis of conflict. The therapist in this model of listening identifies with her refusal to accept herself, with her fear of judgement, and with her hostility as well. By identifying with each aspect of the patient the therapist is able to speak from within her experience. In this vignette, the therapist needed to ask himself, "If I were my patient, what would it be like to feel hostility? What would it be like if I wanted to break things and lose control of myself?" This would be a trial identification with her wish. "What would it be like to live with the fear of hurting people every time I had a feeling or thought?" This would be a trial identification with her fear. "Why would I be unable to accept my hostility? What would it mean to me?" This would be a trial identification with her defense.

Through this trial identification (Fliess 1942) with her wish, fear, and defense, the therapist might be able to form a silent trial reflection of her conflict within himself: "I can't accept [defense] my hostility [wish], because if I do, I might act on it, and hurt someone [fear]. Every word, every thought I have brings me closer to losing control of myself and hurting someone I love. Please stop me before I go too far!" With this intuitive grasp of her conflict, the therapist can then offer responses that will be experience-near (Kohut 1971) and that capture the *subtle, dynamic quality of her emotional movement.*

The hour continues:

Therapist: *It takes time.*

Patient: *Is it normal to feel resentful about someone you love?*

Therapist: [Gestures]

Patient: *I feel resentful toward God for taking mother from me* [Wish, fear, or defense?]. *But then perhaps He does do things in ways we don't understand* [Wish, fear, or defense?].

Write down the patient's wish, fear, and defense, and give your interpretation.

Author's Commentary

Her wish is to express her feelings of resentment toward God, her fear is unclear—perhaps of judgement, and her defense is to use rationalization: "Perhaps He does do things in ways we don't understand."

Interpretation of conflict: *"You know you love God and you also know you resent him for taking away your mother* [wish to express this]. *Is there a fear people would judge you as not normal* [fear] *if they knew you feel both ways about Him?"*

Notice that she is defending against not just her resentment, but against her experience of resenting someone she loves. To state it otherwise would miss the complexity of feelings she is struggling to understand.

The hour continues:

Therapist: *He understands.*

Patient: *Just like the other day, I went to a store I usually avoid because it has so many people in it. I usually go to the one where there aren't many people, but last week I went to the store with the people and it didn't bother me any more than the other store. I felt so ridiculous and so dumb and stupid for having had those feelings about the store. I'm 30 years old. I act like a 1-year-old baby and it makes me feel so childish—I feel as though I'm depending on my family. It makes me feel as though I'm just not right.*

Therapist: *I understand how you feel at times.*

Patient: *I get the feeling that I could just scream to the top of my lungs at times* [Wish, fear, or defense?].

Therapist: [Gestures]

Patient: *Yet, I shouldn't have those feelings. I shouldn't lose control of my emotions* [Wish, fear, or defense?].

Write down the patient's wish, fear, and defense, and give your interpretation.

Author's Commentary

Therapist: *I understand how you feel at times.*

Patient: *I get the feeling that I could just scream to the top of my lungs at times* [Wish].

Therapist: [Gestures]

Patient: *Yet, I shouldn't have those feelings. I shouldn't lose control of my emotions* [Defense].

Her wish is to talk about the feeling that she could scream, her fear is that by expressing her feelings she could lose control of herself, and her defense is to say she shouldn't have such feelings.

Interpretation of conflict: *"It's a terrible struggle. There is so much you want to say but you're afraid that if you start to talk* [wish] *you'll lose control and start to scream* [fear]. *So you feel as if you need to avoid even having those feelings at all* [defense]. *You are wondering how to have feelings and say them without losing control."*

The hour continues:

Therapist: *You're safe here.*

Patient: *I have to hurry and shop as quickly as possible; yet I don't know why I have to hurry. There's nothing to hurry about.* [She is pensive for several moments, then looks up and smiles warmly.] *I'm going to a coffee tomorrow morning. I'm a bit leery of that. It's not the lady that I'm afraid of. I afraid I'll get nervous there, and just lose control of myself* [Wish, fear, or defense?]. *What I want most of all is to have somebody with me all the time that understands* [Wish, fear, or defense?].

Therapist: *I know what you mean.*

Patient: *But it's not right.*

Therapist: *It's okay with me.*

Patient: *Yes, you said that before. I'm just expressing my feelings.*

Therapist: *That's all right.*

Patient: *Monday is my best day. It's because Bill has been with me all day Sunday. If I didn't have him, I'd end up here as a patient again.*

Therapist: *I understand.*

Patient: *Like that article I read in the paper on how to treat a patient who returns from a mental hospital. It said you had to determine if he's violent— that scares me. I'm afraid I could be violent. Like Dr. H said to me, if I started throwing things I wouldn't be able to stop throwing them* [Wish, fear, or defense?].

Therapist: *You couldn't hurt me.*

[Patient laughs.]

Patient: *I don't want to—in fact I'd rather be dead than do that* [Wish, fear, or defense?]. [She becomes anxious.] *Sometimes I feel as though I don't have any place to turn* [Wish, fear, or defense?].

Write down the patient's wish, fear, and defense, and give your interpretation.

Author's Commentary

Therapist: *You're safe here.*

Patient: *I have to hurry and shop as quickly as possible; yet I don't know why I have to hurry. There's nothing to hurry about.* [She is pensive for several moments, then looks up and smiles warmly.] *I'm going to a coffee tomorrow morning. I'm a bit leery of that. It's not the lady that I'm afraid of. I afraid I'll get nervous there, and just lose control of myself* [fear]. *What I want most of all is to have somebody with me all the time that understands.*

Therapist: *I know what you mean.*

Patient: *But it's not right.*

Therapist: *It's okay with me.*

Patient: *Yes, you said that before. I'm just expressing my feelings.*

Therapist: *That's all right.*

Patient: *Monday is my best day. It's because Bill has been with me all day Sunday. If I didn't have him, I'd end up here as a patient again.*

Therapist: *I understand.*

Patient: *Like that article I read in the paper on how to treat a patient who returns from a mental hospital. It said you had to determine if he's violent—that scares me. I'm afraid I could be violent. Like Dr. H said to me, if I started throwing things I wouldn't be able to stop throwing them* [Fear: she is elaborating the fear of losing control and being unable to stop.].

Therapist: *You couldn't hurt me.*

[Patient laughs.]

Patient: *I don't want to—in fact I'd rather be dead than do that* [Defense]. [She becomes anxious.] *Sometimes I feel as though I don't have any place to turn* [Fear].

She elaborates on the theme of wanting to talk to someone but fearing she will lose control of herself. Notice how this vignette describes the same previous conflict with the therapist but now displaced onto her friend. Since the therapist did not offer an interpretation that would have helped the patient with her anxiety earlier in the session, the patient used a defense of displacement to manage her anxiety. Hence, we might interpret conflict within the relationship with the friend.

Conflict #1: wish to talk [conscious], fear of losing control of herself [fantasy partly conscious], defense of wishing self dead so others would not be hurt [content conscious; function unconscious]

Conflict #2: wish to lose control of herself [unconscious], fear of hurting therapist [preconscious], defense of wishing self dead, turning of aggression onto herself [content conscious; function unconscious]

Her wish is to say what comes to mind, her fear is that she would begin to act on her violent impulses and be unable to stop, and her defense is to wish she was dead.

Interpretation of conflict: *"It sounds like you are afraid [fear] that if you give voice to your violent thoughts [wish] that you would start acting on them and be unable to stop yourself [fear]. When you feel that, you feel you have no place to turn [fear] but to wish you were dead. Perhaps, because if you were dead, you couldn't act on those thoughts; nobody would be hurt [defense]."*

The hour continues:

Therapist: *You're perfectly safe here.*

Patient: *You know when I had those feelings that I was going to faint if I looked up in the air.*

Therapist: *Yes.*

Patient: *I don't have them anymore. Those feelings that I had of myself fainting are gone.*

Therapist: [Gestures]

Patient: *Do you remember Mary?*

Therapist: [Gestures]

Patient: *I got a letter from her and she's doing real well. She said my mother was my biggest comfort. The neighbors thought I'd go to pieces when she died, but I didn't.*

Therapist: *Mary is doing all right.*

Patient: *I surprised them. It's this rebellion inside of me. I'm rebelling deep down inside of me about something.*

Therapist: *Let's continue the same time next Monday.*

Patient: *Okay and thank you, doctor.*

Evolution of the Conflict

Having gone through the entire session, let's review the portrayal of her conflicts to see the evolution in the hour. [n.b. we will review only conflicts involving a conscious wish.]

Conflict #1:   wish to tell her friend she missed her, fear? unclear, defense of not telling her friend

Conflict #2:   wish to get her feelings out, fear she will be thought of as hostile, defense of inviting therapist to call her hostile

Conflict #3:   wish to tell husband she wanted to go out with him, fear this would hurt him, defense of feeling hurt: "it hurts me"

Conflict #4:   wish to tell husband she wanted to go out with him, fear this would hurt him, defense of turning that experience on herself and feeling hurt [helps her restrain herself from expressing the wish]

Conflict #5:   wish to speak, fear she will lose control of herself and hurt someone she loves and needs, defense not portrayed in content

Conflict #6:   wish to speak, fear her feelings will turn into actions, defense of controlling her speech

Conflict #7:   wish to speak, fear her feelings will turn into actions, defense of punishing herself so she won't have feelings

Conflict #8:   wish to speak, fear she will remain stuck in self punishment, defense of asking the therapist to speak instead

Conflict #9:   wish to speak, fear she would be judged as hostile, defense of inviting therapist to judge her

Conflict #10:   wish to express resentment and love for God, fear of being judged, defense of asking therapist to judge her

Conflict #11:   wish to talk about feeling she could scream, fear feeling would become an action, defense of saying she shouldn't have feelings

Conflict #12:   wish to speak, fear of losing control/being unable to stop/ hurting someone, defense of wishing herself dead

Notice how each vignette, regardless of the person, place, or time described illustrates the same conflict. By listening for the depiction of conflict, we learn with each successive vignette new details of the wish, fear, and defense that allow us to make fuller interpretations. Each one presents pieces of the puzzle that develop into a picture as the hour unfolds. As this pattern becomes clearer, we better understand conflicts that earlier in the hour were unclear. For instance, notice examples where the fear, unclear in one vignette, becomes obvious several vignettes later. Now we will review the evolution of the wish, fear, and defense, so you can perceive this process of unfolding.

Emergence of the Wish

The depiction of the wish evolved as follows:

- to tell friend she missed her
- to get her feelings out
- to tell her husband she wanted to go out with him
- to describe feelings of wanting to break things, hurt people
- to say she resents and loves God
- to say she wants to scream

The patient's aggressive feelings become increasingly obvious to us. Yet, although the content is conscious in the last three wishes, the person for whom they are intended is unconscious. She resents and loves God, but is unable to make that connection to her husband or friend, people with whom she probably has had the same conflict. Hence, her feelings toward them could emerge because they were displaced onto God. The wish becomes increasingly aggressive during the session. Her wish to scream, preconscious at the beginning, is conscious at the end.

Emergence of the Fear

The depiction of the fear evolved as follows:

- at first unclear
- of being judged hostile
- of hurting her husband
- of committing an unforgivable sin
- of losing control and hurting someone she loves and needs
- of feelings becoming actions
- of remaining stuck in self punishment

The patient's fear, initially vague, evolves into a fear of being judged for a wish to lose control of herself and hurt someone. The fears allow us to infer unconscious wishes as well.

Emergence of the Defense

The depiction of the defense evolved as follows:

- not telling her friend what she thinks
- inviting the therapist to judge her

- of feeling hurt; turning aggression onto herself
- punishing herself
- wishing herself dead

The function of only the first defense is conscious. The patient is aware of the content but not the function of the following defenses. This also clarifies what we interpret in defenses. The content of a defense is usually conscious, e.g., wishing herself dead. What is not conscious, and what we interpret, is the function that thought and feeling serve: to restrain herself from voicing her aggressive thoughts.

As the depiction of the wish becomes clearer and more aggressive, her fear increases as well as the severity of the defense. The last four defenses increase in severity: "hurt me", "I hurt myself", "I must punish myself," "I wish I were dead."

☐ Case #3: A Patient in the Sixth Month of Therapy

Patient: *I don't know if this is good or not. Well . . . Friday night . . . we all went to a party, and then all went to a bar, and I didn't go, and L came back and came into my room. My roommate and I were in bed, he just came into my room. I kept hinting for him to leave but he wouldn't. Then a few more guys came in and they were drunk and he comes up my ladder and talking to me and touching my leg. I was just "no": giving him big signals. When they came in he said, "what's my odds." For him to do that in front of me! They said five to one against you. I just jumped down and went out of my room and went to talk to his roommate. When L came in he said "stay" and it was . . . I said "no" and it was great, like I had no feelings, like I didn't even really want to be with him at all* [Wish, fear, or defense?]. *I was so excited. I never said "no" to him before.*

Therapist: *What was it like this time to be different?*

Patient: *It was nice but I kind of felt bad for him* [Wish, fear, or defense?]. *Like there are certain people you can always talk into doing things, like you make nice. But I just said goodnight. The next day he wouldn't talk to me, like he got the hint. Then on Valentine's day, they're laughing at him and saying he wants to ask me out. Well I was sitting with K, watching him play Nintendo. Well last semester K and I had a bet that if I didn't have a date all semester he'd have to take me to [a restaurant]. Well I didn't, and he had to take me. Everyone knew about it and it was funny. Well on Valentine's day, L said to me, "why don't you go to the E party with me and let K get his free meal at [the restaurant]" and I said no. And he said, "Don't you want to let K get his free meal?" and I said, "No, I don't want to go out with you."*

Therapist: *That sounds like a real different place for you.*

Patient: *Yeah, it was weird. He walked out and he was mad and I followed him out because it was mean to say in front of others and I said, "Look. I really don't want to go out with you." He said, "Why?" I said, "This may sound really mean but you're probably one of the last people I'd want to spend Valentine's day with."* [Wish, fear, or defense?] *It was nice but I felt bad* [Wish, fear, or defense?] *because I'm not a person who would want to hurt him in any way* [Wish, fear, or defense?].

Based on this material, what are the wish, fear, and defense? What are possible interpretations?

Author's Commentary

Patient: *I don't know if this is good or not. . . . When L came in he said "stay" and it was . . . I said "no" and it was great, like I had no feelings, like I didn't even really want to be with him at all* [This expresses her wish to say no to L.]. *I was so excited. I never said "no" to him before.*

Therapist: *What was it like this time to be different?*

Patient: *It was nice but I kind of felt bad for him* [This may be unclear to you now, but the later material reveals that this is a defense.]. *. . . And he said, "Don't you want to let K get his free meal?" and I said, "No, I don't want to go out with you."*

Therapist: *That sounds like a real different place for you.*

Patient: *Yeah, it was weird. He walked out and he was mad and I followed him out because it was mean to say in front of others and I said, "Look. I really don't want to go out with you." He said, "Why?" I said, "This may sound really mean but you're probably one of the last people I'd want to spend Valentine's day with."* [This is an expression of her wish to say no. Now observe what happens.] *It was nice but I felt bad* [This is her defense against saying no which is stimulated by the fear which she states next.] *because I'm not a person who would want to hurt him in any way* [This is what she fears happens if she says no.].

Conflict: a wish to tell L that she did not want to go out with him; a fear that she might hurt him and be thought of as mean; and a defense of feeling bad about herself as a hurtful person. She knew she wanted to tell him no and did not want to hurt him. She is not aware, however, that feeling bad has a defensive function.

Possible interpretation of conflict: *"I wonder if fearing that you might have hurt him [fear] interfered with your feeling good about having said no*

[wish]." Or, "*It sounds like as soon as you sensed that he felt bad when you said no, that you started to feel bad too* [defense]. *It's as if there was some danger* [fear] *if you felt good when he felt bad* [wish]."

Possible reflections: "*You wish you could say what you want without hurting someone.*" This statement would infer her wish. Or, "*You just wanted to say no, not to hurt him.*" This would reflect her wish but would not explore her fear. Or, "*You wanted to say no but felt bad that he might be hurt.*" This statement would reflect her wish, defense, and fear, but it would not infer the relationships between these three feelings. For example, feeling bad is not explored as a defense against a wish. Reflection tends to explore implicit feelings without interpreting how they are structured, i.e., their relationships to each other.

In contrast, analysis of conflict guides and structures our inferences. When analyzing a problem, the therapist tries to infer three groups of feelings and how they relate to one another. In this example, the therapist would focus on understanding more fully the patient's wish to say no, her fear of doing so, and her defenses against asserting herself. At this point, the patient is aware of her wish to say no and her anxiety, but is unaware of the defensive function of feeling bad. This illustrates how reflections infer preconscious feelings that the therapist intuits, whereas analysis of conflict makes us look for three different feelings (wish, fear, and defense). These feelings may be preconscious or unconscious. And, if unconscious, the therapist focuses on the preconscious feelings first *and waits for unconscious feelings to emerge later.*

Now on to the unconscious conflict. Given how rude and exasperating this boy was, the patient could well have felt angry and resentful with him. So she may have wanted to hurt him by telling him he was one of the last people she would want to go out with. If so, then we might infer that she felt guilty because rejecting him felt good. Her fear was that she would be judged by others as mean, and her defense was to judge herself.

Notice how these two conflicts are layered:

Conflict #1: wish to say no[conscious], fear of hurting him[conscious], defense of feeling bad [function unconscious]

Conflict #2: wish to hurt him[unconscious], fear of being judged [conscious], defense of feeling bad, hurt [function unconscious]

She is aware of conflict number one, including feeling bad. Feeling bad is conscious, its *function* is not conscious. In conflict number two, she is unaware of the wish. But even so, if we are aware of this wish, we gain a deeper understanding of her conflict. Her wish to say no is doubly conflictual because it symbolizes the wish to hurt him. This is important because frequently a patient will present a problem that seems obvious. For example, "Why can't she say 'no'? After all, it's no big deal. She has a right to assert herself." Absolutely correct. Therefore, her inability to say no should lead us to wonder what that wish symbolizes, what other feelings are implicit. If her wish to say no also symbolizes a wish to hurt him then her guilt becomes more understandable.

The fear in the first conflict is also a wish in the second conflict. This is an example of a concept you may have read about: a conscious fear is often also an unconscious wish. The feeling that someone might be hurt has two functions at the same time. This illustrates the complexity of conflict.

These two levels of conflict also illustrate a principle of timing for interpretations. In general, interpret conscious and preconscious feelings before proceeding to unconscious conflict. It is easy to infer the patient's anger at this obnoxious boy. However, if she is afraid to say no because he could get hurt, she will be unable to entertain the possibility that she wanted to hurt him.

The hour continues:

Therapist: *What kind of person is that?*

Patient: *When you say "no." I don't know.* [laughed] *I usually just go with the flow.* [Wish, fear, or defense?]

Therapist: *When you think of someone "like that" who doesn't go with the flow, what is that person like?* [Wish, fear, or defense?]

Patient: *I don't know. Not that it's bad.* [Patient is unable to elaborate and instead minimizes the judgement.]

Therapist: *Maybe part of you does think it's bad.*

Patient: *Yeah. Well, yes I do. I know what you're getting at. It's not that it's bad but I'm not a person who causes problems. Any added tension I avoid. It's my personality.* [Wish, fear, or defense?]

Note the wish, fear, and defense that are illustrated in this passage.

Author's Commentary

The patient is beginning to describe her defense more fully. The wish is to say no, the fear is that she will cause problems and additional tension, and the defense is to avoid conflict by "going with the flow." At the same time, the therapist's comments are not as facilitative as they might be. Rather than describe the patient's conflict she pushes for the patient's anxiety. In response, the patient is unable to elaborate much; neither her feeling nor her understanding deepens. She merely becomes more anxious. This illustrates two principles when listening for conflict: 1) listen to the patient's responses to see if your comments are helpful, and 2) if a patient is unable to respond to your focus, change and broaden it.

Static, non-dynamic comments state only one part of a conflict, failing to capture the movement and tension between different feelings. For instance, here are three static comments that would be unhelpful because they focus on only one feeling:

- Static comment on her defense: "You go with the flow."
- Static comment on her fear: "You're afraid of the tension."
- Static comment on her wish: "You didn't want to go out with him."

Each of these statements is true but useless for the patient. She already knows that she has each of these feelings. But she does not know how they are *related* to each other. She knows the *content* of each of these feeling states, but she does not know or understand their *function*. She knows she has each of these feelings, but she does not perceive how she *moves* from one feeling to another and why. In this sense, the psychodynamic listener does not think of a patient as having a feeling, but as moving from one feeling to another, or feeling torn between urges to move in contradictory directions.

A comment that explores her conflict between several feelings would be more dynamic than the therapist's static comments.

Possible interpretation of conflict: *"So although sometimes you want to say "no" [wish], you're afraid that this might cause tension [fear]. So you say "yes" and go with the flow [defense]. But then this "no" is still rattling around inside you."*

This kind of interpretation illustrates the principle of reflecting the dynamic movement of conflict. It tries to capture the tension between wanting, fear, not wanting, and yet still wanting.

The hour continues:

Therapist: *Has it always been that way for you?*

Patient: *Yeah, definitely. I'd know that someone would want to do something and I wouldn't but I'd do it for that person* [Wish, fear or defense?]. *But finally I was saying "NO, I DON'T WANT TO!"* [Wish, fear, or defense?]

Therapist: *Where do you think that you learned to go along?*

Patient: *I guess, I don't know. My mom's totally not like that. She's a real dominating person. She's a real control freak.*

Therapist: *You were in reaction to her.*

Patient: *I guess my dad is accommodating. I have a car. My dad really wanted a truck* [wish, fear, or defense?] *and it was his turn (they take turns), but she was really complaining* [wish, fear, or defense?] *so they bought what she wanted* [wish, fear, or defense?]. *She doesn't threaten but you get that sense you do whatever she wants* [wish, fear, or defense?]. *She's not horrible or anything.*

Write down the patient's wish, fear, and defense, and give your interpretation of the conflict in the past.

Author's Commentary

Therapist: *Has it always been that way for you?*

Patient: *Yeah, definitely. I'd know that someone would want to do something and I wouldn't but I'd do it for that person* [Defense]. *But finally I was saying "NO, I DON'T WANT TO!"* [Wish].

Therapist: *Where do you think that you learned to go along?*

Patient: *I guess, I don't know. My mom's totally not like that. She's a real dominating person. She's a real control freak.*

Therapist: *You were in reaction to her.*

Patient: *I guess my dad is accommodating. I have a car. My dad really wanted a truck* [Wish] *and it was his turn (they take turns), but she was really complaining* [Fear] *so they bought what she wanted* [Defense]. *She doesn't threaten but you get that sense you do whatever she wants* [Defense]. *She's not horrible or anything.*

Earlier she outlined her conflict about saying no to the boy. Now she describes the same conflict she and her father had when saying no to her mother. Her father wanted to buy a truck but apparently feared what would happen if he persisted with his desire in the face of the mother's anger, so he went with the flow and got a car instead.

Possible interpretation of conflict in the past: *"So it sounds like he wanted to buy a truck* [Wish], *but gave in to her and went with the flow* [Defense] *to end the tension with her. I wonder what he might have been afraid of if that tension had persisted* [Fear]?"

Exploring a conflict in the past allows us to gain more information about her conflicts in the present so we can link this conflict with her mother to her current conflict with L. With the appearance of the last sentence, the patient reveals another conflict: the wish to describe her mother, an unspecified fear, and a defense of downplaying the severity of the mother's behavior.

The hour continues:

Therapist: *What was it like growing up with that kind of person as your mother?*

Patient: *I was terrified.* [Wish, fear, or defense?] *A lot of other things. She's a lot better than when I was young.* [Wish, fear, or defense?] *She's great with my sister.*

Therapist: *What was she like for you when you were young?*

Patient: *She was very tough. She hit maybe too much* [Wish, fear, or defense?]. *Her parents were really bad. She doesn't even speak to them. I would never hit a kid because of how my mom was.*

Therapist: *How badly did she hit you?*

Patient: *Not like I did things to warrant being hit, but she didn't know when to stop. My father had to intervene and tell her to stop.*

Therapist: *Did she ever beat you up pretty badly?*

Patient: *Not that I ever had scars. It was more like yelling would have been enough. She's not evil but she didn't realize that just talking to me or hitting me once was enough but she didn't realize it. I don't know if I'm making sense. She wanted to make sure I got the point; but I did the first time. She couldn't differentiate how much was required. She had her own problems. She was abused. Not that it gives her the right.*

Write down the patient's wish, fear, and defense, and give your interpretation of the past conflict with her mother. How does it relate to the patient's current conflict?

Author's Commentary

In the three previous vignettes, she has described her conflict about saying no, how this is related to her father's conflict with her mother, and her fear of being hit by her mother in the past. We can infer that she wanted to say no to her mother, feared she would be hit, so she went along with the flow, like her father.

Possible interpretation of conflict in the past: *"Perhaps when you disagreed with your mother as a little girl* [wish], *you were afraid of getting hit* [fear], *so to avoid the risk of saying no and upsetting her, you kept quiet like your dad* [defense]."

Since she is still unaware of the defensive function of feeling bad and of her wish to hurt L, it is not yet possible to interpret these feelings. At a later stage in therapy, however, when she is aware of a wish to hurt him, one might be able to provide **a possible interpretation (in**

the future) of the defensive function of her identification with her mother: *"It sounds like you were afraid you would get hit* [fear] *if you said no* [wish]*, so you would go along with your mother so she wouldn't get upset and hurt you. I wonder if that was part of what happened with L. Maybe you were afraid if your saying no hurt him, that you would be acting like your mother who hurt you* [fear] *and that image holds you back* [defense] *from saying no* [wish] *when you need to."*

We can infer a bit more about her unconscious conflict that we described earlier:

Conflict #1: wish to say no, fear of hurting L [like mother hurt her and father], defense of feeling bad

Conflict #2: wish to hurt L [like mother hurt her and father], fear of being judged as mean [like her mother], defense of judging self [perhaps as she judged her mother]

Based on the conflicts she described just above, her fear of hurting him and her wish to hurt him may be related to an identification with her mother. It's as if she says to herself, "I'm afraid that if I assert myself and someone gets hurt, then I am like my mother, someone who does not give in and who in fact wants to hurt people." Why is there an identification with her mother just now?

She just began to describe her mother as a domineering, physically abusive person. In the previous section when she began to criticize her mother, she was in conflict. She immediately softened her criticism or denied its importance by focusing on how wonderful her mother is now. Hence, we might infer another conflict at a deeper level.

Conflict #3: wish to criticize mother in session as a hurtful person, fear that is unspecified, defense of criticizing self as hurtful

Her capacity to empathize with her mother may serve a defensive function. She stops criticizing her mother by identifying with her.

The hour continues:

Therapist: *It made it feel normal to her.*

Patient: *Yes, and she finally realized. When I was twelve she hit me really hard and I never said anything. Then one day she hit my sister and I thought she was hitting her too much that if she didn't stop, I'd call my father. And that was the last time she ever hit anyone. I think she realized then it was wrong. We've never talked about it, but my dad and I talked. She's so much more calm. She's a different person.*

Therapist: *Did she seem out of control?*

Patient: *Yes, definitely. Sometimes when she hit me I don't think she even knew she was.*

Therapist: *That must have been so frightening for you.* [Therapist explores wish, fear, or defense?]

Patient: *I was terrified of my mother* [wish, fear or defense?]. *I'd drop a book and my papers would fall out and I'd look to see if she'd get mad.*

Therapist: *You'd always have to watch her.*

Patient: *Now recently my dad and I were talking about how much better she is.*

Therapist: *What was it like for you to share that with your dad?*

Patient: *It was good. When she'd hit me she'd say bad things and it would hurt and I'd go into my room and my dad would come in and make it better and convince me to go out and make up.*

Therapist: *It's tough when parents are like that because they're the most important people in the world when you're little.*

Patient: *My father was hit too, but he completely turned the other way.* [Wish, fear, or defense?] *She didn't. She never realized until I confronted her.*

Therapist: *How was that for you to confront her like that?*

Patient: *After I ran into my bedroom crying, I thought she wouldn't speak to me* [wish, fear, or defense?]. *She was the total authority figure.*

Therapist: *I wonder if at that moment you were afraid it would be a permanent rupture.* [Therapist addresses wish, fear, or defense?]

Patient: *I thought she'd never speak to me again* [wish, fear, or defense?]. *But since I was thirteen, we've gotten along great. I have a new mom* [wish, fear, or defense?]. *I didn't want you to think she hit me all the time, just every four months* [wish, fear, or defense?].

Therapist: *What would it mean if I pictured her worse?* [Therapist addresses wish, fear, or defense?]

Patient: *I say those things* [wish, fear, or defense?] *and I don't want you to think they are horrible people* [wish, fear, or defense?].

What is her conflict at this very moment? Write down the patient's wish, fear, and defense.

Author's Commentary

Therapist: *That must have been so frightening for you* [Fear].

Patient: *I was terrified of my mother* [Fear]. *I'd drop a book and my papers would fall out and I'd look to see if she'd get mad.*

Therapist: *You'd always have to watch her.*

Patient: *Now recently my dad and I were talking about how much better she is.*

Therapist: *What was it like for you to share that with your dad?*

Patient: *It was good. When she'd hit me, she'd say bad things and it would hurt and I'd go into my room and my dad would come in and make it better and convince me to go out and make up.*

Therapist: *It's tough when parents are like that because they're the most important people in the world when you're little.*

Patient: *My father was hit too, but he completely turned the other way.* [This was his defense.] *She didn't. She never realized until I confronted her.*

Therapist: *How was that for you to confront her like that?*

Patient: *After I ran into my bedroom crying, I thought she wouldn't speak to me* [Fear]. *She was the total authority figure.*

Therapist: *I wonder if at that moment, you were afraid it would be a permanent rupture.* [Therapist addresses fear.]

Patient: *I thought she'd never speak to me again* [Fear].

She describes her conflict in the past: a wish to confront her mother, a fear her mother would never speak to her again, and a defense of running away and staying in her room. Revealing this conflict, she becomes anxious and uses another defense.

Patient: *But since I was thirteen, we've gotten along great. I have a new mom* [Defense: she shifts to good experiences in the present, moving away from bad memories in the past.]. *I didn't want you to think she hit me all the time, just every four months* [Defense].

Therapist: *What would it mean if I pictured her worse?* [Therapist addresses fear.]

Patient: *I say those things* [Wish] *and I don't want you to think they are horrible people* [Fear].

This new conflict involves a wish to describe her parents, a fear the therapist would think they were horrible, and a defense of describing them as good in the present rather than bad in the past.

Possible interpretation of conflict: *"So when you talk about them in the past* [wish], *you're afraid I might think they were like that all the time* [fear]. *I wonder if describing how good they are today helps you feel less anxious than when you describe how they were in the past* [defense]."

This kind of interpretation focuses her attention on her defense: the function served by talking about her parents' good points. Or we might address her conflict in another way. Insofar as she fears the therapist would think such thoughts about her parents, this may be the patient's projection. Rather than wonder with her if she has such thoughts (which would just be ping-pong, batting the projection back at her), we might invite her to speculate on such thoughts in us.

Possible interpretation of conflict without interpreting the defense of projection: *"That I might want to understand them* [wish] *but feeling confused with the complexity* [fear], *I might just label them as horrible to avoid facing that complexity* [defense]." Or, *"What might make it difficult for me to see their good qualities?"* This would be an indirect reference to the patient's fear of what she would feel if she faced her parents' flaws.

When analyzing this vignette you may have inferred that the patient wants the therapist to think her parents were horrible. If so, this wish is unconscious. The patient is aware only of her fear. So let's pause for a moment and infer two conflicts active at this moment in the session:

Conflict #1: wish to describe parents [conscious], fear therapist would think they were horrible [conscious], defense of focusing on present good qualities and denying the importance of past bad memories [function unconscious]

Conflict #2: wish therapist would think her parents were horrible [unconscious], fear of some judgement [preconscious], defense of reaction formation and denial (now my parents are great), focus on the present and ignore mother's past actions; identification with mother [content is conscious; function is unconscious]

We would focus on conflict #1 first because the wish is conscious, as well as the fear. By helping her deal with her conflict over describing her parents and understanding her defense against that, we would be prepared to hear what wishes and fears she will become aware of next. If our inference of her unconscious feelings is correct, they will come up after our interpretations of the first conflict.

The hour continues:

Therapist: *What if they are or were?* [Is the therapist addressing her wish, fear, or defense?]

Patient: *It would change my image of them. If you could tell that someone's bad, what does that say about you?* [Wish, fear, or defense?]

Therapist: *I think you can tell. I think sometimes it's hard to just say it out loud.*

Patient: *Yeah. I don't know.*

Therapist: *Do you feel like you're being disloyal?* [Is the therapist addressing her wish, fear, or defense?]

Patient: *Yes. I don't want to say bad things about her* [Wish, fear or defense?]. *She's incredible now. I'm not afraid anymore.*

Therapist: *How long did it take for that to disappear?*

Patient: *Through high school. We talk now. It's really nice. It's great to see her.* [Described an incident where mother did not get angry at her sister.] *And I thought, 'aren't you supposed to get angry, aren't you supposed to hit her?" I was happy.*

Therapist: *Part of you felt glad for your sister but part of you felt that you had to get through it when she didn't.* [Wish, fear, or defense?]

Patient: *Yes and I felt really bad for feeling that.* [Wish, fear, or defense?]

What might have been the patient's conflict during this incident? Write down the patient't wish, fear, and defense now.

Therapist: *It's pretty natural what you thought. You don't have to beat yourself up for it.*

Patient: *That's when I realized she really changed.*

Therapist: *It sounds like you had a lot of really tough years.*

Patient: *Oh, I don't know. She had her good days too. She was great at other times. And I learned to stay out of her way.* [Describes telling her father for the first time of the beatings and realizing how much it affected him because she never said anything to him before.]

Therapist: *Why do you think you never talked to your dad about it?*

Patient: *I don't know. Mom never dealt with her parents. Cut off all contact with them. She didn't deal with them. Wouldn't feel comfortable talking about things. She deals with the feelings by pushing them away* [Describes mother in terms of wish, fear, or defense?].

Therapist: *Which is exactly what you tried to do* [Therapist addresses wish, fear, or defense?].

Patient: *Which is exactly what I tried to do. Yeah you're right. Maybe it works for her. I don't know her family at all. When my sister asks about them* [wish, fear, or defense?] *I tell her to stop* [wish, fear, or defense?].

Therapist: *What do you think would happen if you didn't stop her?* [Therapist is pushing for what part of conflict: wish, fear, or defense?]

Patient: *I think my mom would walk out of the room* [Wish, fear, or defense?]. *She didn't even tell me her father died. In her family, no one talks about the past. They say this is us now. I can't imagine not speaking to them for years. I could never do that. It's not that I'm angry with her. It's that I feel*

I lost something because I don't have all that extra family. My sister is more like my mom. I'm more like my father. I hate to start fighting [wish, fear, or defense?] *and disappear with people* [wish, fear, or defense?].

What is the conflict as it is described in the patient's last two passages? Write down the patient's wish, fear, and defense, and give your interpretation.

Author's Commentary

Therapist: *What if they are or were?* [The therapist is pushing for the anxiety the patient would feel if she gave in to her wish to criticize her parents.]

Patient: *It would change my image of them. If you could tell that someone's bad, what does that say about you?* [She fears that if she criticizes them she might deserve to be criticized. She turns her criticism of others back onto herself.]

Therapist: *I think you can tell. I think sometimes it's hard to just say it out loud.* [Rather than interpret her conflict over expressing her wish, the therapist presses her to express it. The patient says, "what does it mean?" And the therapist replies, "I think you can tell." She implies that the patient is being deceitful. If this were true, it would be more useful to try to understand why a patient is being deceitful rather than subtly accuse her of lying. The patient feels criticized.]

Patient: *Yeah. I don't know.* [The patient shuts down.]

Therapist: *Do you feel like you're being disloyal?* [The therapist tries to infer her anxiety of being criticized as disloyal if she criticized her parents.]

Patient: *Yes. I don't want to say bad things about her.* [The patient confirms the therapist's description of her anxiety and then describes her defense: "I don't want to say bad things."] *She's incredible now. I'm not afraid anymore.*

Therapist: *How long did it take for that to disappear?*

Patient: *Through high school. We talk now. It's really nice. It's great to see her.* [Described an incident where mother did not get angry at her sister.] *And I thought, 'aren't you supposed to get angry, aren't you supposed to hit her?" I was happy.* [The conflict may be that when she recognized this new kind of relationship her mother was capable of having [wish], that she began to experience anger and sadness over not having had that relationship [fear of experiencing anger and sadness], and as a defense against those feelings she reports only her happiness.]

Therapist: *Part of you felt glad for your sister* [defense], *but part of you felt that you had to get through it when she didn't* [gentle allusion to her defense of resentment: the wish to express her anger].

Patient: *Yes, and I felt really bad for feeling that.* [Patient confirms this interpretation and responds with a defense against her resentment: feeling bad.]

Therapist: *It's pretty natural what you thought. You don't have to beat yourself up for it.* [The therapist tries to reassure the patient rather than analyze her guilt over resenting her sister and the sadness over the relationship she did not get to have with her mother.]

Patient: *That's when I realized she really changed.*

Therapist: *It sounds like you had a lot of really tough years.*

The therapist invites the patient to express her feelings of loss. But this is a mistake because we know now that the patient fears this feeling so much that she has to ward it off. A reflection that could go in any direction within the conflict might have been more useful. For instance, *"That something was going to be possible now that had not been possible before."* This reflection infers a thought implicit in her last statement and allows her to expand on her awareness of this difference, her feelings of loss, or her resentment.

Patient: *Oh, I don't know. She had her good days too. She was great at other times. And I learned to stay out of her way.* [Patient defends against describing her feelings of loss.] *(Describes telling her father for the first time of the beatings and realizing how much it affected him because she never said anything to him before.)*

Therapist: *Why do you think you never talked to your dad about it?* [Why do you use this defense? The question aims at the patient's anxiety over telling her father.]

Patient: *I don't know.* [She is unable to answer directly. However, she begins to describe how her mother used this same defense.] *Mom never dealt with her parents. Cut off all contact with them. She didn't deal with them. Wouldn't feel comfortable talking about things. She deals with the feelings by pushing them away.*

Therapist: *Which is exactly what you tried to do.*

The therapist addressed the defense, but not the anxiety or wish. An interpretation which addresses only the defense is often experienced as criticism by the patient. In the next statement, the patient is unable to describe herself more fully.

It might have been more helpful if the therapist wanted to intervene at this moment to say, *"Given that your mother might have wanted to be with her family* [wish], *the fact that she kept her distance* [defense] *suggests that she was afraid of what she would feel* [fear] *if she tried to deal with them* [wish]." This would direct the patient's attention to her mother's anxiety, which drove her defense and indirectly to the patient's anxiety. In this sense, we might interpret conflicts outside the patient as a pathway to understanding her own. It is like interpreting within the metaphor. It's as if the patient is saying, *"I can't talk about this conflict in myself, but I can talk about it in my mother."* The therapist, by interpreting the conflict within the mother, implicitly says, *"I realize you can't talk about this conflict within yourself right now, so I'll follow your lead and interpret conflicts within whoever you talk about."*

Patient: *Which is exactly what I tried to do. Yeah you're right. Maybe it works for her. I don't know her family at all. When my sister asks about them* [Wish], *I tell her to stop* [Defense]. [Although the patient confirms that she uses the same defense her mother uses, there is no elaboration of meaning, new understanding, or deepening of affect. The patient mentions only her wish and defense, but not the anxiety.]

Therapist: *What do you think would happen if you didn't stop her?* [Therapist's question is aimed at the patient's fear.]

Patient: *I think my mom would walk out of the room* [Fear: the therapist's allusion to the patient's anxiety enables her to elaborate a great deal now. Precisely because the patient mentioned the wish and defense in her previous statement, the therapist can inquire about the missing part of the conflict.] *She didn't even tell me her father died. In her family, no one talks about the past. They say this is us now. I can't imagine not speaking to them for years. I could never do that. It's not that I'm angry with her. It's that I feel I lost something because I don't have all that extra family.* [This is her fear of what will happen if she brings things up to her mother.] *My sister is more like my mom. I'm more like my father. I hate to start fighting* [Fear] *and disappear with people* [Defense].

She would like to talk to her mother, fears her mother would be so upset that she would leave, so the patient remains quiet and insists her sister do so as well.

Possible interpretation of conflict in the past: *"It sounds like you may have wanted to say things to your mother too* [wish], *but feared that she might leave the room* [fear]. *And given that you had already lost so much with her, you couldn't afford to take that chance, so you disappear* [defense] *rather than have her disappear from you* [fear]." If this interpretation were confirmed, one might follow up with an allusion to her feelings of desire and loss with something like, *"And yet, since part of you has to disappear so you don't lose her, that part of you is still longing and waiting to be with her too."*

The hour continues:

Therapist: *So what was it like to stand up to L that way?* [Therapist's comment aims at wish, fear, or defense?]
Patient: *Well, I felt good. Well, I didn't feel bad. Well, I don't like anyone to feel bad but I knew I had to do it. My dad says I think of others too much.*

Based on the patient's comments, what might have been a good interpretation at this point that would explain why she must think of others too much?

Therapist: *It sounds like it feels like there are two choices, bad like your mother or an accommodation like your dad.* [What aspects of conflict are being addressed?]
Patient: *I don't want to hurt people.* [Wish, fear, or defense?]

Author's Commentary

Therapist: *So what was it like to stand up to L that way?* [The therapist's comment aims at the feelings aroused by expressing her wish to L: her fear of hurting L and her guilt over the fact that it felt good to hurt him. We would anticipate that she will describe her fear of hurting him and her guilt over wanting to hurt him. Notice how facilitative this open ended question is. The patient is free to describe the feeling of expressing the wish, the fear it evoked, or the feeling resulting from the defense.]
Patient: *Well, I felt good.* [For expressing herself, and perhaps also for hurting him.] *Well, I didn't feel bad. Well, I don't like anyone to feel bad but I knew I had to do it.* [Now we hear her guilt over making him feel bad.] *My dad says I think of others too much.*

Possible interpretation of conflict in the past: *"It sounds like you had to. If you said no* [wish], *someone might feel hurt and disappear* [fear]. *So you felt you needed to think of others so you would know how much of you should disappear* [defense]."
Possible follow-up interpretation to link conflict in the past to one in the present: *"And maybe that was at work with L. Maybe you were so afraid of how hurt he might feel* [fear], *that you would feel tempted to make your no disappear with him too* [defense]. *But if you did, you would have been defenseless."*

The hour continues:

Therapist: *It sounds like it feels like there are two choices, bad like your mother or an accommodation like your dad.*

Patient: *I don't want to hurt people.*

Offer a possible interpretation now.

Author's Commentary

Therapist: *It sounds like it feels like there are two choices, bad like your mother or an accommodation like your dad.* [When she wants to assert herself, she fears she is becoming like her domineering mother, so she wards off those wishes by being like her submissive father. Although the therapist addresses two feelings, they are not understood as in tension with one another. The comment ends up being static.]

Patient: *I don't want to hurt people.* [Fear. And, on an unconscious level, we can also view this as a denial of her wish to hurt L.]

Possible future interpretation of conflict focused on the unconscious wish: *"It sounds like it felt good to say no and getting him to stop. This was a new step forward and it took courage. But maybe what troubles you is that this legitimate feeling of accomplishment is contaminated with another feeling. Perhaps you're afraid* [fear] *that after all the misery you went through with him that it also felt good because he felt bad for a moment* [wish]. *And maybe that's what you feel guilty* [defense]: *not just that you wanted to say no* [conscious wish], *but that you wanted him to hurt a little bit for everything he put you through."* [unconscious wish]

Evolution of the Conflict

Conflict #1:   wish to tell L he was one of the last people she'd want to go out with, fear of hurting him, defense of feeling bad

Conflict #2:   wish to say 'No I don't want to!', fear she causes additional tension and problems, defense of going with the flow [Notice how the fear in Conflict two is a milder form of the fear in Conflict one; perhaps reflecting a defensive move.]

Conflict #3:   wish of father to buy a truck, fear of mother's complaining, defense of doing what mother wanted

Conflict #4:   wish to describe her parents, fear therapist would think they were horrible, defense of denying they are horrible, and shifting from bad in the past to good in the present

Conflict #5:   fear of being hit by mother

Conflict #6: wish to confront mother, fear mother would never speak to her again, defense of running to her room

Conflict #7: wish to describe her mother in the past, fear therapist would think she always hit the patient and was horrible, defense of focusing on the good mother of the present

This is an excellent example of how one truth can function as a defense against another truth. Her mother may be really great now. That should not be in dispute. Our concern would be that she focuses on this current truth to avoid looking at another truth in the past. The issue is not whether something is true, but what function a particular truth serves at this moment.

Conflict #8: wish to describe her mother, fear if mother is bad this reflects on the patient, defense of not wanting to say horrible things about her mother

Conflict #9: wish to face loss of relationship with mother, fear of pain(?), defense of resenting her sister

Conflict #10: wish to describe resentment of sister, fear(?), defense of feeling bad

Conflict #11: wish of sister to ask mother a question, fear mother would walk out, defense of telling sister to stop

Conflict #12: wish to ask mother, fear of starting a fight, defense of disappearing

Conflict #13: wish to say no to L, fear of hurting him, defense of thinking of others too much

Emergence of the Wish

The wish evolved in the hour as follows:

- to tell L he was the last person she would go out with
- to say 'No, I don't want to!'
- to say 'I want this, not what you want' [father's conflict]
- to describe her parents
- to confront her mother
- to describe her mother
- to face loss of relationship with her mother
- to ask mother about the past [sister's wish]
- to say no to L

We can see the clear evolution of her wish to say no, first to L and then to her mother. We can infer from this pattern of evolution that she wanted to say no to her mother's withdrawal, to confront her, and to ask her about the past and deal with the loss that their relationship involved.

Emergence of the Fear

The fear evolved in the hour as follows:

- of hurting L
- of causing problems and additional tension
- of mother's complaining
- of therapist thinking mother was horrible
- of being hit
- of mother never speaking to her again
- of therapist thinking mother always hit her
- of reflection upon her if mother is bad
- of mother walking out
- of starting a fight
- of hurting L

Her fears evolve from a fear of hurting L to being hit to being in a fight. Her fear of hurting L is a reversal of being hurt by her mother.

Emergence of the Defense

The defense emerged in the hour as follows:

- feeling bad
- going with the flow
- doing what mother wanted
- denying mother was horrible
- running to her room
- focusing only on the good in mother and ignoring the bad
- not wanting to say horrible things
- resentment of sister
- feeling bad
- telling sister to stop asking mother questions
- disappearing
- thinking of others too much

We can see the evolving picture of her defenses as depicted in her family (going with the flow, doing what mother wanted, withdrawing) and as depicted in the therapy (denying mother was horrible, focusing only on the good in mother, and telling her sister not to say things). In addition, she turns aggression against herself by feeling bad. She makes her desires and anger disappear to avoid conflict and turns anger upon herself.

CHAPTER

Theory of the Analysis
of Transference

In the previous chapters, we listened for the conscious, or manifest content of the patient's associations [what the patient is aware of]. Now we will focus on the symbolic, unconscious, or latent content. Let's look at a vignette from these two perspectives to demonstrate how to listen for transference.

☐ Listening for Manifest Content

Patient: *I'm jittery as usual today. I get that way every time I drive down that road that leads to the main gate.*

Therapist: *I know you are frightened.*

Patient: *But I shouldn't be. I see my neighbor regularly now. She helps my loneliness. I think she helps me most with her understanding. She's very patient with me and she told me it will take time. I do get to feeling lonely and blue, though, in spite of her.*

Therapist: *She'll always be around for you.*

Patient: *Her hours of work change around now and then so I'm not quite sure of her work schedule. I didn't see her for two weeks last month and I missed her, but I didn't tell her as I felt angry at her.*

Manifest Content

Manifest content refers to the content that is obvious to the listener or reader. In the previous vignette, the manifest content is that the patient is nervous. She has a friend whom she sees regularly who helps her with her understanding. After the friend had been gone for two weeks, she missed her but didn't tell her because she felt angry. From a reflective point of view, the therapist might summarize back to her some of these themes. From a conflict point of view, the therapist might organize this vignette into an interpretation: her wish to speak to the friend, a fear of what would happen if she revealed her anger over the missed time, and a defense of keeping quiet about her feelings.

Latent Content

Latent content refers to the unconscious meanings that are symbolized in the associations (Gill and Hoffman 1982; Langs 1973a, 1973b, 1975, 1976, 1985). To decode those unconscious meanings, we adopt a playful frame of mind and listen *as if* every association refers to the therapy and the therapist. Here is a translation of the latent content:

Patient: *I'm jittery as usual today. I get that way every time I drive down that road that leads to the main gate* [every time I come to therapy].

Therapist: *I know you are frightened.*

Patient: *But I shouldn't be. I see my neighbor* [you] *regularly now. She* [You] *helps my loneliness. I think she* [you] *helps me most with her* [your] *understanding. She's* [You're] *very patient with me and she* [you] *told me it will take time. I do get to feeling lonely and blue, though, in spite of her* [you].

Therapist: *She'll always be around for you.*

Patient: *Her* [Your] *hours of work change around now and then so I'm not quite sure of her* [your] *work schedule. I didn't see her* [you] *for two weeks last month* [therapist was out of town] *and I missed her* [you], *but I didn't tell her* [you] *as I felt angry at her* [you].

We put this latent content together into an interpretation with the hope that the patient can begin to explore her conflicts within the therapy relationship.

Possible reflections: *"How could I tell her that?" "You were feeling torn between wanting to tell her you missed her and fearing she might find out you were also angry."*

Possible interpretation of conflict: *"It sounds like you wanted to tell your friend that you missed her* [wish], *but were afraid to tell her for fear* *your anger might come out* [fear]. *So you kept quiet* [defense]. *What were you afraid would happen if she knew you were angry* [fear]?"

Possible transference interpretation: *"You mention how important your friend has been and that although you were angry with her when she was gone, you didn't tell her. I wonder if there is a parallel here. Is it possible that you were upset with me for going on vacation last month? Maybe you feared what would happen if you told me, and so you have tried not to mention it ever since?"* Notice how a transference interpretation takes a conflict in the manifest content and analyzes it within the therapy relationship.

The key difference between transference analysis and reflection and analysis of conflict (as described earlier) is the focus on *latent, unconscious* content, not simply the manifest, conscious content. This difference in focus poses a great obstacle to beginning therapists. As a rule, most conversation involves listening only for manifest content. As a result, listening for latent content feels unnatural and unempathic. So, before we talk further about listening for transference, we need to reflect on the nature of language and interpretation.

☐ The Poetry of Therapy

Listening for transference often seems like an alien approach for therapists because it makes us think about what words mean and what patients means by their words. How do we figure out what patients mean? Through close study and attention to the associations.

Many therapists argue, however, that the close study of the patient's words is inappropriate. They suggest that, instead, we need only sit back dreamily and let the patient's words flow over us and affect us. Sometimes simple messages with an immediacy all their own require no analysis. But with more complex sessions, how can we possibly grasp the rich, compact, and highly charged meanings with merely a relaxed, passive attitude? To glean the full richness of meaning, whether from a musical masterpiece, a poem, or a session with a patient, we need to exercise not less but more attentiveness (Brooks and Warren 1938).

Some therapists object that close study of the patient's words destroys the feel of the hour. Through close examination, they argue, the parts are observed but the whole is destroyed in the process. But if that happens, that is not the fault of transference analysis but of the therapist who fails to generate a broad, integrated understanding of the whole person. Clearly, analysis for the sake of analysis, noting a variety of meanings as isolated, unrelated events, would be inappropriate. We use close study of the patient's associations to contribute to an understanding of a whole person. We are not interested only in the words of this person; we want to understand the person who uttered these words.

What Do Words Mean?

If we closely study the patient's words, we must understand a little about the nature of language, especially figurative language. When listening to a poem, for instance, we go beyond the literal meaning of the words in order to catch all the meanings the poet offers us. If we hear only the literal meanings, we miss everything and completely misread the poem. For instance, in Andrew Marvell's "To His Coy Mistress," we find the phrase:

> But at my back I always hear
> Time's winged chariot hurrying near.

Marvell is not suggesting that he needs to get better medical insurance because he is about to be run over by a chariot (a possible literal meaning). Instead, he is trying to convey how quickly time passes, how he can never escape from time, how death is approaching and he is aware of it every moment of his life (figurative meanings). He is not really talking about a chariot but about the passage of time, awareness of mortality. He could have talked literally about mortality. For instance:

> But all the time I notice
> that time passes quickly.

Mundane, isn't it? Poetry is richer because figurative language allows us to evoke so much more feeling and richness of meaning. The poet uses a word or phrase that refers to one thing—to stand for the idea or feeling he is trying to communicate. As Robert Frost said, "Poetry provides the one permissible way of saying one thing and meaning another." Yet therapists have found that all of us use metaphor unconsciously to enrich our communication, and to engage our emotions, our imagination, and our intellect. Hence, the patient's associations have both important literal and figurative meanings. To glean both of these meanings, we need to listen for both the literal and the figurative. If we listen only for literal meanings, we will miss the figurative meanings and vice versa. Since we usually listen for only the literal meaning, we need to train ourselves to listen for the figurative or transference meanings. It is the equivalent of needing two eyes for binocular vision by which we achieve depth perception.

When we listen for transference, we listen for the poetry in the patient's words. Suppose a patient talks about a boyfriend who has been giving her the silent treatment recently. She tries to get him to talk about it, but he always bounces the questions back to her and reveals nothing about himself. She tells you that unless he gets it together, she may dump him and start going out with someone else.

The literal meaning of this passage is obvious: she is upset with her boyfriend's silence and may soon leave him. You may think to yourself that this sounds like a good idea too. And in doing so you would be listening, as we generally do in everyday life, for the literal meaning.

The next week she does not show up for her session. You call her and she says she wants to stop therapy. You're shocked, thinking to yourself that she never mentioned it before. You mention feeling a bit surprised and convince her to come in for at least one final session. Meanwhile, you are still puzzled.

As you review the previous hour for its poetic, transference meaning, you discover that her feelings about the boyfriend may have also been a metaphor about her feelings about you: "You have been giving me the silent treatment recently. I try to get you to talk about it but you always bounce the questions back to me and reveal nothing about yourself. Unless you get it together, I may dump you and begin therapy with someone else."

Now you understand that, in addition to the literal meaning of the hour, there was a transference meaning as well. She experiences you as too silent and withholding, so she wants to leave the therapy rather than tell you directly. In case you think this example unusual, almost every time a patient ends a therapy precipitously, you can find the clues hidden in the previous sessions if you listen for the transference meanings.

This figurative or symbolic meaning allows us to hear something we would have missed if we listened only to the literal meaning. Sometimes at this point, therapists will question this approach: "Are you saying that this is what the patient is saying?" Or, "Are you saying that the patient's feelings about her boyfriend are irrelevant?" Questions such as these reveal the difficulty we have understanding the complexity of communication and meaning. The patient feels this way about her boyfriend *and* her therapist. Both sets of feelings exist and are expressed at the same time. Neither is more real than the other, although one may be more in her awareness. Both are real and relevant. As a therapist, you might always listen to the transference, not because that meaning is more real than other feelings for the patient, but because those feelings allow you to get a richer understanding of the patient and her experience. They augment your understanding of the literal meanings. All the meanings you can glean from an hour are important and legitimate. The question becomes one of discerning how they are woven together into the complex tapestry of meaning.

Listening for Transference

You have no doubt read that transference refers to our tendency to take feelings for someone in our past and transfer them onto someone else in the present. A simple example might be a child who, having been beaten by his parents, fears he will be beaten again when he hears his school teacher yell. The feelings and fears with his parents are transferred upon the teacher. Or a young woman whose father abandoned the family may fear that her boyfriends will leave her.

These obvious examples from everyday life can give the incorrect impression, however, that we discover transference only in obvious behaviors. In fact, transference during therapy is discovered most often in the symbolic meanings of the patient's associations (Langs 1973a, 1973b, 1975, 1976, 1985). When listening for transference, we listen to the patient's associations for symbolic references to the therapy. By this, we don't simply mean when the patient talks about you directly. We mean when the patient refers to you and the therapy directly or indirectly. From a transference point of view, we listen as if every association and vignette could refer to the therapy. Using those possible references to the therapy, we try to create a vision of what the experience of therapy is like for the patient.

Hence, a major focus of much psychodynamic therapy involves listening for and interpreting the unconscious feelings the patient expresses about you and the therapy (Brenner 1976, 1982; Freud 1912a, 1914, 1915b; Langs 1973a, 1973b, 1975, 1976, 1985; Strachey 1934). Since this book focuses primarily on skill development, we will not discuss the different kinds of transference or styles of interpretation. Instead, we will focus on some basic guidelines for listening for transference.

Displacement

When we listen for the transference we adopt a playful frame of mind, entertaining the possibility that anything the patient says might refer to the therapy. In the beginning of therapy, a patient may talk about a new relationship or new roommate. We would listen carefully, knowing that the therapy is also a new relationship, and in this office you are also, in a manner of speaking, a new roommate. As we listen, we want to hear how the patient is experiencing us.

Often at this point a student will say, "Are you saying that transference meanings are the only meanings?" No, of course not. Many meanings coexist in any therapy hour and it would be impossible to address them all, even if it were advisable—which it never is. When a patient talks about her new roommate, we entertain the possibility that what she says about the roommate is real, and that these comments at the same time may refer to the therapy: both are possible. In this way, therapists listen to the patient's words much like they listen to a poem, where words have many potential meanings simultaneously.

"Well suppose you are right, that she is describing this relationship with you. If she's not aware of it, why bring it up? Wouldn't it be an empathic lapse to discuss something of which she is unaware?" This raises two questions: timing and plausibility. A therapist almost never interprets all the transference meanings of an hour. To adopt such a mechanistic stance would be to comply with a therapist's compulsion rather than respond to the patient's need. The therapist tries to interpret the transference when it is interfering with the patient's ability to speak freely. Further, we do not interpret the transference as soon as we figure it out. It is usually wise to listen to several vignettes that elaborate the same theme so we can weave together a kind of story that helps explain to the patient what is going on (Gill and Hoffman 1982; Langs 1973a, 1985). As each vignette develops, the theme will become increasingly clear, making it possible for you to interpret more accurately.

For instance, a patient may talk about a new roommate whom she is having some trouble getting used to. You hear the reference to her difficulty getting used to you. But if you were to ask what she has trouble getting used to with you, she might feel puzzled and be unable to answer your question. So you listen rather than interpret. She continues, saying that she went out with her boyfriend on Saturday night and although she enjoyed being with him, talking with him was hard. He seemed preoccupied, uncommunicative. She could hardly get him to talk. As you listen, you realize that she may be having trouble getting used to your silence and that she is trying to figure you why you say so little. Then she goes on to talk about a class where the teacher says so little that is new that she is thinking about dropping the class and doing something else with her time. At this point you might interpret, which brings us up to the issue of plausibility.

As we listen to the hour of therapy as a symbolic portrayal of how the patient feels about you, she is talking and not hearing what we hear. If we simply say out of the blue "Maybe you want to drop this therapy, too," she will wonder where in the world that came from.

Many interpretations, though correct, are rejected by patients because they are presented in an implausible manner (Gill and Hoffman 1982) without giving the patient an inkling how the therapist got these ideas from what she said. Instead, summarize what the patient has said first, then wonder with her if the following interpretation is possible (Gill and Hoffman 1982; Langs 1973a, 1985).

A possible transference interpretation: *"You've been talking about a new roommate whom you are having trouble getting used to; a boyfriend who says very little; and a class you want to drop. There's a new person in your life whom you are having trouble getting used to because he is so quiet and a theme of dropping something you recently started. I wonder if these thoughts might be related here. Perhaps you are having trouble getting used to me because of how silent I am. If that's so, you might find yourself wondering if you'll stay in therapy."*

This form of interpretation allows you to bring up something the patient was not aware of at the moment while allowing her to see how it might be implicit in what she said. Then it is up to her to say what comes to mind. This brings us to the next issue: confirmation of a transference interpretation.

An interpretation is not offered based on some fantasy of the therapist. It is based on the decoded associations of the patient. In transference analysis, all interpretations are based on the patient's associations. However, no matter how wonderful we think our interpretations are, the proof is not in our conviction but in the interpretation's effectiveness: Does the patient confirm the interpretation? Is the patient freer to discuss previously difficult material? Does the patient develop a more mature and complex relationship with the therapist?

Confirmation of Interpretations

When we interpret, we are interested in whether the patient responds "Yes!" or "No!"; however, but we can't rely on that alone (Freud 1925). We continue to look for confirmation or non-confirmation in the following associations (Langs 1973a, 1973b, 1975, 1976, 1985). A patient might say "yes," but the following associations might describe a person who doesn't listen and utters irrelevant comments. This would suggest that the patient experienced the interpretation as irrelevant and an example of not listening to her. Or a patient might say "no," but then describe a doctor who diagnosed a health problem that other people had not noticed. Here we would see the interpretation being confirmed as an accurate diagnosis of her situation.

A conscious "yes" or "no" tells us only that the patient agrees or disagrees consciously. To find out the unconscious experience of our interpretation, we listen further to the associations for validation in the latent content. For instance, suppose the patient says "yes," and then describes a doctor who diagnosed her condition appropriately. This would be confirmation. Then she continues, saying that when her boy-friend was so silent on the date that she thought he didn't love her anymore and that he was thinking about another girlfriend but was afraid to tell her. Now she has not only confirmed the interpretation, but has gone further. In the displacement she says that she feared your silence meant that you no longer found her interesting and that you were thinking about someone or something else. This tracking of associations allows you to gain a deeper understanding of what she thinks and feels when she is in therapy. Here you could follow up with another interpretation: *"So maybe when I'm silent here, you wonder if I have lost interest in listening to you too."*

The following associations will show you not only whether you were correct or not but also which issues you need to address that your interpretation left out (Langs 1973a, 1975, 1976, 1985). Again, all this information comes out in the displacement through the latent content. Therapists often mistakenly assume that confirmation always takes place in conscious awareness. However, those who work with the transference rely upon both manifest and latent content for validation.

It is impossible to address all the approaches to transference analysis today in this book. But all those approaches depend on a capacity to understand the latent content and decipher the patient's unconscious communications. That is the skill the following exercises will help you with.

☐ Further Readings

The following readings include session transcripts that allow you to see how analysts decode transference meanings in sessions.

Gill, M. and Hoffman, I. (1982). Session transcripts with the authors' analysis.

Hill, D. and Grand, C. (eds.). (1966). Chapters 3–5 include process notes of sessions illustrating three approaches to transference analysis.

Langs, R. (1976, 1985). Langs provides a clear approach to the validation of interpretations. To further develop your ability to hear unconscious communication, see his workbook, volume 3.

Raney, J. (ed.). (1984). Some of the articles offer clinical vignettes with the authors' translations of unconscious meaning.

Rosenfeld, H. (1987). A Kleinian interprets the latent content in a session in chapter 3.

7

Transference Studies

To him who opens himself without reservations to symbols, their meaning will gradually become clear of itself. The Chinese who hears mere noise in our music has not yet given the symbols sufficient opportunity to impart to him the significance they contain. But if the opportunity has been present and still nothing happens, the only conclusion that can be drawn is that, as the result of some obstructive circumstance or other, this one person although physically his hearing is unimpaired, cannot share in the community of those who hear musically. His musical deafness says neither more nor less against the existence of the dynamic qualities than blindness says against the existence of light, or an absence of metals against the reality of magnetism.

Zuckerkandl (1956:70)

This chapter contains studies designed to help you hear and interpret the transference. Clinical material will be interrupted with questions to answer. You will be asked many times to create a transference interpretation precisely so you will have many chances to hone your listening skills. But keep in mind that you would almost never interpret the transference as frequently as we will in these studies.

As mentioned before, there are many ways to approach a clinical hour. This chapter will focus only on listening for the unconscious references to the therapy. As you read, play with the possibility that each association symbolizes feelings about the therapy or the therapist. Where instructed, translate the previous associations of the patient as if they refer to the therapy and see what further understandings you can gain about the patient.

☐ Case #1

The tenth session of a depressed female patient (Shave 1968). The therapist missed a session two weeks previously.

Patient: *I'm jittery as usual today. I get that way every time I drive down that road that leads to the main gate.* [She feels anxious when she comes to therapy. We listen to find out why that might be.]

Therapist: *I know you are frightened.*

Patient: *But I shouldn't be. I see my neighbor* [you] *regularly now. She* [you] *helps my loneliness. I think she* [you] *helps me most with her* [your] *understanding. She's* [You're] *very patient with me and she* [you] *told me it will take time. I do get to feeling lonely and blue, though, in spite of her* [you].

Silent Interpretation

I'm jittery as usual today. I get that way every time I come to see you. But I shouldn't be frightened of seeing you. I see you regularly now. You help my loneliness. You're very patient with me and you told me it will take time. I do get to feeling lonely and blue, though, in spite of you.

As we decode the latent content we wonder why the patient has these feelings? To what event is she responding? Langs (1973a, 1985) refers to the event as the *adaptive context*, and the encoded meanings as the *derivative communications*. So far, we know she feels jittery and lonely. As her therapist, we would wonder what has happened recently to make the patient have these feelings: an intervention, a failure to intervene, an empathic failure, or a violation of the frame? Although we don't have any evidence for it in the material so far, we might wonder if these feelings are related to the missed session two weeks earlier. Now let's listen to find out what the adaptive context might be.

The hour continues:

Therapist: *She'll always be around for you.*

Patient: *Her hours of work change around now and then so I'm not quite sure of her work schedule. I didn't see her for two weeks last month and I missed her, but I didn't tell her as I felt angry at her.*

See if you can translate this paragraph into its transference meaning. If the woman symbolizes the therapist, what might you infer?

Author's Translation

Therapist: *She'll always be around for you.*

Patient: *Her* [Your] *hours of work change around now and then so I'm not quite sure of her* [your] *work schedule. I didn't see her* [you] *for two weeks last month and I missed her* [you]*, but I didn't tell her* [you] *as I felt angry at her* [you].

Silent Interpretation

Your hours of work change around now (like a couple weeks ago), so I'm not quite sure of your work schedule. I didn't see you for two weeks last month (the missed session) and I missed you, but I didn't tell you as I felt angry at you.

The time is not yet ripe for an interpretation. One way we assess ripeness is by offering silent interpretations. By thinking of possible interpretations, we can see if we have enough to work with, if we are clear enough, if anything important is missing.

Now the adaptive context is clear: the missed session. And the theme of feelings organizes itself clearly around this context: she is afraid to tell the therapist she missed him when he was gone because she feels angry at him. Of course, the topic of the missed session, her feelings towards the therapist, and her fear of expressing those feelings to the therapist are all out of the patient's awareness. So how do we decide from a transference point of view to interpret these unconscious feelings and thoughts?

There are many schools of thought on this topic. At one extreme, some interpret the transference as soon as it is clear to the therapist with the belief that there is always a part of the patient's mind that can receive the interpretation and work with it even if the patient appears to deny it. At the other extreme are those who do not work with the transference at all when it is symbolized in the displacement. We will use the work of Langs (1973a, 1985) and Gill and Hoffman (1982) to illustrate a middle of the road approach for timing of interpretations. But keep in mind that different theorists operate with different guidelines for timing.

Langs (1973a, 1985) suggests that we not interpret until we know three things: 1) the adaptive context: what is the patient responding to?, 2) a meaningful derivative complex: a series of vignettes that when decoded, yield meaningful, coalescing images of the therapist's activities, and 3) a problem that is apparent in the manifest content such as a resistance, an emotional symptom, or an interpersonal difficulty that could be understood as a response to the adaptive context.

In this vignette so far, we have a reference to an adaptive context: the missed session. However, there is no reference to therapy or a doctor in the manifest content that might provide a bridge from the latent content to the therapy situation. So far we have one vignette that provides images describing the therapist's missed session. We haven't heard a series of images that might add richness to our understanding. The problem the patient provides is her feelings of jitteriness and loneliness. Hence, we would wait for further transference images and an image that might provide the bridge to the therapy.

The hour continues:

Therapist: *We'll go on very regularly.*

Patient: *I sure would hate to feel like I used to. It's that awful fear of being alone. That's why I go and visit this neighbor so much. It keeps my mind off my loneliness when Bill is away. I don't know why I have this loneliness—other housewives don't have it. And Bill is the best husband a woman could hope for. He never seems nervous or afraid. That fear shouldn't be with me if I only knew of a way to get it out. I wish I could get those feelings out. Dr. H told me once that I was hostile deep down within me, but I don't think I'm hostile at all. I'm not hostile when I talk to you.*

Again, translate this into the transference meaning, playing with the possibility that the feelings she has about the neighbor, Bill, and Dr. H might refer to the therapist.

Author's Translation

Therapist: *We'll go on very regularly.*

Patient: *I sure would hate to feel like I used to* [when you were gone]. *It's that awful fear of being alone. That's why I go and visit this neighbor* [you] *so much. It* [Therapy] *keeps my mind off my loneliness when Bill is* [you are] *away. I don't know why I have this loneliness—other housewives don't have it. And Bill is the best husband* [you are the best therapist] *a woman* [I] *could hope for. He* [You] *never seems nervous or afraid. That fear shouldn't be with me if I only knew of a way to get it out* [with you in therapy]. *I wish I could get those feelings out* [here]. *Dr. H told me once that I was hostile deep down within me* [maybe you would too], *but I don't think I'm hostile at all. I'm not hostile when I talk to you.*

Silent Interpretation

I sure hate to feel that awful fear of being alone like when you were gone. That's why I visit you so much. Therapy keeps my mind off my loneliness when you are here and visiting her keeps my mind off my loneliness when you are away. I don't know why I have this loneliness. You are the best therapist a woman could hope for. You never seem nervous or afraid. That fear shouldn't be with me if I only knew of a way to get it out with you here. I wish I could but I'm afraid you would think I was hostile deep down within me, but I don't think I'm hostile at all. At least I try not to be when I talk to you.

These vignettes deepen our understanding. She would like to share her feelings with the therapist about his vacation but is afraid he would think she was hostile. The reference to a doctor suggests that her feelings about the therapist [another doctor] are close to her awareness. The image of the doctor who commented on her feelings can serve as a bridge from the manifest content to the latent content. This bridge makes it easier to show the patient how the latent content is related to this doctor: the therapist. Hence, from this perspective, a bridge is an unconscious cue that the patient is ready for an interpretation.

When the transference is depicted in the displacement, the degree of displacement indicates how close feelings are to awareness. The more obscure, distant, or distorted the displacement, the more these feelings are out of the patient's awareness. This reference to the doctor is an indication of "ripeness" for interpretation. Another factor indicating her readiness is her stated wish to get her feelings out. We would hear that as an unconscious message to the therapist that she is ready for his help to get them out.

In summary, timing of a transference interpretation is an art, but we can be guided by several factors: 1) a level of displacement that is relatively transparent, 2) a symbolic *indication* of readiness for interpretation, 3) an adaptive context that can be linked to the transference feelings, and 4) a series of coalescing images of the therapist's activities that are organized around the adaptive context.

Those criteria have now been met, and so we need to create an interpretation. Within the field this has been an area of tremendous controversy. Some advocate direct interpretations of the transference, assuming that bringing the patient into direct contact with the unconscious meanings will be useful. Others counter that this runs the risk of relying upon suggestion. The patient unaware of unconscious feelings can only take what the therapist interprets on faith without gaining any additional capacity for self analysis. Responding to these concerns, Gill and Hoffman (1982) insist that transference interpretations be plausible to the patient. Langs (1973a, 1985) agrees, suggesting that an interpretation play back the manifest themes first, then loop back and use the bridge theme to wonder about the possible latent meanings. In this way, the patient can see where your interpretation came from and the patient is then invited to look back at her own associations and wonder about their possible symbolic meanings.

A transference interpretation from this model is based only on the material the patient presents in this hour. It attempts to describe the nature of the relationship at this moment. The interpretation will include a reference to the adaptive context: what caused the feelings, the derivative complex: the symbolic portrayal of the therapy, and the patient's symptoms that are a response to what caused the feelings.

When making a transference interpretation with this patient, we reflect back the manifest themes: her concern about what would happen if she told people what she felt and the conflict with her friend and Dr. H. Then we wonder with the patient if those themes are linked to the therapy.

Possible transference interpretation: *"But it sounds like you're concerned about what will happen if you tell people what you feel. You missed your friend when she was gone, but you didn't tell her because you were angry. And you told Dr. H what you felt, and he told you you were hostile. You know, I'm reminded that I also was gone last month, just like your friend. I wonder if you missed me too but were hesitant to bring it up for fear of how I might respond."*

Notice that the interpretation didn't say that she was afraid "that I might criticize your anger like Dr. H did." We need first to see if she is aware of having had feelings about the missed session, and if she is aware of having been in conflict about it. If she can play with this possibility, then we could go further and add the fears that were linked to Dr. H. We will always hear more in the transference than the patient will be able to work with. The art of interpretation is giving voice to something just outside her awareness that she can work with. Then, in listening to her responses, we can titrate the dosage of what we add depending on her increased ability to think symbolically and to voice her feelings and thoughts about the therapy.

Her following associations will bring up those feelings and thoughts in the latent content that are available for the next interpretation. Rather than push our own fantasies about the transference, we instead follow her lead, interpreting only those images she brings up. "The therapist should add virtually nothing that the patient has not communicated in the hour at hand." (Langs 1985:18) Although this comment may seem overly restrictive to many clinicians, it is a useful corrective. Far too often, therapists imagine that transference interpretations can be based on the patient's history, relationships with parents, and other theoretical biases. However, interpretations based on what the patient has just said will be the most responsive to the patient's state at this moment.

The hour continues:

Therapist: *We can handle it.* [There is knocking at the door.]

Patient: *Is there someone at the door?*

Therapist: *It's okay. You're more important.*

Patient: *Tuesday evening Bill has to bowl, and last time I asked to go along with him as I didn't want to stay home, but I think I hurt him—that's his night out. His chance to get away from me for a while. It hurts me to know I wouldn't let him go alone. I think of things that might happen to him when he's away from home. I worry that he might be hurt in some way or that some thing could happen to him because of me. Some people think that I am looking better. Maybe I do on the outside, but it's on the inside that really hurts. I think a lot about religion; it seems all mixed up to me. God gave me a mind and a body for good things, yet I think such awful thoughts.* [She grimaces, breaks down, and then cries for several minutes.]

Therapist: *I understand.*

Patient: *It says in the Bible, "Fear not for God is with you," but I can't fear not. Therefore He's not with me.*

Again, translate the transference meaning. Remember to play in your mind as if Bill and "some people" symbolize the therapist. Provide a possible transference interpretation assuming we had made the earlier interpretation addressing the missed session.

Author's Translation

Therapist: *We can handle it.* [There is knocking at the door.]

Patient: *Is there someone at the door?*

Therapist: *It's okay. You're more important.*

Patient: *Tuesday evening Bill has to bowl* [recently you had to leave me], *and last time I asked to go along with him* [you] *as I didn't want to stay home* [here alone], *but I think I hurt him* [you]—*that's his* [your] *night out. His* [Your] *chance to get away from me for a while. It hurts me to know I wouldn't let him* [you] *go alone. I think of things that might happen to him* [you] *when he's* [you're] *away from home. I worry that he* [you] *might be hurt in some way or that some thing could happen to him* [you] *because of me. Some people* [You may] *think that I am looking better. Maybe I do on the outside, but it's on the inside that really hurts* [because of the time you were gone]. *I think* *a lot about religion; it seems all mixed up to me. God gave me a mind and a body for good things, yet I think such awful thoughts* [about you]. [She grimaces, breaks down, and then cries for several minutes.]

Therapist: *I understand.*

Patient: *It says in the Bible* [You say to me now], *"Fear not for God is* [I am] *with you," but I can't fear not. Therefore He's* [you're] *not with me.* [You aren't understanding me. Just because you are physically with me now doesn't mean that you were here then nor that you are present emotionally now.]

Silent Interpretation

When you left me and were gone for that session, I wanted to go along with you as I didn't want to have to stay here, but I think I hurt you. That was your chance to get away from me for a while. It hurts me to know I wouldn't let you go alone. I think of things that might happen to you when you're away from me. I worry that you might be hurt in some way, or that some thing could happen to you because of me. You think I am looking better since you returned. Maybe I do on the outside, but it's on the inside that really hurts. I think a lot about therapy; it all seems mixed up to me. God gave me a mind and a body for good things, yet I think such awful thoughts about you. You think I shouldn't feel fear because you are with me. But emotionally you aren't with me, that's why I am so scared.

Possible transference interpretation (assuming you made the previous interpretation addressing the missed session): *"It's so hard when people are gone and you are left alone. Some people think you are looking better but on the inside you are still hurting. In fact, you're still afraid and dealing with this feeling of aloneness. Perhaps this is also connected to my missed session. Although you look good on the outside, that missed time in therapy may still be hurting you on the inside. Because not only did you feel God wasn't with you—I wasn't with you."*

The hour continues:

Therapist: *You aren't alone now.*

Patient: *They say the devil tempts a person. I wonder if that's what is happening now. God doesn't help a person—he has to be able to help himself. God helps those that help themselves and I just can't seem to do it.* [She cries.] *I don't have normal fear. It used to be unbearable, but it doesn't seem to bother me so much now. It's still there, though—I fear its being there. I fear fear itself and what it can do to me. It is like I told Sandra, I don't feel I'm a good*

Christian. I don't feel good in God's sight. It's as if I've committed some unforgivable sin.

Again, translate the transference meanings using the different figures here as symbols of the therapist. Also, since the therapist has made a comment here, analyze the patient's response to see if you can hear the unconscious meanings.

Author's Translation

Therapist: *You aren't alone now.*

Patient: *They say the devil tempts a person.* [You are tempting me now to say and think awful things.] *I wonder if that's what is happening now* [with you]. *God doesn't help a person—he has to be able to help himself.* [You aren't helping me now; I will have to help myself. Your last comment that I'm not alone now shows again that you aren't with me. I get so exasperated that you are like a devil tempting me to let you have it.] *God* [Therapy] *helps those that help themselves and I just can't seem to do it.* [She cries.] *I don't have normal fear. It used to be unbearable but it doesn't seem to bother me so much now. It's still there, though—I fear its being there. I fear fear itself and what it can do to me. It is like I told Sandra* [you], *I don't feel I'm a good Christian. I don't feel good in God's* [your] *sight. It's as if I've committed some unforgivable sin.*

Silent Interpretation

You are tempting me to let you have it since you are not helping me with an interpretation that would relieve my distress. I have to help myself as a result. But I just can't seem to do it. I don't have normal fear. It is like I told you, I don't feel I'm a good Christian. I don't feel good in your sight. It's as if I've committed some unforgivable sin by being angry with you when you were gone and now that you have come back. Although maybe I'm also feeling that your absence was an unforgivable sin.

   Possible transference interpretation (if nothing had been interpreted yet): *"You've been talking about missing your friend but not saying anything because you were angry. And how Dr. H thought you were hostile when he heard about your anger. You feel lonely and aren't sure how to talk about it to other people without doing something wrong. I wonder if this may be related to some feelings here. I remember that I was also gone like your friend. Maybe you missed me and were angry too but are afraid of what I would think if I knew how you felt."*

Unconscious Supervision of the Therapist

This passage illustrates how the patient's associations respond to the therapist's comments with either confirmation or invalidation. In this case, the patient is not only letting the therapist know that he is not helpful, she is telling him how he is not being helpful and what she needs. This illustrates that not any interpretation or comment will be helpful. Indeed, the patient will let us know on conscious and unconscious levels whether our comments help or not.

Although some therapists imagine that there is a rule that we should never reassure patients ["you're not alone now"], the issue is more complex. The question is not whether one should reassure the patient. Rather, we should ask: what response would be most helpful right now? No matter what we imagine before we interpret, the proof of an interpretation's usefulness will be found in the patient's following associations. In this case, the patient experiences the therapist as ignoring her feelings when he reassures her. He refuses to be with her. She experiences him as not doing therapy, and later in the session as being dead. When the unconscious meanings of the patient's associations reveal that she found a reassurance helpful, we defer to the patient. We are guided not by adherence to arbitrary rules but by observance and following of the evidence: the symbolic, latent meanings of the patient's associations (Hoffmann 1983; Langs 1973a, 1973b, 1985; Searles 1979).

The hour continues:

Therapist: *God can accept you just the way you are.*

Patient: *Yes, but people don't go around thinking they might hurt someone or even kill them. It seems as though I'm fighting the feeling of hurting someone; that I might lose control and hurt someone I love and need. Does that make sense? Do you know what I mean?*

Translate the transference meaning. Her final questions suggest she is ready for an interpretation of the transference. What might you say? Remember to review what she has said and then link that to her feelings about the therapist.

Author's Translation

Therapist: *God can accept you just the way you are.*

Patient: *Yes, but people don't go around thinking they might hurt someone [you] or even kill them [you]. It seems as though I'm fighting the feeling of hurting someone [you]; that I might lose control and hurt someone I love and need [you]. Does that make sense? Do you know what I mean?*

Silent Interpretation

But how can you possibly accept me if you find out that I think about how I might hurt or even kill you? I'm fighting the feeling of hurting you; that I might lose control and hurt you when I love and need you as my therapist. Does that make sense to you? Do you know what these unconscious feelings mean?

Possible transference interpretation: *"You mentioned how you wanted to tell your friend that you missed her when she was gone but decided against saying anything because you were angry. Then you talked about your husband and your reluctance to tell him about your feelings when he goes away. I wonder if you also felt upset by my going away but were afraid to let me know."*

In this interpretation, notice how we use those vignettes that most clearly illustrate her conflict. By summarizing the themes, we invite her to observe the pattern. And if we had not interpreted earlier, we would add the vignette of Dr. H to serve as the bridge to this doctor-therapist, which would make it possible for her to entertain a link between the feelings towards other people and feelings towards the therapist.

If she confirmed this interpretation, then you might follow up with another **possible interpretation:** *"Perhaps like with Bill, you were afraid you would hurt my feelings if you told me but also that I might hurt yours. That I might be like Dr. H and judge you rather than understand that you were lonely and scared. And so ever since the vacation, you've been struggling to keep those feelings to yourself."*

The hour continues:

Therapist: *I understand.*

Patient: *It frightens me. Sitting here, I get very anxious that the fear will come back to me.*

Therapist: *I can accept your feelings.*

Patient: *I can't accept them.*

Therapist: *We'll go on together.*

Patient: *Sometimes I think I don't want to go on. Yet I don't know why. I have everything a woman could want. I pray every day I won't be afraid. I pray that nothing can take me from Bill and children.* [Here she breaks down and cries for several minutes. She then blows her nose, recovers, and smiles warmly.] *I feel as though I could throw things at times. That I could smash up things if I let myself go. I rebel against these feelings and have to fight myself to keep control.*

Therapist: *It's okay to have feelings.*

Patient: *I pray that if I ever do anything like that I do it here and not at home.*

Therapist: *We can handle it.*

Patient: *I don't know why I have to be so afraid. I feel as though I have to punish myself.*

Therapist: *You don't seem bad.*

Patient: *Then why do I feel the way I do?*

Therapist: [Gestures.]

Patient: *I don't want my life to end.*

Therapist: *We have a way to go together.*

Patient: *I know, but I don't want to keep coming back here to this place all my life.*

Therapist: *You're stuck with me.*

[The patient laughs and then smiles warmly.]

Patient: *It's like when I was working here as a patient, I wanted to work but it frightened me and didn't want to work at the same time.*

Therapist: *I understand.*

Translate the transference implications of this material playing as if her thoughts symbolize her conflicts about the therapy. Assuming you made the interpretation suggested above, what might be a follow-up interpretation of transference at this point?

Author's Translation

Therapist: *I understand.*

Patient: *It* [Your response] *frightens me. Sitting here, I get very anxious that the fear will come back to me* [because you have offered me no evidence of what you understand].

Therapist: *I can accept your feelings.*

Patient: *I can't accept them.* [So what if you can! I can't. That's what you should explore with me.]

Therapist: *We'll go on together.*

Patient: *Sometimes I think I don't want to go on* [with you]. *Yet I don't know why. I have everything a woman could want. I pray every day I won't be afraid. I pray that nothing can take me from Bill and children* [you]. [Here she breaks down and cries for several minutes. She then blows her nose, recovers, and smiles warmly.] *I feel as though I could throw things* [at you] *at times. That I could smash up things if I let myself go. I rebel against these feelings and have to fight myself to keep control.*

Therapist: *It's okay to have feelings.* [The therapist's reassurance is out of tune with the patient's anxiety at this moment. As a result, the patient's following comments become brief and static as if she is waiting until the therapist shows evidence of understanding.]

Patient: *I pray that if I ever do anything like that* [make a reassuring comment that misses the point], *I do it here and not at home.*

Therapist: *We can handle it.*

Patient: *I don't know why I have to be so afraid. I feel as though I have to punish myself.*

Therapist: *You don't seem bad.*

Patient: *Then why do I feel the way I do?* [Pay attention to what I actually feel and why I feel it! Don't reassure me, help me analyze this problem!]

Therapist: [Gestures.]

Patient: *I don't want my life* [therapy] *to end* [but by your unhelpful comments the therapy right now has ended, and I don't know when you will start to do therapy again.]

Therapist: *We have a way to go together.*

Patient: *I know, but I don't want to keep coming back here to this place all my life.* [I don't want to have to keep waiting for you. Help me figure this out.]

Therapist: *You're stuck with me.*

[The patient laughs and then smiles warmly.]

Patient: *It's like when I was working here as a patient, I wanted to work but it frightened me and didn't want to work at the same time.* [You are working here as a therapist, you want to work but it frightens you and so you don't want to work at the same time. That's why we're stuck.]

Therapist: *I understand.*

Silent Interpretation

Your response frightens me. I get very anxious that the fear will come back to me because you have offered me no evidence of your understanding. I can't accept my feelings. So what if you can! I can't. That's what you should explore with me. Now I think I don't want to go on with you. And actually, you are refusing to go on with me by your not understanding. I don't know why. You have everything a therapist could want. I pray I won't be afraid. I pray that nothing can take me away from you even though something already has. I feel as though I could smash things if I let myself go here. I rebel against these feelings and have to fight myself to keep control with you. I feel as though I could throw things at you at times. That I could smash up things if I let myself go. I rebel against these feelings and have to fight myself to keep control.

I pray that if I ever misunderstand anyone like that I do it here and not at home. I don't know why I have to be so afraid. I feel as though I have to punish myself. Perhaps to keep from letting you have it. Pay attention to what I actually feel and why I feel it! Don't reassure me, help me analyze this problem. I don't want this therapy to end but by your unhelpful comments the therapy right now has ended and I don't know when you will start to do therapy again. I don't want to have to keep waiting for you. You are working here as a therapist, you want to work but it frightens you and so you don't want to work at the same time. That's why we are stuck.

Possible transference interpretation (based on the assumption that you made the previous interpretation): "*Maybe the same thing is true now too. You obviously want to work hard here, which is why you come. But it sounds like you are so afraid of the angry feelings and thoughts that might come out here that you find yourself holding back. You hope it comes out here instead of at home so you won't lose your family, yet I sense you're afraid that if it came out here you might lose me instead.*"

Possible transference interpretation (if the previous interpretation had not been made): "*On the other hand, maybe there is some work I have not done. I've been telling you it's ok to have and accept these feelings rather than help you understand why you have them and why you can't accept them. Maybe we need to back up to something you said earlier to put this together.*" [Now you would address the themes mentioned in earlier interpretations.]

These two interpretations illustrate differences in approach between those who believe transference is intrapsychically generated and those who believe that both patient and therapist contribute to and shape the evolution of the transference.

The hour continues:

Patient: *I rebel against my own mind—against breaking things, or hurting people, and against harsh feelings. Does that mean I feel that way deep down? Am I really that way? Am I actually hostile?*

Therapist: *I find you're quite acceptable.*

Patient: *But I can't. I never could watch mysteries on TV before, but you know, this past week I actually watched a couple. I wasn't completely relaxed. It takes time, Bill says.*

Therapist: *It takes time.*

Patient: *Is it normal to feel resentful about someone you love?*

Therapist: [Gestures.]

Patient: *I feel resentful toward God for taking mother from me. But then perhaps He does do things in ways we don't understand.*

Provide a possible transference interpretation now.

Therapist: *He understands.*

Patient: *Just like the other day, I went to a store I usually avoid because it has so many people in it. I usually go to the one where there aren't many people, but last week I went to the store with the people and it didn't bother me any more than the other store. I felt so ridiculous and so dumb and stupid for having had those feelings about the store. I'm 30 years old. I act like a 1-year-old baby and it makes me feel so childish—I feel as though I'm depending on my family. It makes me feel as though I'm just not right.*

Therapist: *I understand how you feel at times.*

Patient: *I get the feeling that I could just scream to the top of my lungs at times.*

Translate the transference implications.

Author's Translation

Patient: *I rebel against my own mind—against breaking things, or hurting people* [you], *and against harsh feelings. Does that mean I feel that way deep down* [toward you]? *Am I really that way? Am I actually hostile?*

Therapist: *I find you're quite acceptable.*

Patient: *But I can't. I never could watch mysteries on TV before, but you know, this past week I actually watched a couple.* [We seem to have a hard time looking at the mystery of my feelings.] *I wasn't completely relaxed.* [I'm not relaxed with you.] *It takes time, Bill* [you] *says.*

Therapist: *It takes time.*

Patient: *Is it normal to feel resentful about someone you love?* [Like resenting you for having left me?]

Therapist: [Gestures.]

Patient: *I feel resentful toward God* [you] *for taking mother* [therapy] *from me. But then perhaps He does* [you] *do things in ways we don't understand.*

Therapist: *He understands.*

Patient: *Just like the other day, I went to a store I usually avoid because it has so many people in it. I usually go to the one where there aren't many people, but last week I went to the store with the people and it didn't bother me any more than the other store. I felt so ridiculous and so dumb and stupid for having had those feelings about the store. I'm 30 years old. I act like a 1-year-*

old baby and it makes me feel so childish—I feel as though I'm depending on my family [therapy]. It makes me feel as though I'm just not right.

Therapist: *I understand how you feel at times.*

Patient: *I get the feeling that I could just scream to the top of my lungs at times* [at you].

Silent Interpretation

I rebel against my own mind—against breaking things, or hurting you, and against harsh feelings towards you. That's how I feel deep down, that I am hostile. But I can't accept those feelings. Neither can you. I never could look at mysterious aspects of myself before in here, but you know, this past week I actually was able to look at a couple. I'm not completely relaxed with you, but you say it takes time. Is it normal to feel resentful and loving towards you? I feel resentful towards you for the therapy we lost. But then perhaps you do things for reasons I don't understand. Just like the other day, I went into something I usually avoid and it didn't bother me as much as I thought it would. I felt so ridiculous and so dumb and stupid for having those feelings. Childish—I feel as though I'm depending on you. It makes me feel as though I'm just not right.

Therapist: *I understand how you feel at times.*

Patient: *I get the feeling that I could just scream to the top of my lungs at times like this, I'm so irritated by that comment.*

   Possible transference interpretation: *"You wonder if it's normal to resent someone you love, to have such harsh feelings when something is taken away from you. Perhaps this is related to feeling upset with your friend who was gone, and I suspect it's related to my absence too. Maybe you were upset when I was gone and found yourself resenting me for being gone, yet also wanting to be with me, wondering how to balance both feelings at once."*

The hour continues:

Therapist: [Gestures.]

Patient: *Yet, I shouldn't have those feelings. I shouldn't lose control of my emotions.*

Therapist: *You're safe here.*

Patient: *I have to hurry and shop as quickly as possible; yet I don't know why I have to hurry. There's nothing to hurry about.* [She is pensive for several moments, then looks up and smiles warmly.] *I'm going to a coffee tomorrow morning. I'm a bit leery of that. It's not the lady that I'm afraid of. I* *afraid I'll get nervous there, and just lose control of myself. What I want most of all is to have somebody with me all the time that understands.*

Provide a possible transference interpretation.

Therapist: *I know what you mean.*

Patient: *But it's not right.*

Therapist: *It's okay with me.*

Patient: *Yes, you said that before. I'm just expressing my feelings.*

Translate the transference meaning now.

Author's Translation

Therapist: [Gestures.]

Patient: *Yet, I shouldn't have those feelings* [about you]. *I shouldn't lose control of my emotions* [in therapy].

Therapist: *You're safe here.*

Patient: *I have to hurry and shop* [look for what I need here] *as quickly as possible; yet I don't know why I have to hurry.* [Apparently you don't either since you said I'm safe.] *There's nothing to hurry about.* [I'm not going to find understanding here.] [She is pensive for several moments, then looks up and smiles warmly.] *I'm going to a coffee* [therapy] *tomorrow morning. I'm a bit leery of that. It's not the lady* [you] *that I'm afraid of. I afraid I'll get nervous there* [here], *and just lose control of myself. What I want most of all is to have somebody with me all the time that understands.* [I want you to do that now. Understand me.]

Therapist: *I know what you mean.*

Patient: *But it's not right* [for me to want you with me all the time].

Therapist: *It's okay with me.*

Patient: *Yes, you said that before* [I heard that, now listen to me]. *I'm just expressing my feelings* [that it does not feel right for me to want you with me all the time].

Silent Interpretation

I shouldn't have these angry feelings about you. I shouldn't lose control of my emotions in therapy. I have to hurry and look at these issues and what I need but I don't know why I have to hurry. When I come to see you, I feel leery because I'm afraid I'll get nervous and lose control of myself. I wish I could have you with me all the time understanding me. But it's not right for me to want that.

Although it was possible to interpret earlier in the session, we see the patient continue to offer more vignettes that symbolize her feelings about the therapist. These images of her friend, her husband, Dr. H, the coffee klatch, and God coalesce into a theme of feelings of resentment over loss and the fear of those feelings coming out. This also illustrates that if the therapist misses a transference theme, it will keep recurring in the session until it is interpreted.

Possible transference interpretation: *"You're leery of the coffee because you're afraid you could lose control of your emotions. So you wish somebody could be with you and help you understand so you wouldn't lose control. Whether it's with your husband or your friend or at the coffee there's a fear of these feelings coming out. And when they did come out with Dr. H, he judged you as hostile. I wonder if you may be struggling with feelings here too. I was gone last month like your friend, and perhaps you were upset about that but afraid to tell me for fear I might judge you like Dr. H."*

The hour continues:

Therapist: *That's all right.*

Patient: *Monday is my best day. It's because Bill has been with me all day Sunday. If I didn't have him, I'd end up here as a patient again.*

Therapist: *I understand.*

Patient: *Like that article I read in the paper on how to treat a patient who returns from a mental hospital. It said you had to determine if he's violent—that scares me. I'm afraid I could be violent. Like Dr. H said to me, if I started throwing things I wouldn't be able to stop throwing them.*

Therapist: *You couldn't hurt me.*

[Patient laughs.]

Patient: *I don't want to—in fact I'd rather be dead than do that. [She becomes anxious.] Sometimes I feel as though I don't have any place to turn.*

Therapist: *You're perfectly safe here.*

Patient: *You know when I had those feelings that I was going to faint if I looked up in the air.*

Therapist: *Yes.*

Patient: *I don't have them anymore. Those feelings that I had of myself fainting are gone.*

Therapist: [Gestures.]

Patient: *Do you remember Mary?*

Therapist: [Gestures.]

Patient: *I got a letter from her and she's doing real well. She said my mother was my biggest comfort. The neighbors thought I'd go to pieces when she died, but I didn't.*

Therapist: *Mary is doing all right.*

Patient: *I surprised them. It's this rebellion inside of me. I'm rebelling deep down inside of me about something.*

Therapist: *Let's continue the same time next Monday.*

Patient: *Okay and thank you, doctor.*

Translate the transference meanings.

Author's Translation

Therapist: *That's all right.*

Patient: *Monday is my best day. It's because Bill has been with me all day Sunday. If I didn't have him* [you], *I'd end up here* [in the hospital] *as a patient again.*

Therapist: *I understand.*

Patient: *Like that article I read in the paper on how to treat a patient who returns from a mental hospital. It said you had to determine if he's violent— that scares me. I'm afraid I could be violent* [with you]. *Like Dr. H said to me, if I started throwing things I wouldn't be able to stop throwing them.* [The patient is hinting that she is ready for a transference interpretation by offering a number of bridge themes: patient, mental hospital, a doctor. These are all indications of readiness to talk about this treatment, this patient, and this doctor.]

Therapist: *You couldn't hurt me.*

[Patient laughs.]

Patient: *I don't want to—in fact I'd rather be dead than do that.* [She becomes anxious.] *Sometimes I feel as though I don't have any place to turn.* [I am afraid I will become violent and hurt you. But your refusal to engage my feelings shows me that this is not a place I can turn to right now.]

Therapist: *You're perfectly safe here.*

Patient: *You know when I had those feelings that I was going to faint if I looked up in the air.* [If you are going to deny the fact that I feel in danger, I will deny it too.]

Therapist: *Yes.*

Patient: *I don't have them anymore. Those feelings that I had of myself fainting are gone.*

Therapist: [Gestures.]

Patient: *Do you remember Mary?* [Do you remember me? When you ignore my anger and anxiety I don't know what you remember.]

Therapist: [Gestures.]

Patient: *I got a letter from her and she's doing real well. She said my mother was my biggest comfort. The neighbors thought I'd go to pieces when she died, but I didn't.* [You were my greatest comfort and I thought I'd go to pieces when you were gone, but I didn't. You have been dead to me today, but I didn't fall apart as I had feared.]

Therapist: *Mary is doing all right.*

Patient: *I surprised them. It's this rebellion inside of me. I'm rebelling deep down inside of me about something.*

Therapist: *Let's continue the same time next Monday.*

Patient: *Okay and thank you, doctor.*

Silent Interpretation

I do best when I have been with you. If I didn't have you I'd end up back in the hospital. Like that article I read in the paper on how to treat a patient who returns from a mental hospital. You should pay attention to my fear of my violence. If I started throwing things I wouldn't be able to stop.

Therapist: *You couldn't hurt me.*

[Patient laughs.]

Patient: *I don't want to—in fact I'd rather be dead than do that, because I would turn my anger against myself before I would express it towards you.* [She becomes anxious.] *I feel like I don't have any place to turn to for understanding right now because you can't seem to talk about my anger and my fear of it coming out. If you are going to deny the fact that I feel in danger, I will deny it too. My feelings of anxiety no longer exist. Do you remember me? By saying I am safe you seem to have forgotten that I don't feel safe, that I am angry and terrified of my feelings coming out in a hurtful manner. This part of me, that I think you have forgotten, thought you were my biggest comfort. That part of me thought I'd go to pieces when you were gone, but I didn't. I surprised myself. It's this rebellion inside of me by which I keep all my dangerous feelings hidden.*

In this hour, we see a shift from her transference feelings being organized around the missed session to being organized around the therapist's failure to understand the patient.

☐ Case #2

The previous hour illustrated how images of the therapist evolved in response to an adaptive context: a missed session. This hour will illustrate the therapist's intervention becoming an adaptive context and the patient's unconscious supervision of the therapist. Listen for the transference and see how the patient's conflict about trust and intimacy evolves.

Patient: *I don't know where to start. . .*

Therapist: *One thing that I need for us to talk about . . . I was thinking about something you said last week about how long therapy would go on. I don't know if they made it clear to you, but I'm a student, and I'm only scheduled to be here until the end of this school year. There is a possibility that I will be here next year, but we have to work on the assumption that we will be ending in May, and I'm wondering what your feelings are about that.*

Patient: *I guess it's fine. I don't think I'd have a problem with another person. I think that the only problem would be telling everything that had gone on.*

Therapist: *At the point we stopped, if you wanted I could talk to the new person and I could tell them where we were and what we had talked about.*

Patient: *That would be really good. I'm really glad that you told me that. I'm in a really good mood. Nothing is really wrong. I don't know what to say.*

Therapist: *Is that a different place for you?*

Patient: *I don't know. I just got a package from my mom, $50. Last night I found out that guy L, well, a group of us are going to the Bahamas over Spring break, and I just found out that he's going too. I'm not worried, but I know that I'll have to see him and talk to him. He keeps coming into my room and I assume that he's coming to see my girlfriend, not me.*

Therapist: *It sounds like you have mixed feelings about him.*

Patient: *I think ok, but then I remember all the things he said about me and I realize that I can't get involved with him.*

Therapist: *So you can't really trust him.*

Patient: *No. Not even nothing. I can't even sit in the room alone with him.*

Therapist: *Is it him or any guy?*

Patient: *I don't know. I think a lot of it is him because I told him everything and gave him all of me. It could be the same with other guys.*

Translate this passage into its transference meanings.

Author's Translation

Patient: *I don't know. I just got a package from my mom, $50* [I just received some information from you]. *Last night I found out that guy L, well, a group of us are going to the Bahamas over Spring break, and I just found out that he's* [you're] *going* [away] *too. I'm not worried, but I know that I'll have to see him* [you] *and talk to him* [you]. *He keeps coming into my room and I assume that he's coming to see my girlfriend, not me.* [We keep meeting, but I assume you would rather see someone else.]

Therapist: *It sounds like you have mixed feelings about him.*

Patient: *I think ok, but then I remember all the things he* [you] *said about me and I realize that I can't get involved with him* [you in therapy, now that I know you will be leaving me].

Therapist: *So you can't really trust him.*

Patient: *No. Not even nothing. I can't even sit in the room alone with him* [you].

Therapist: *Is it him or any guy?*

Patient: *I don't know. I think a lot of it is him* [you] *because I told him* [you] *everything and gave him* [you] *all of me. It could be the same with other guys.*

Silent Interpretation

I realize you and I will be together for now, but I assume you would rather see someone else since you'll be leaving. I realize I can't get involved with you or the therapy because I can't even trust you enough to sit in the room alone with you now that I know you'll be leaving. I told you everything about myself last time and let you know too much.

Although the patient said it's "fine" that the therapist is leaving, the transference material gives us a very different story. In fact, the following material indicates that the adaptive context is the therapist's announcement that she will leave at the end of the year. All the transference statements are organized around this event. Now we need to wait for a bridge comment that will allow us to link her feelings in the latent content to the therapy.

The hour continues:

Therapist: *What do you think still connects him to you that you still have these feelings?*

Patient: *He's the first person I told all what happened to me. I mean I told my roommates and K, but it meant more telling him. I expected him to be* *concerned and sympathetic, and be there for me, but of course he didn't do that.*

Therapist: *You sound like you think those expectations were unreasonable.*

Patient: *Well, I wonder. He didn't talk to me for a while and then threw all this stuff on me, and he still feels I told him to get him to feel sorry for me. Once he said that everything with S I caused. I couldn't stand to hear him say that. I believed that for a long time and I finally had got so that I no longer believed, so he really upset me to think that maybe I'd been right before. When I asked him more about it, he said that what he means was that if I had talked about it right away, then I'd be all ok with things now and he wouldn't have to deal with all this stuff. That I'd have no problem any more and wouldn't have to tell him. "Why didn't you straighten yourself up before so that I wouldn't have to deal with it?" But I don't think that was all. I think he thinks that what S did wasn't so wrong. I would never think that I would go out with a guy who would think that was ok that another guy took advantage of a girl, but that's what he thinks so I wonder what to say to him.*

Translate the passage and write down a possible transference interpretation.

Author's Translation

Therapist: *What do you think still connects him to you that you still have these feelings?*

Patient: *He's [you're] the first person I told all what happened to me. I mean I told my roommates and K, but it meant more telling him [you]. I expected him [you] to be concerned and sympathetic, and be there for me, but of course he didn't [you won't] do that [since you'll be leaving].*

Therapist: *You sound like you think those expectations were unreasonable.*

Patient: *Well, I wonder. He [You] didn't talk to me for a while [about your leaving] and then threw all this stuff [the fact that you're leaving] on me and he [you] still feels I told him [you] to get him [you] to feel sorry for me. Once he [you] said that everything with S I caused. I couldn't stand to hear him [you] say that. I believed that for a long time and I finally had got so that I no longer believed, so he [you] really upset me to think that maybe I'd been right before. When I asked him [you] more about it, he [you] said that what he [you] means was that if I had talked about it right away, then I'd be all ok with things now and he [you] wouldn't have to deal with all this stuff [my feelings about your leaving]. That I'd have no problem any more and wouldn't have to tell him [you]. 'Why didn't you straighten yourself up before so that I wouldn't have to deal with it.' But I don't think that was all. I think he*

[you] *thinks that what S did* [you are doing to me] *wasn't so wrong. I would never think that I would go out with a guy who would think that was ok that another guy* [you] *took advantage of a girl* [me], *but that's what he* [you] *thinks so I wonder what to say to him* [you].

Silent Translation

You are the first person I told all of what happened to me. I've told others, but it means more telling you. I expected you to be concerned and sympathetic, but of course you won't do that since you are going to leave me. You didn't tell me for a while and then you suddenly throw all this stuff on me and say I told you to get you to feel sorry for me. If you did know you were going to leave all this time without telling me, I wouldn't be able to stand to hear you say that. I believed that for a long time and I finally had got so that I no longer believed, so you would really upset me if you made me think that maybe I'd been right before. I'm also critical of you for not having talked about it right away. If you had, I'd be all ok with things now and you wouldn't have to deal with all this stuff. I'd have no problem and wouldn't have to tell you. Why didn't you straighten yourself up before so that I wouldn't have to deal with it? But that's not all I'm afraid of. I'm also afraid you will think that what you did wasn't so wrong. I would never have worked with you if I had thought you would take advantage of me like this, but that's what you did so I wonder what to say to you.

Although the images of the therapist continue to coalesce, we still don't have an obvious reference to the therapy in the manifest content. References to the announcement are getting very close to the surface, however, as can be seen in the references to discussions with the boyfriend. At this point, we would probably wait and listen.

Silent transference interpretation: "*You mention that there was something he didn't tell you for a while and then he suddenly sprung it on you. You had mistrusted him at first, then trusted him, and then with this you were upset that maybe you had been wrong to trust him all along. He didn't seem to think it was wrong to do that to you, to take advantage of your trust. I wonder if that may be happening here. There was something I didn't tell you for a while too: that I will leave at the end of the year. And, in fact, I did spring it on you suddenly today. I think that upset you too and made you wonder if you were wrong to trust me. If I knew all this time that I was leaving, you might feel I had taken advantage of you, gaining your trust, only to leave you. And what's worse, you may be afraid that I don't care about how my leaving hurts you.*" This statement is longer than anything you would ever say, but it summarizes our understanding at this point.

The hour continues:

Therapist: *It sounds like you don't trust yourself with him.*

Patient: *I've done so many things that didn't turn out the way I expected.*

Therapist: *I don't think anyone could have anticipated the thing that happened with you and S.*

Patient: *I don't know. I think about so many things that I shouldn't have done. I know it wasn't right, but there were many things I shouldn't have done, like driving there with my dad. I never smoked pot in the day. Why did I do that? It was always at night.*

Therapist: *What do you think it means that you did that?*

Patient: *I don't know. Sometimes I think like it was going to happen, like I had no chance. All these random things happened. Usually there were always people at his house but weren't that time. I didn't think about it then, but I've gone over it and over it.*

Therapist: *It's hard not to go back and look for clues and look for things.*

Patient: *And then sometimes I think that it just happened, but when I look at all the things I really think about it. Do you understand what I mean?*

Translate the passage and write down a possible transference interpretation.

Author's Translation

Therapist: *It sounds like you don't trust yourself with him.*

Patient: *I've done so many things that didn't turn out the way I expected.* [Like this therapy, since I didn't expect you to leave me.]

Therapist: *I don't think anyone could have anticipated the thing that happened with you and S.*

Patient: *I don't know. I think about so many things that I shouldn't have done. I know it wasn't right, but there were many things I shouldn't have done, like driving there with my dad* [or coming here to therapy and telling you so much, or you keeping this a secret and springing it on me now]. *I never smoked pot in the day. Why did I do that?* [Why did I let go and tell you so much? Why did you do this?] *It was always at night.*

Therapist: *What do you think it means that you did that?*

Patient: *I don't know. Sometimes I think like it was going to happen, like I had no chance.* [You were going to leave anyway.] *All these random things happened. Usually there were always people at his house but weren't that time* [I'm alone here with you because I already see you as a person who will not be here and a person who is not here understanding my pain.]. *I didn't think about it then, but I've gone over it and over it.* [I should have seen this coming, that you would leave, but I didn't see any clues.]

Therapist: *It's hard not to go back and look for clues and look for things.*

Patient: *And then sometimes I think that it just happened, but when I look at all the things I really think about it. Do you understand what I mean?* [Do you understand how devastated I am?]

Silent Interpretation

This therapy will not turn out the way I expected because I didn't expect you to leave me. I think about so many things you shouldn't have done. It wasn't right. You shouldn't have led me into therapy knowing you would leave. Why did you do that? I had no chance. You were going to leave anyway. You used to be here with me but now I feel alone: you will not be here to understand my pain. I should have seen this coming but I didn't see any clues. Do you understand how devastated I am by your telling me you will leave?

She continues to describe her feelings about the announcement in the latent content. With the direct question to the therapist, the patient is offering unconscious supervision: do you understand me now? It's time for an interpretation.

Possible transference interpretation: *"So many things didn't turn out the way you expected. Things were done that shouldn't have been done. He held back for a while and suddenly threw all this stuff at you. And then you realized you were all alone. You know I wonder if that's happened here too. Therapy is also not turning out the way you expected because I told you that I'll be leaving. And since I didn't tell you last time it probably felt like a surprise to hear it all of a sudden today; you didn't see this coming at all."*

This interpretation leaves out a number of references and feelings. Rather than address everything, I chose those feelings that I thought would be most plausible to her, that she mentioned most recently in the hour, and that she would remember most easily. The interpretation is incomplete; it leaves out some images of the therapist in the latent content and it does not refer to her symptoms that arise in this context. However, we don't have to throw everything into one interpretation, just enough for her work with. This is where the art of interpretation enters. It's best to be brief and to the point. Later interpretations can fill in the rest of the pieces.

The hour continues:

Therapist: *I'm not sure.*

Patient: *He knew I never smoked in the afternoon, he was much more into it than I was, I did it just socially. I wonder if he planned it all, and that makes it even worse. At first I thought it was something that just got out of hand, but if he planned it, it would be so much worse.*

Therapist: *What would make it worse that way?*

Patient: *That would mean he really had no respect for me and that I had no control, and that I was completely vulnerable, that he could think I could do this for him. Do you understand what I'm saying?*

Therapist: *Yes, I do.*

Patient: *I don't know if this makes any sense. I feel like cheaper, like I always held on that he did care about me but now I think that he really didn't care about me if he could do that to me.*

Therapist: *How is that for you thinking that he really didn't care?*

Patient: *It really hurts. My friends all make fun of me. When I told them all the things that L said to me, they say "that's guy lines." S was the first person who said nice things to me that complimented me, that said what you want a guy to say when you were younger. He said them and he didn't mean that. Then L said that too and he didn't mean them either. If another guy said them to me I'd just laugh in his face, like "nice try, good job."*

Translate the passage and write down a possible transference interpretation.

Author's Translation

Therapist: *I'm not sure.*

Patient: *He knew I never smoked in the afternoon, he was much more into it than I was, I did it just socially. I wonder if he* [you] *planned it all* [that I would reveal so much when you knew you would leave me] *and that makes it even worse. At first I thought it was something that just got out of hand* [revealing so much to you] *but if he* [you] *planned it, it would be so much worse.*

Therapist: *What would make it worse that way?*

Patient: *That would mean he* [you] *really had no respect for me and that I had no control and that I was completely vulnerable, that he* [you] *could think I could do this for him* [you]*. Do you understand what I'm saying?* [Do you understand how furious I am that I feel you took advantage of my trust without letting me know you would leave me? The patient is unconsciously urging the therapist to make an interpretation.]

Therapist: *Yes, I do.*

Patient: *I don't know if this makes any sense* [to you]. *I feel like cheaper, like I always held on that he* [you] *did care about me but now I think that he* [you] *really didn't care about me if he* [you] *could do that to* [make me trust you when you were going to leave] *me.*

Therapist: *How is that for you thinking that he really didn't care?*

Patient: *It really hurts. My friends all make* [You have made] *fun of me. When I told them all the things that L* [you] *said to me, they say "that's guy lines."* [You have been leading me on, seeming to care, but just feeding me lines.] *S was* [You were] *the first person that said nice things to me that complemented me, that said what you want a guy to say when you were younger. He* [You] *said them and he* [you] *didn't mean that. Then L* [you] *said that too and he* [you] *didn't mean them either. If another guy* [you] *said them to me* [now] *I'd just laugh in his* [your] *face, like "nice try, good job."*

Silent Interpretation

I wonder if you planned it so that I would reveal so much when you knew you would leave me. That makes it even worse. At first I thought it was something that just got out of hand but if you planned it, it would be so much worse. It would mean you really had no respect for me and that I had no control, and that makes it even worse. I don't know if this makes sense to you. I feel cheaper, like you never really cared about me. It really hurts. Now I won't believe you.

   Possible transference interpretation: "*You have the sense that he knew this all along and had planned it, which means he didn't really respect you and wanted to keep you in a vulnerable position. So that in the end you realize he said what he thought you wanted to hear, he was just using lines on you. I wonder if that's how you experience me now too. I let you be vulnerable and trust me, knowing the whole time that I would leave you. So that now you may not want to believe what I say either.*"

The hour continues:

Therapist: *It's real hard to see yourself trusting a guy.*

Patient: *If a guy really felt that way. L was my first love and I really made him up to be more than he was and that was really bad.*

Therapist: *Why do you think that you made him up to be more than he was? So wonderful, ideal?*

Patient: *I don't know. It was my own fault. My friend K said a lot of things in the beginning like the first time we were together freshman year and he comes to my room and he pours his heart out to me and it's hard to trust him.*

Therapist: *It sounds like it's hard to know what's real and what's not.*

Patient: *I mean, I don't know. I've been raised to be a very trusting person but every time I do it I get stabbed in the back. It's like a joke, but it really hurts. It makes me want to never trust a guy again. It's ok for a friendship but not if it's more than that. I remember with S everyone said that he's a nice guy, maybe I'm the one that has the problem. I don't know what I'm doing wrong. If I know, I can fix it, but I don't know.*

Therapist: *Maybe you're not doing anything wrong.*

Patient: *Then why is it all happening to me? You have to question it. If everyone thinks that these people are nice and they end up doing terrible things to me, maybe the problem is me. I sometimes don't understand, can't differentiate when someone is being sincere or only doing it to get something.*

Translate the passage and write down a possible transference interpretation.

Author's Translation

Therapist: *It's real hard to see yourself trusting a guy.*

Patient: *If a guy* [you] *really felt that way. L was* [You were] *my first love* [the first person I trusted since the rape] *and* [as your leaving shows me] *I really made him* [you] *up to be more than he was* [you are] *and that was really bad.*

Therapist: *Why do you think that you made him up to be more than he was? So wonderful, ideal?*

Patient: *I don't know. It was my own fault. My friend K* [I] *said a lot of things in the beginning like the first time we were together freshman year* [during our first therapy sessions] *and he* [I] *comes to my room* [therapy] *and he* [I] *pours his* [my] *heart out to me* [you] *and it's hard to trust him* [you].

Therapist: *It sounds like it's hard to know what's real and what's not.*

Patient: *I mean, I don't know. I've been raised to be a very trusting person but every time I do it I get stabbed in the back* [just as you did today by telling me you will leave]. *It's like a joke, but it* [your leaving] *really hurts. It makes me want to never trust a guy* [you] *again. It's ok for a friendship but not if it's more than that* [like therapy is]. *I remember with S* [you] *everyone said that he's* [you're] *a nice guy, maybe I'm that one that has the problem.* [Now she identifies with the therapist to direct her criticisms at herself.] *I* [You] *don't know what I'm* [you're] *doing wrong. If I* [you] *know, I* [you] *can fix it, but I* [you] *don't know.*

Therapist: *Maybe you're not doing anything wrong.*

Patient: *Then why is it all happening to me? You* [the therapist] *have to question it. If everyone* [you] *thinks that these people* [you] *are nice and they* [you] *end up doing terrible things to me* [like leaving], *maybe the problem is me. I sometimes don't understand, can't differentiate when someone is* [you are] *being sincere or only doing it to get something.*

Silent Interpretation

You were the first person I trusted since the rape but your leaving shows me I made you up to be more than you are and that was really bad. It was my own fault. I said a lot of things during our first therapy sessions when I came here and poured my heart out to you and now it's hard to trust you. I did but you stabbed me in the back. It really hurts and makes me want never to trust you again. It would have been ok if this were a friendship, but not in therapy. You think you're nice, but you don't know what you've done to me. If you knew, you could fix it but you don't know. You have to question how you've handled telling me you're going to leave. If you think you are nice and yet you can still leave me like this, maybe the problem is me. Now I don't know if you are being sincere or lying to me to get something.

    Possible transference interpretation: "*L was the first person you really trusted but you discovered you had made him up to be more than he really was. You felt stabbed in the back, hurt, and didn't want to trust anyone again. You also have trusted me, but perhaps you're feeling betrayed by me today, by telling you I will be leaving. And maybe that is making you wonder if you can trust me to be sincere with you.*"

The hour continues:

Therapist: *A guy thing?*

Patient: *Yeah. I don't know. I think that's my main problem. I never say anything that I don't mean. I'd never say "I love you" to a guy if I didn't mean it. That's what really hurts me.*

Therapist: *It's tough when you're at the age when some guys are cutting notches in their belt competing with other guys. It's hard when some girls get the brunt of that.*

Patient: *It's weird. My guy friends—I could never see them do that, but then I think that K is a really good friend of L so maybe he would do that too.*

Therapist: *You think K would do that?*

Patient: *Now he went out with my roommate, so I know that he wouldn't do that. But it makes me question that maybe it is me. I don't know what to think.*

Therapist: *When something bad happens to you sometimes it's hard not to look at yourself and think that you might be to blame somehow.*

Patient: *I understand that a lot of things happen that aren't my fault, but I don't know how to deal with it. I need an answer to what happened.*

Therapist: *Do you need an answer or do you want a way that you can anticipate and not just be blindsided the way you were?*

Patient: *I want to have better judgement. I want to know when it's coming.*

Translate the passage and write down a possible transference interpretation in response to the patient's last two statements.

Author's Translation

Therapist: *A guy thing?*

Patient: *Yeah. I don't know. I think that's my main problem. I never say anything that I don't mean* [like you did]. *I'd never say "I love you" to a guy* [patient] *if I didn't mean it. That's what really hurts me.* [You lied to me and led me on.]

Therapist: *It's tough when you're at the age when some guys are cutting notches in their belt competing with other guys. It's hard when some girls get the brunt of that.*

Patient: *It's weird. My guy friends—I could never see them do that, but then I think that K is a really good friend of L so maybe he* [you] *would do that too.* [Maybe getting patients to reveal their inner secrets then dumping them is a competitive thrill for you too.]

Therapist: *You think K would do that?*

Patient: *Now he went out with my roommate, so I know that he wouldn't do that.* [Hint: K wouldn't, but you would.] *But it makes me question that maybe it is me. I don't know what to think.*

Therapist: *When something bad happens to you sometimes it's hard not to look at yourself and think that you might be to blame somehow.*

Patient: *I understand that a lot of things happen* [like how you handled your leaving me] *that aren't my fault, but I don't know how to deal with it. I need an answer to what happened.* [Why are you leaving me and why are you only telling me now after all this time?] Again, she is unconsciously urging the therapist to make an interpretation.

Therapist: *Do you need an answer or do you want a way that you can anticipate and not just be blindsided the way you were?*

Patient: *I want to have better judgement* [in therapy]. *I want to know when it's* [an abandonment is] *coming.*

Silent Interpretation

Your dishonesty with me is my main problem. I never say anything that I don't mean like you did. I'd never say "I love you" to a patient if I didn't mean it. That's what really hurts. You lied to me and led me on. I wasn't able to see you doing it but now I think maybe you would too. Maybe getting patients to reveal their inner secrets then dumping them is a competitive thrill for you too. K wouldn't do it, but you would and did. I understand that your leaving and the way you dealt with it aren't my fault but I still don't know how to deal with it. Why are you leaving me and why are you only telling me now after all this time? I want to have better judgement in therapy so I'll know when I'm going to be abandoned.

Possible transference interpretation: *"Perhaps you also wished you could have seen this coming when I told you I'll be leaving. You realize it's not your fault but you're probably still not sure how to deal with it. It was a surprise."*

Notice how the patient's last comment provides a smooth bridge to the latent content. I used the word *surprise* to see what what feelings the patient might bring up. However, others might prefer to directly interpret her feelings of anger and betrayal mentioned in the latent content.

The hour continues:

Therapist: *I think that you probably couldn't have known that was going to happen, but maybe there were things that you could have noticed. You said that you realized afterwards that this was a pretty lousy crowd, you could see that nobody really cared about anyone else; maybe you couldn't know that he would do that, but maybe you could have known that he would be self absorbed and not really caring about you. Like with K, you know from how he's acted that he would never really do anything harmful to you. But with another kind of person where you aren't so sure, you may say "well, I don't know. I guess I have to be more careful."*

Patient: *When you start to question that maybe he could do something bad, but you're still close. Like with L, I wondered was it just a little problem? When do you need to cut it off? Maybe he wasn't what I wanted, but I didn't want to start all over again and have to tell it to someone else. What's the chances of me, at college, finding a nice guy?*

Therapist: *Even though part of you recognized that this was not the right guy, a part of you was still afraid to let him go. What do you think is going on that's so hard to do?*

Patient: *It's scary that maybe I'll never find the right one. Maybe he's the best I'll find. Because of what happened.*

Therapist: *Last week you said that your mother said that you shouldn't* *settle, but maybe you got other messages from her or your dad that said that you would have to settle.*

Patient: *Not from my parents.*

Therapist: *Last week you said that your parents didn't see the real you, that they thought that you were perfect. What was the real you like?*

Translate the passage and write down a possible transference interpretation.

Author's Translation

Therapist: *I think that you probably couldn't have known that was going to happen, but maybe there were things that you could have noticed. You said that you realized afterwards that this was a pretty lousy crowd, you could see that nobody really cared about anyone else, maybe you couldn't know that he would do that, but maybe you could have known that he would be self absorbed and not really caring about you. Like with K, you know from how he's acted that he would never really do anything harmful to you. But with another kind of person where you aren't so sure, you may say "well I don't know. I guess I have to be more careful."*

Patient: *When you* [I] *start to question that maybe he* [you] *could do something bad but you're still close. Like with L* [you], *I wondered was it* [how you handled the leaving] *just a little problem? When do you* [I] *need to cut it* [the therapy] *off? Maybe he wasn't* [you aren't] *what I wanted but I didn't* [don't] *want to start all over again and have to tell it to someone else* [another therapist]. *What's the chances of me, at college, finding a nice guy* [therapist after you leave]?

Therapist: *Even though part of you recognized that this was not the right guy, a part of you was still afraid to let him go. What do you think is going on that's so hard to do.*

Patient: *It's scary that maybe I'll never find the right one* [therapist]. *Maybe he's* [you're] *the best I'll find. Because of what happened.*

Therapist: *Last week you said that your mother said that you shouldn't settle, but maybe you got other messages from her or your dad that said that you would have to settle.*

Patient: *Not from my parents.* [From you. I'm afraid you think I should just settle for this situation of knowing you are leaving and ignore all the feelings it raises for me. After all, I will have to settle for another therapist when you leave.]

Therapist: *Last week you said that your parents didn't see the real you, that they thought that you were perfect. What was the real you like?*

Silent Interpretation

I start to question that you could do something bad but I'm still close to you. I wonder if your leaving me is a little problem. But when do I need to stop the therapy? Maybe you aren't what I wanted, but I don't want to start all over again with a different therapist. What are the chances the next therapist would be any better? It's scary that maybe I'll never find the right therapist. Maybe you're the best I'll find, because of what happened. I'm afraid though that you think I should just settle for you and ignore my doubts and concerns about therapy.

Possible transference interpretation: *"With L you wondered, was it was a little problem or was it big enough that you ought to end the relationship? Even though he wasn't what you wanted, you also didn't want to have to start over with somebody else. Perhaps you're also wondering if my leaving is a little problem or is it big enough that you would like to end this relationship too? Even though you don't want a therapist who will leave you at the end of the year, you also don't want to have to start over with another therapist."*

The hour continues:

Therapist: *Does your family not talk about things when things are going wrong?*

Patient: *No, I think that it's completely me. I just didn't want them to know. I don't know why I didn't. I think if I would have told them, it would have made it worse. Without telling, I thought I could make it go away. It took coming here to make me realize that wasn't true. It's not them but me not wanting to deal with it at all. Sometimes I think that my parents are so old-fashioned that they would never let me do anything. Because I did so well in school and was so good, they really trusted me. When I got to high school, they gave me a lot of freedom.*

Therapist: *They didn't protect you.*

Patient: *I don't know if "protect" is the right word. I sometimes wish they hadn't let me go out that much. I know no kid would ever say that, but it's not that they are easy going. I had to work. But they saw the responsible part and never saw the irresponsible part. I wish they had considered that part that I was too. I don't think "protecting me" is the right word.*

Translate the passage and write down a possible transference interpretation.

Author's Translation

Therapist: *Does your family not talk about things when things are going wrong?*

Patient: *No, I think that it's completely me.* [I am the only one talking about how this therapy is going wrong.] *I just didn't want them* [you] *to know. I don't know why I didn't. I think if I would have told them* [you]*, it would have made it worse. Without telling I thought I could make it* [this problem of your leaving] *go away. It took coming here to make me realize that wasn't true. It's not them but me not wanting to deal with it at all. Sometimes I think that my parents* [you] *are so old fashioned that they* [you] *would never let me do anything. Because I did so well in school and was so good, they* [you] *really trusted me* [in the therapy]. *When I got to high school* [here]*, they* [you] *gave me a lot of freedom.* [Perhaps a reference to the freedom to say whatever comes to mind in therapy.]

Therapist: *They didn't protect you.*

Patient: *I don't know if "protect" is the right word. I sometimes wish they* [you] *hadn't let me go out that much* [into dangerous topics while knowing you would leave me. Also could be heard as "I wish I hadn't let you leave me."]. *I know no kid would ever say that, but it's not that they are easy going. I had to work. But they* [you] *saw the responsible part and never saw the irresponsible part. I wish they* [you] *had considered that part that I was too. I don't think protecting me is the right word.*

Silent Interpretation

We aren't talking about how this is going wrong. I don't know why. I think if I told you, I thought it would have made things worse. Without telling you, I thought I could make it go away. It took coming here to make me realize that wasn't true. It's my not wanting to deal with it at all. Sometimes I think you are old-fashioned and won't let me do anything. Yet you also really trust me and give me a lot of freedom here to say anything I want. But I sometimes wish that you didn't give me that much freedom. I'm afraid you see only my responsible side and not my irresponsible side. I wish you considered that part of me too.

    Possible transference interpretation: *"Maybe it's more that you wish they had been more responsible and aware of the impact their decisions might have on you. I suspect that you may want that here too. That you need me to be aware of the impact my leaving is having on you right now. Like with them, you may be afraid to say what you think because it might make things worse. And yet my encouraging you to say what comes to mind right now might feel like too much freedom: freedom to say things you're afraid could get you into trouble. Maybe you wish I had prevented this whole thing from happening in the first place so you wouldn't have all these feelings and so you wouldn't have to struggle with whether to say them."* This interpretation is long, but it can be broken down into parts and shared with the patient piece by piece.

The hour continues:

Therapist: *You wish they had more understood where you really were.*

Patient: *Yes. I wish my mom were a lot more aware. I used to go to Manhattan and say we were just going to eat there. My mom always said you are a good kid, you'll never do anything wrong. She believed because I was so good until I was 16, I never lied before and they thought I never would.*

Therapist: *You wish they had seen through you.*

Patient: *Yes. They just figured that when my friends came over, my friends talked to them. They believed them.*

Therapist: *It's real hard because you want your parents to believe you and let you do what you want, but another part knows that terrible things can happen and wishes they had done something so that they didn't happen.*

Patient: *I think too that I realize that when they moved from Manhattan to where we now live, they didn't realize that the same things that were happening back there were also happening where we moved. I had the same things that they had grown up with. They thought that I would be fine, that I had it different. I'll tell you something that happened. When I went home for Christmas, my parents were away for the weekend and I was home with my sister. She wanted to go to this party and my mom said "no" because she is in seventh grade and the person giving the party was in ninth grade. So I said "I'll drive you and all your friends and I'll pick you up in three hours." When I picked them up, I could completely smell pot. She had no clue that it was on her clothes. When we got home, I was just screaming at her. She said that she didn't smoke and I believe her, and she said all the kids were doing it and she didn't. It really scared me that she was doing in seventh grade what I was doing at 16. It scares me. It really scared me. My friends at school were laughing, but I was really scared.*

Translate the passage and write down a possible transference interpretation.

Author's Translation

Therapist: *You wish they had more understood where you really were.*

Patient: *Yes. I wish my mom [you] were a lot more aware. I used to go to Manhattan and say we were just going to eat there. My mom [you] always said you are a good kid, you'll never do anything wrong. She [you] believed* *because I was so good until I was 16* [now], *I never lied before and they* [you] *thought I never would.*

Therapist: *You wish they had seen through you.*

Patient: *Yes. They just figured that when my friends came over, my friends talked to them. They believed them.* [You don't see beneath the surface.]

Therapist: *It's real hard because you want your parents to believe you and let you do what you want, but another part knows that terrible things can happen and wishes they had done something so that they didn't happen.*

Patient: *I think too that I realize that when they moved from Manhattan to where we now live* [when you told me you will be leaving], *they* [you] *didn't realize that the same things that were happening back there were also happening where we moved* [that what happened earlier in the hour is still upsetting me now]. *I had the same things that they had grown up with.* [I have the same upset feelings that I had earlier.] *They* [You] *thought that I would be fine, that I had it different* [that I would feel differently now than earlier because I am a different person from the one you told]. *I'll tell you something that happened. When I went home for Christmas, my parents were away for the weekend and I was home with my sister. She wanted to go to this party and my mom said "no" because she is in seventh grade and the person giving the party was in ninth grade. So I said "I'll drive you and all your friends and I'll pick you up in three hours." When I picked them up I could completely smell pot. She had* [You have] *no clue that it was on her clothes* [what is in the air]. *When we got home* [When I am here] *I was* [am] *just screaming at her* [you]. *She said that she didn't smoke* [You think you haven't done anything wrong] *and I believe her* [you], *and she said* [you figure] *all the kids* [other people] *were doing it* [wrong things] *and she* [you] *didn't. It really scared me that she was* [you are] *doing in seventh grade what I was doing at 16* [such a dangerous thing]. *It* [Your leaving] *scares me. It really scared me. My friends at school were laughing* [you might laugh] *but I was* [I'm] *really scared* [of what could happen here].

Silent Interpretation

I wish you were a lot more aware. You believe me and imagine I am a good girl who would never lie to you. So you take me at face value and don't look beneath the surface. When you told me you will be leaving, you didn't realize that it upset me so much and still does now. You thought I would be fine, that I would quickly get over it. But you see the idea of someone going away is connected with something wrong being done. You have no clue that you have done something wrong. I could scream at you for what you've done. You don't think you've done anything wrong and I believe you. But you're doing something dangerous now. Your leaving scares me. You might laugh but I'm really scared now.

The hour continues:

Therapist: *What was that like for you to be in the parent role with your sister?*

Patient: *I always did some parent things, like going to school plays or driving her places, but never anything like this. I wanted to hit her so hard. It was really hard. It really scared me to death. My parents are talking about moving and when I was in school, I always said "no," but now I say move, move. It's scary that somehow I want to stop what happened to me from happening to her.*

Therapist: *You want to protect her.*

Patient: *It's really scary.*

Therapist: *You don't want bad things to happen to her like they happened to you.*

Patient: *No. She's worse than me. She's starting a lot younger than me. I don't know what to tell my mom.*

Therapist: *What do you want to tell your mom?*

Patient: *That's the point that I think that I might tell my mom about what happened to me. But I don't know what they could have done different. They are really good parents and I'm afraid they might freak and never let her out. It's not that they weren't home or that they didn't care. I'm scared that if I say that they should have been more aware, then they'll really question everything. I don't think that's fair. That's not fair to her.*

Translate the passage and write down a possible transference interpretation.

Author's Translation

Therapist: *What was that like for you to be in the parent role with your sister?*

Patient: *I always did some parent things, like going to school plays or driving her* [taking you to psychological] *places, but never anything like this* [the impending loss]. *I wanted* [want] *to hit her* [you] *so hard. It was* [is] *really hard. It* [telling me about your leaving] *really scared me to death. My parents* [you] *are talking about moving* [leaving] *and when I was in school* [therapy], *I always said "no," but now I say move, move.* [Get this over with as soon as possible!]. *It's scary that somehow I want to stop what happened to me from happening to her* [me again here in the therapy].

Therapist: *You want to protect her.*

Patient: *It's really scary.*

Therapist: *You don't want bad things to happen to her like they happened to you.*

Patient: *No. She's worse than me. She's starting a lot younger than me. I don't know what to tell my mom* [you].

Therapist: *What do you want to tell your mom?*

Patient: *That's the point that I think that I might tell my mom* [you] *about what happened to me. But I don't know what they* [you] *could have done different. They* [you] *are really good parents* [therapist] *and I'm afraid they* [you] *might freak and never let her* [me] *out. It's not that they* [you] *weren't home* [aren't available] *or that they* [you] *didn't care. I'm scared that if I say that they* [you] *should have been more aware* [of the impact of your leaving], *then they'll* [you'll] *really question everything. I don't think that's fair. That's not fair to her* [you].

Silent Interpretation

I have always been responsible for taking you to emotional places but never anything like this impending loss. I want to hit you so hard. It is really hard. Telling me you would leave really scares me to death. When you talked about leaving, I thought no, don't. But now I say move, move, get it over with as soon as possible. It's scary that I want to stop a repetition of this abandonment and betrayal. It's really scary. I'm worse off than you think, I feel a lot younger than you realize. I don't know what to tell you. I might tell you what happened here but I don't know what you could have done differently. You are a good therapist and I'm afraid you might freak if I told you and never let me out. It's not that you weren't available or that you didn't care. I'm scared that if I say that you should have been more aware of the impact of your leaving, you'll question everything. I don't think that's fair to you.

    Possible transference interpretation: *"It sounds like it's been really hard taking care of your sister and trying to keep her from doing dangerous things. It would be such a relief if you could share with your mother what risk your sister is in and what you've gone through but you're afraid she would overreact and doubt herself too much. I wonder if you're in a similar bind here. I have a hunch that my leaving is scary too, but that you may be afraid to share that with me for fear of how I would react. So you keep those feelings to yourself at the same time that you probably feel the urge to let them out."*

The hour continues:

Therapist: *It sounds like you want to tell, are afraid that they will clamp down too much on your sister, but don't just want to do nothing.*

Patient: *I wish I could know how they'll react.*

Therapist: *It's the same issue isn't it? You want to know when you start here, how it will all turn out.*

Patient: *It would make it so much easier, because I don't know what to do.*

Therapist: *My guess is that you've been doing a lot of thinking about this.*

Patient: *I don't think it would help to talk to my mom.*

Therapist: *If you had a sister eight years older, who went through what you did, what would you have wanted her to do?*

Patient: *Sometimes I think of not telling my parents, but telling my sister. After the party, I pointed out friends of mine that are really in trouble. Of course, they did more than just smoke pot. My roommate smokes sometimes, and when she does I get really nervous. I hold it as the root of all evil. If I didn't smoke, I wouldn't have hung out with that crowd. It's stuck in my head. I want to tell her sometimes so she'll understand.*

Therapist: *How would you feel about telling her?*

Patient: *Actually, I would be, well, "embarrassed" isn't the right word. It's that she really idolizes me, and I don't know how she'd handle it. I don't know if she'd respect me like she does now. I don't think she'd be angry. I don't know how she'd react. And she's so young, in seventh grade. If I had an older sister who told me, I'd be "Huh? What are you talking about?"*

Translate the passage and write down a possible transference interpretation.

Author's Translation

Therapist: *It sounds like you want to tell, are afraid that they will clamp down too much on your sister, but don't just want to do nothing.*

Patient: *I wish I could know how they'll* [you'll] *react* [to what I tell you].

Therapist: *It's the same issue isn't it? You want to know when you start here, how it will all turn out.* [Nice allusion to the transference, which the patient promptly confirms.]

Patient: *It would make it so much easier, because I don't know what to do* [with my fear of your reaction]. [The therapist misses this opening to discuss the patient's fear of what might happen.]

Therapist: *My guess is that you've been doing a lot of thinking about this.*

Patient: *I don't think it would help to talk to my mom* [you]. [Your last comment did not indicate to me that you can talk about this.]

Therapist: *If you had a sister eight years older, who went through what you did, what would you have wanted her to do?*

Patient: *Sometimes I think of not telling my parents, but telling my sister* [you]. *After the party* [Right now], *I pointed* [am pointing out to you] *out friends of mine that are* [I am] *really in trouble. Of course, they did more than just smoke pot.* [My problem is more serious than just smoking pot.] *My roommate* [therapist] *smokes* [does troubling things] *sometimes, and when she does* [you do like right now] *I get really nervous. I hold it as the root of all evil. If I didn't smoke, I wouldn't have hung out with that crowd. It's stuck in my head. I want to tell her* [you] *sometimes so she'll* [you'll] *understand.*

Therapist: *How would you feel about telling her?*

Patient: *Actually, I would be, well, "embarrassed" isn't the right word. It's that she* [you] *really idolizes me, and I don't know how she'd* [you'd] *handle it. I don't know if she'd* [you'd] *respect me like she does* [you do] *now. I don't think she'd* [you'd] *be angry. I don't know how she'd* [you'd] *react. And she's* [you're] *so young* [unaware], *in seventh grade. If I had an older sister who told me I'd be* [maybe you'd be] *"Huh? What are you talking about?"*

Silent Interpretation

I wish I could know how you'll react to what I tell you. It would make it so much easier because I don't know what to do with my fear of your reaction. I don't think it would help to talk to you. Sometimes I think of telling you everything I've done so you'll understand. I am pointing out to you that I am really in trouble. I want to tell you so you'll understand. I'm not embarrassed about telling you. But you idolize me as someone who isn't affected by this loss and I don't know how you would handle knowing that this upsets me. I don't know if you'd respect me like you do now. I don't think you'd be angry. I don't know how you'd react. And you're so unaware, naive. If I told you, you'd be puzzled, wondering what I was talking about.

    Possible transference interpretation: *"You'd like to tell your sister what risks she is taking so she will understand. But you're afraid of her reaction if you told her your feelings. She might not respect you, or she might be so naive that she wouldn't understand at all. Maybe you're also afraid I may not realize how scary it is for you knowing that I'll be leaving. You probably* *wanted to tell me but wondered if I would lose respect for you or if I wouldn't understand at all. If I would understand how much it hurt when I told you I'll be leaving and how much it hurts even now."*

The hour continues:

Therapist: *It's hard for you to see her identifying and saying, "if it happened to my sister, then I'd better be more careful."*

Patient: *It's hard because I think of her social skills like when I was sixteen, but she just got into junior high, and I wouldn't know what she could handle. Her penmanship just got all right, and when I go home I have to help her with long division. It really scares me. Was I slow or is the environment just different for her? I have a real problem figuring out what to do.*

Therapist: *What's your relationship been with her?*

Patient: *Of course I'm eight years older, but when I go home I'd rather be with her than with my friends. So I guess we are pretty close. I like her a lot, we're pretty good friends.*

Therapist: *I can see why you're so worried about her.*

Translate the passage and write down a possible transference interpretation.

Author's Translation

Therapist: *It's hard for you to see her identifying and saying, "if it happened to my sister, then I'd better be more careful."*

Patient: *It's hard because I think of her* [your] *social skills like when I was sixteen, but she* [you] *just got into junior high* [aren't as aware as I am], *and I wouldn't* [don't] *know what she* [you] *could handle. Her penmanship just got all right, and when I go home I have to help her with long division.* [Some skills you have learned but others I have to help you with; skills having to do with "division."] *It really scares me. Was I slow or is the environment* [the therapy situation and experience of loss] *just different for her* [you]? *I have a real problem figuring out what to do* [with you].

Therapist: *What's your relationship been with her?*

Patient: *Of course, I'm eight years older* [more aware than you], *but when I go home* [here] *I'd rather be with her* [you] *than with my friends. So I guess we are pretty close. I like her* [you] *a lot, we're pretty good friends.*

Therapist: *I can see why you're so worried about her.*

Silent Interpretation

It's hard because I don't know what you can handle. Some things you still don't get at all. You have learned some skills but others I have to help you with. It really scares me. Am I slow or is this problem just different for you? I have a problem figuring out what to do with you. Of course, I'm more aware than you, but I'd rather be with you than with my friends. So I guess we are pretty close. I like you a lot, we're pretty good friends.

CHAPTER

Theory of Defense Analysis

☐ Listening for Process

Previously, we learned to listen for conflict—the wish, fear, and defense—by focusing on the content of the patient's associations and looking for patterns in current and past relationships as well as in the transference. In the following two chapters, we will be looking for defenses not in the content of the patient's associations, but in the *process*. What do the terms "content" and "process" mean? Content simply means *what* the patient tells you. Process is *how* the patient tells you. For example, let's look at the following vignette from a content perspective and then from a process perspective.

Patient: *I was talking to Jane yesterday, and I realized that I have been staying in my AA group for a long time even though I wanted to leave. I realize they have not really liked me and I have never fit in. And really, as I think about it I think I'm going to leave. Do you think that's a good idea?*

From a content perspective, the conflict is as follows:

- wish: to leave the group
- fear: of what will happen if she leaves
- defense: staying with the group and doubting herself

Possible interpretation of conflict: *"It sounds like you are afraid of what would happen [fear] if you did leave the group [wish], so you are tempted to stay [defense]. What is it you are afraid would happen if you did leave?"*

From a process perspective, a different picture emerges. The patient is talking about a wish to leave the group, but at the very moment she says she will leave, a defense occurs: she invites your voice into the room. We see a shift *in the way she tells the story*. She shifts from voicing her thoughts to inviting you to voice yours. From a process perspective the conflict is as follows:

- wish: to give voice to her own thoughts
- fear: of what would happen if she does so
- defense: inviting you to offer your thoughts instead

Possible defense interpretation: *"You are inviting my voice into the room just now* [defense] *after you were speaking with your own voice* [wish]. *Was there something risky just then* [fear] *when you voiced your own thoughts that led you to want me to speak instead?"*

In this kind of defense analysis, we seek to understand not only the content of her question, but its function. Why did she ask that question at that moment? What became so risky about saying she wanted to leave that she had to ask you for your thoughts? From a process point of view, we are looking for defenses *as they occur in the hour with you* (Gray 1995).

Unlike the earlier approach of listening for conflict in the content of the associations, here the therapist listens for conflict as manifested in the process. As the patient freely associates, the therapist listens for any shifts that could indicate an inhibition in the patient's ability to associate to a given topic. As the intensity of a topic, thought, or feeling increases, the therapist observes how the patient handles this increasing intensity. Will she be able to continue exploring this topic? If not, when does she shift? How does she shift? (Davison et al. 1986)

Here is another example to illustrate listening for process.

Patient: *I was supposed to go for a date with Jim last Saturday night. He was going to pick me up at seven, but when it was 7:30 he still hadn't come. I was worried. Wondered if he had forgotten. And that bugged me. Finally, about 8:30 he shows up drunk and apologized for being late. I was upset. I was going to tell him I was irritated, <u>but then I remembered that I've been late a lot of times, and who am I to criticize him</u>?*

The patient expresses increasingly critical feelings about Jim until the underlined passage, where she begins to criticize herself instead. Her critical feelings would be considered an id derivative, that is, an expression of an unconscious fantasy, feeling, or thought that is somewhat concealed within a conscious thought. For example, we might speculate that the patient had some very angry feelings about the boyfriend, but only these mild expressions would be tolerable in her conscious awareness. As these mild expressions become stronger, we would wait until the moment when they have become so strong that the patient can tolerate them no longer and needs to ward them off. That occurs at the underlined passage.

What do we interpret? It is obvious this woman would have been angry with her boyfriend and we might feel tempted to say that. We might be tempted to interpret the content of her feelings and perhaps infer deeper feelings than what was stated. From a process point of view, however, we would interpret *not the unconscious content of her feelings, but rather the process of how she handles those feelings that have become conscious.* Whereas transference and conflict perspectives focus on the meaning of a statement, defense analysis focuses on the function or use of a statement. We would not speculate on what unconscious, more intense, and more dangerous feelings might lurk beneath the surface. Instead, from a process point of view we are interested in the *conscious thoughts and feelings that provoked a defense.* Notice in the excerpt that the woman did not suddenly criticize herself because she had expressed a murderous fantasy. Merely saying she wanted to tell him she was irritated was enough to provoke a defense.

Defenses do not occur only when violent fantasies are stated. They can be provoked by even the mildest of statements. Rather than speculate about the fantasies these statements symbolize, we simply point to the conscious statement that provoked a defense. Then we begin to explore the anxiety that even so mild a statement might have aroused. From a process oriented focus we listen to increasingly intense conscious statements, note when a defense occurs, then examine what the anxiety was that arose as she was talking that brought up the defense (Gray 1995).

Possible defense interpretation: *"You are describing yourself just now* [defense] *when a moment ago you were describing Jim as late* [id derivative: wish to talk about Jim]. *Was there some feeling of risk as you were describing him just now?"* [anxiety]

This is a common structure for a process oriented defense interpretation: first mention the defense, then the the wish, then inquire into the anxiety that evoked the defense. Why this structure to the interpretation? By starting with the last thing the patient said, we start with what is in the patient's immediate awareness. Then we note what the patient said previously, also in the patient's awareness. Then we note that this constitutes a shift and ask the patient if she noticed the shift. This step is essential early in treatment because we cannot analyze a defense together unless the patient can observe it. The vast majority of defenses are outside the patient's awareness until the therapist points them out (Davison et al. 1990).

These defenses are usually so smooth and unobtrusive that their defensive function is not obvious to the patient. For instance, the patient above who was irritated at her tardy boyfriend would not have been aware that she was warding off her anger. In fact, if you pointed out the shift to her she might counter, "But I am late a lot!" She would see the fact that she is late a lot, but she would not see the *function* of mentioning that fact: mentioning her lateness shifts her attention away from her feelings about his lateness. One might respond to her: *"Well, it is true that you are late a lot. We might wonder though if the fact of your lateness distracts you from describing another fact: his lateness."*

The smoothness of defenses can sometimes masquerade as insight. Here is an example from from work with a borderline patient:

Patient: *I realized these women hated me in the support group but I didn't do anything about it. And Grace said I should get out. And I agree. You know they really have not been kind. One woman disinvited me from her wedding. That is so rude I can hardly believe it. <u>But you know I remember that I have been really paranoid in the past and I don't know if I can trust my judgment.</u>*

For this woman to be able to observe her past paranoia with some insight is indeed an advance in the work. However, the insight functions as a defense. By referring to her paranoia, she shifts the focus from the group to herself, from criticizing them to criticizing herself, from feelings she has now to feelings she has had in the past. My response to her: *"Well, it is true you have been paranoid in the past. But I wonder if that fact is getting enlisted here to restrain you from describing how the group has treated you."* She began to speak more freely about how she perceived the group and said she was going to quit the group and announce that fact at the next meeting. She described what she would say then asked, "What do you think about that?"

This is another example of a very smooth defense which would ordinarily escape her notice. She shifts from expressing her thoughts to soliciting mine. And by asking me to critique her thoughts, she invites me to help her put on the brakes and inhibit her from expressing her perceptions. I replied: *"You're inviting my voice in here just after you gave expression to your own. I wonder what felt risky about saying what you want to do."* She realized that she felt anxious when criticizing women and went on to explore that anxiety. This vignette illustrates how smooth defenses can be and how important it is to focus not only on the content of the patient's associations but the process, i.e., the function of statements. What is the function of the patient's statements: to further the free expression of her feelings, thoughts, and perceptions, or to restrain them?

☐ Free Association

What is meant by free association? Early in Freud's work, one of his patients changed his work forever by informing him that this was to be a "talking cure." She would talk, he should listen. By listening to and learning from his patients, Freud came to a deeper understanding of what it meant to listen. He encouraged patients to say whatever came to mind just as if they were riding in a train and reporting whatever sights happened to pass by. By saying whatever came to mind without censoring their thoughts, patients would say things that would reveal the unconscious feelings and thoughts that motivated their otherwise inscrutable and irrational problems.

Freud discovered, however, that none of us is able to say whatever comes to mind without defenses coming up. Initially, he detected resistance to this fundamental rule of "say whatever comes to mind" when the patient fell silent or became openly oppositional. And as his work progressed, he detected ever more subtle means by which free association could be derailed. For instance, a patient could talk continuously in therapy without any silences or obvious opposition and yet not be freely associating at all. She might talk about a difficult topic and keep talking, but shift to a different tone of voice, or a different topic, or a different perspective. By these means, the patient would no longer be associating to the difficult topic; she would be associating *away from* the topic. Remember the patient who talked about rude people then shifted to her previous paranoia? Talking about herself allowed her to associate away from the rudeness of other people. Or consider the patient who was angry at her tardy boyfriend. Talking about her lateness allowed her to associate away from his lateness. She was still talking about lateness, but from a different perspective (Kris 1990).

Freud realized that he would need to focus both on what the patient said and on the problems the patient had saying it. He would need to talk about defenses that interfered with free association in the session. This raises the question of timing of defense interpretations.

Timing

We interpret when a defense occurs (Davison et al. 1986, 1990; Gray 1995). How do we recognize a defense? As you listen to the patient's comments, you listen for a change in function, i.e., when is the patient less able to follow a train of thought? When does the patient become less able to talk about something? For example, reread the following passage.

Patient: *[#1] I realized these women hated me in the support group but I didn't do anything about it. [#2] And Grace said I should get out. [#3] And I agree. [#4] You know they really have not been kind. [#5] One woman disinvited me from her wedding. [#6] That is so rude I can hardly believe it. [#7] But, you know, I remember that I have been really paranoid in the past, and I don't know if I can trust my judgment.*

In the first sentence, the patient talks about the fact that she knew people hated her, and then she shifts to not doing anything about it. But in the next sentence, she focuses on the idea of doing something after all. Sentence #3 continues that theme. Sentences #4, 5, and 6 elaborate on her anger: people who were "not kind," an example, and then a reference to someone who was "so rude I can hardly believe it." Notice the increase of her anger and criticism. Then in sentence #7, we see a shift.

Let's now describe the nature of this shift so we can better understand how we observe defenses in a process oriented approach. In sentence #7, she shifts in several ways: 1) she shifts from describing how she perceives others to how she perceives herself; 2) she shifts from criticizing others to criticizing herself; 3) she shifts from how she feels at this moment to how she has felt in the past. These are shifts in the direction of her perception, of her aggression, and in time (from a focus on the present to a focus on the past). She is no longer talking about how other people have been rude to her. Hence, it is time for an interpretation.

Now we will review a series of vignettes to illustrate shifts in process.

Patient: *I almost think I wanted N around because he was always, always there for me, and that made me feel safer. But the other part of me didn't want to need him. It was like a double sided thing.*

From a content perspective, this woman suffers from both a wish to be with N and a prohibition against that wish. From a process point of view, we would be wondering: what made the patient so anxious *just a moment ago* while she was talking about feeling safe with N that she shifted to describing not wanting to need him? What prevented her from elaborating further about the feeling of safeness?

Patient: *I feel like I've been talking a long time and I wish you would say something. I don't like what I'm getting into here and I really don't want to say more about this right now. [pause] I'm thinking, "Ok, Jack, what are you feeling now? What is going on in your mind?" You know, trying to figure out what is going on in me right now.*

From a content perspective, we might perceive the patient as simply trying to figure out his conflict. From a process point of view, we would notice that the patient has shifted from expressing his desire not to talk to trying to talk. He moves from an external focus [the demand that the therapist speak] to an internal focus [what is going on in me?].

You might counter, however, that the patient is overcoming his resistance to the therapy by making himself talk. From a process point of view, we would agree. However, from a process point of view, we are interested in facilitating free association: even if it means helping the patient more freely express resistance to the therapy.

The vignette continues:

Therapist: *You seem to be trying to make yourself talk right now* [defense] *when a moment ago you said you would prefer not to talk* [wish]. *Was there something uncomfortable* [fear] *about simply saying you didn't want to talk here* [wish]?

Patient: *Well, yes. But you know what do I do then? Simply stop talking or get up and leave the room?* [The patient enlists the danger that he might act on a thought to block himself from voicing more thoughts.]

Therapist: *Well, if we leave action out of it for the moment, we can wonder what is uncomfortable about simply having the thought here, even without the action.*

Patient: *That's interesting, because I often have these weird thoughts of taking a knife and hurting M. And then I really get worried.*

Therapist: *So the idea of action gets you worried and helps you put a lid on those thoughts.*

Patient: *Exactly. It's weird. You know when you bring up the idea here that I could tell you I don't want to talk, I remember my mother and her rejecting me and being unable to tolerate different opinions.*

Therapist: *So that there is some fear here too that I might reject you if you said you didn't want to talk.*

Patient: *Yes. I'm so pliable or compliant. It's like I feel I have to reveal all of myself whether I want to or not.*

Therapist: *And at the same time, there seems to be a taboo against revealing certain parts of yourself, such as your wish not to reveal, to say no.*

Patient: *It's true, it is selective. As if I am figuring out what you can tolerate and what you can't.*

This vignette illustrates the interpretive sequence (Goldberger 1996): 1) state what the patient is saying now, and 2) state how that seems to shift the patient away from what she was saying earlier. Then check to see if the patient can see and understand that shift. If so, then 3) ask what might have felt risky or dangerous while the patient was holding the first thought or feelings. Listen for feelings, fantasies, or thoughts [transference] about you that might have been a stimulus for defense, and 4) review those feelings, fantasies, and thoughts about you.

Now let's review the above vignette to understand the interpretive sequence.

1. State what the patient is saying now.

   Therapist: *You seem to be trying to make yourself talk right now when a moment ago, you said you would prefer not to talk.*

   The underlined section starts with what the patient said. This provides an obvious example of a defense that the patient can observe. He can see, once we point it out, that he is indeed trying to make himself talk. What he is not aware of yet is the function of his doing that.

2. State how that seems to shift the patient away from what she was saying earlier, then check to see if the patient can see and understand that shift.

   Therapist: *You seem to be trying to make yourself talk right now when a moment ago you said you would prefer not to talk.*

   The underlined section starts with what the patient had moved away from: the previously stated words. Since this patient had been in therapy for several months, it was not necessary to check if he could understand the shift. Otherwise, I might have had to follow up with something like: "Can you see that shift?"

3. Ask what might have felt risky or dangerous while the patient was holding the first thought or feelings. Listen for feelings, fantasies, or thoughts [transference] about you that might have been a stimulus for defense.

   Therapist: *Was there something uncomfortable about simply saying you didn't want to talk here?*
   Patient: *Well, yes. But you know what do I do then? Simply stop talking or get up and leave the room?*
   Therapist: *Well, if we leave action out of it for the moment, we can wonder what is uncomfortable about simply having the thought here, even without the action.*

4. Review those feelings, fantasies, and thoughts.

The underlined passages above show how I inquired about the anxiety. Now we are listening for feelings, fantasies, or thoughts [transference] that might have stimulated the defense. We are looking for what Anna Freud (1936) referred to as the transference of defense. She observed that when a wish enters the room [such as not wanting to talk], patients will project some image onto you to help restrain themselves from saying more. Therefore, patients may speak freely, but as their thoughts become more powerful, they may project an image onto you [a transference] to help them use a defense and inhibit themselves. It's as if the superego has a storehouse of images that it can project onto you so that by creating a forbidding image of you, patients will be able to stop speaking dangerous thoughts. It is similar to the child who is tempted to steal a cookie from the cookie jar but tells himself he mustn't because "mommie would kill me." Of course his mother wouldn't, but precisely because his temptation is so great he needs to imagine dire consequences to keep from acting on his forbidden wishes. Now, notice where the transferred superego images enter the associations.

Patient: *That's interesting because I often have these weird thoughts of taking a knife and hurting M. And then I really get worried.*

Therapist: *So the idea of action gets you worried and helps you put a lid on those thoughts.*

Patient: *Exactly. It's weird. You know, when you bring up the idea here that I could tell you I don't want to talk, I remember my mother and her rejecting me and being unable to tolerate different opinions.*

The therapist makes the link to the transference here and now:

Therapist: *So that there is some fear here too that I might reject you if you said you didn't want to talk.*

Patient: *Yes. I'm so pliable or compliant. It's like I feel I have to reveal all of myself whether I want to or not.*

Therapist: *And at the same time there seems to be a taboo against revealing certain parts of yourself, such as your wish not to reveal, to say no.*

Patient: *It's true, it is selective. As if I am figuring out what you can tolerate and what you can't.*

Once the defense has been pointed out, we try to discover what transference occurred while the patient was talking that led him to shift to a different topic. When the patient said he didn't want to talk any more, he apparently became afraid that I would be like his mother and reject him for saying this wish; and out of fear of my reaction and to protect the relationship he quickly changed topics. Retrospectively in the process, we can see the emergence of a wish to stop talking, the emergence of transference feelings about me (that I would reject him like his mother), which in turn stimulated the defense of trying to make himself talk about something else.

Enhancing Self Observation

To interpret defenses effectively to a patient, the patient must be able to see a defense in action (Gray 1995; Searl 1936; Sterba 1934). But initially in treatment, most patients are unaware of their defenses. So first we must help them learn to perceive patterns in their speech that indicate a defense at work. Patients cannot analyze defenses they don't see.

Imagine that you point out a shift in the patient's associations and she is unable to see the shift. Rather than go further to wonder about any anxiety she might have felt, we must first help her see the shift. The problem often involves an inability to recognize the symbolic function of their language. "I'm often late," can mean just that. Or, if it comes up just after the patient complains about her boyfriend's lateness, it can have the function of changing the focus from his lateness to her lateness. But for the patient who experiences herself as talking naturally and freely, this shift in function is out of her awareness. Hence, we have to help her step back, look at the sequences of her thoughts, and think about those sequences. We have to help the patient develop a capacity for self observation.

Therefore, when noting a defense, we first point it out, then we ask if the patient noticed that shift, and then we finally can ask the patient what she felt before the shift. For example, one might say, "You seem to be talking about your lateness now, but a moment ago you seemed freer to describe the lateness of your boyfriend. Did you notice that?" If she did not, then you can ask, "Can you see how that is a shift now?" Usually she can. Then having observed the shift together, we can then ask, "Do you have any sense what you were feeling or thinking just before you shifted from his lateness to yours?" Often in the early phases the patient cannot answer this question. However, by observing her shifts and focusing her attention on what she feels before she shifts, she will begin to understand what the anxiety is that motivates her defenses.

Language and Self Regulation

In this form of defense analysis, we focus on the process rather than the content. We analyze the defense and anxiety before we analyze the wish. And finally, we analyze only that part of the wish that has emerged into awareness. In contrast to transference analysis, which directly interprets thoughts outside the patient's awareness, this kind of defense analysis interprets conflicts about wishes that have emerged into awareness. For example, if we look at the vignette of the girl whose boyfriend arrived late, we could hypothesize that she was quite irritated with him. But she has not said that. She merely said that he was late and then a defense arose. So from this approach, we would focus on her ability to describe his lateness without going for the assumed anger that perhaps is buried underneath. We focus only on that part of the wish that has been expressed and has triggered a defense.

Not only that, but when we address the wish we often will understate it or present it in more abstract terms (Davison et al. 1986, 1990; Gray 1995). In defense analysis, we are not simply interested in the wish, but also in the anxiety and defense that interfere with its expression (A. Freud 1936; Freud 1923, 1926)). If we simply restate the patient's wish [her wish to talk about his lateness], we will simply provoke her to engage in the same defense she used before because the anxiety will not have been analyzed. Instead, we may understate the wish so as not to stir up her anxiety and leave the ego free to analyze her conflict, rather than have to engage in a defense (Sterba 1934). For instance, one might use any of the following phrases to understate her wish: 1) "I notice you are describing yourself now, but a moment ago you seemed freer to describe your boyfriend," 2) "I notice the camera is focused on you now, but a moment ago it was focused on him," or 3) "I wonder if talking about yourself now is blocking you from talking more about him."

Much more theory could be discussed, but since the purpose of this book is to develop your capacity for perceiving and interpreting defenses, we will move on to the exercises. All the theoretical material presented here can be found in the following books elaborated on in much more detail.

☐ Further Readings

Busch, R. (1996). Busch builds on the work of Gray and suggests ways his approach may be integrated with others.

Davison, W., Bristol, C., and Pray, M. (1986, 1990). These two articles by this group of authors are among the clearest articles ever written on the activity of defense analysis. Essential reading.

Goldberger, Marianne (ed.). (1996). For an introduction to this approach that is extraordinarily clear, see chapters 1, 2, and 4 by Davison, Bristol, Pray, and Hutchinson.

Gray, Paul (1994). The most thorough description of the theory of this kind of defense analysis by its pre-eminent practitioner. This book is essential reading for anyone interested in this approach to defense analysis.

Levy, S., and Inderbitzen, L. (1990). An introduction to the concept of an analytic surface.

9
CHAPTER

Defense Analysis Studies

☐ Monitoring of Process

The following passages from clinical hours illustrate defenses occuring in clinical material. After studying these passages, go on to the case studies and analyze them in the same manner. In actual practice, one never interprets every defense that occurs in an hour. However, for learning purposes, you will be asked to identify each defense as it occurs in the process and formulate an interpretation.

☐ Example 1

Patient: *At my high school, I didn't feel comfortable telling people. When I came here, my boyfriend here wanted to have sex and I finally told him and he didn't react well. We did get close. I had to tell him why I kept jumping away, getting nervous. He was ok when I first told him, but then he couldn't handle it. Said I told him to make him feel sorry. A month later he said he was really sorry. I'd probably be the same way. I don't know that I could handle it. Senior year, I dated a guy that was so nice and I treated him so badly. I was really bad to him. If I told him what Tom did to me but I didn't tell him. I never let him in. I feel real bad.*

The underlined passage marks the defense. She shifts from describing her boyfriend to describing herself. This shift in the focus is a common defense against criticizing others. She gently criticizes him by noting that he had something to feel sorry for. Then she identifies with the criticized figure, thereby turning the criticism and aggression onto herself: *"I'd probably be the same way."*

Ideally, you would interpret this defense as soon as it occurred. For example, as soon as you heard *"I'd probably be the same way. I don't know that I could handle it,"* you might intervene.

Possible defense interpretation: *"You are describing yourself* [defense] *now just after you were describing him* [wish]. *Was there some discomfort* [fear] *when you mentioned his regret?"*

This interpretation draws her attention first to her defense, describing herself, then to what she defends against, describing him, and finally to her anxiety about describing him, the discomfort that we presume led to the defense.

☐ Example 2

Patient: *I mean I don't know. I've been raised to be a very trusting person, but every time I do it I get stabbed in the back. It's like a joke, but it really hurts. It makes me want to never trust a guy again. It's ok for a friendship but not if it's more than that. I remember with S everyone said that he's a nice guy, maybe I'm that one that has the problem. I don't know what I'm doing wrong. If I know, I can fix it, but I don't know.*

The defense begins after she says "It makes me want to never trust a guy again. The next statement dilutes the impact and the following statement shifts the focus from someone who stabs her in the back to herself as the one who has a problem. She turns the focus of perception from the other to herself.

Possible defense interpretation: *"You wonder what you are doing wrong now* [defense], *but just a moment ago you seemed freer to describe what you thought* [wish] *these guys had done wrong. Did you notice that?"* If the patient can see that, you might go on to ask if she was aware of what she felt [fear] when she said she didn't want to trust a guy again.

☐ Example 3

Patient: *When you start to question that maybe he could do something bad but you're still close. Like with L, I wondered was it just a little problem? When do you need to cut it off? Maybe he wasn't what I wanted but I didn't want to start all over again and have to tell it to someone else. What's the chances of me, at college, finding a nice guy?*

The defense begins when she says *"but I didn't want to start all over again. . . ."* She shifts from describing her desire to the consequences if she acted on that desire. In other words, "I would like to leave him, but I better not have this thought because if I have it, I may act on it, and if I act on it, I will leave him and be alone." Here one needs to interpret the defense but also help the patient begin to think about her thoughts.

Possible defense interpretation: *"You mention what would happen if you left him [defense] and this came up just after you thought he wasn't what you wanted [wish to say this]. Maybe in thinking about this it might be helpful to think of your mind as a sort of room where we leave the door to thought open so that thoughts can come in and we can think about them. But the other door, the door to action, we could keep shut. That way we could look at your thoughts for a while so that you can think about what might be an appropriate action [Pray, personal communication]. Right now you seem afraid if you have a thought that it might run through the room and out the door to action."* If the patient responds well to this, then we could continue. *"Well, then, let's look at this doubt about whether he would be what you wanted. What comes to mind?"*

☐ **Example 4**

This vignette is taken from Dahl et al. (1988).

In fact, regarding myself, I find decisions extremely hard. And if I do make one, even if it's just a minor thing like for instance, with my husband, what we're going to do for an evening if we want to go out, then I, if I do make that decision, then I have, then it has to be that way and it can't be any other way. And, I c—, I can't seem to adjust it if something makes a change in plans necessary. [Sniff] Or something that he used to do a lot, Dave used to do a lot, would be to, in talking about whether we'd go away for a weekend or not, he'd say, "Well, I can't be sure I can get away." And then we'd decide, well, we won't be going. And then on Thursday he'd say, "OK, we're going." And I would just find I—there was no reason I couldn't go—but I would just find that I practically could not get myself together and go away for a weekend that involved little more than just packing a few clothes.

Comparisons in interpretive approach:

Reflection: *"And you probably wondered, 'Gee, if it's so easy to pack, why am I making such a big deal?'"*

Analysis of conflict: *"I wonder if you were irritated by his sudden decision [wish] but were afraid to say anything [fear], so that it came out in your delay [defense]."*

Analysis of transference: *She finds the therapist to be indecisive and is tempted to be a bit oppositional, or if she goes along with the therapy, she does so only half-heartedly.*

Possible defense interpretation: *"You're describing your problem making decisions [defense] just after you were describing what it was like to deal with his indecision [wish]. It's as if you've turned the camera focus from him back onto yourself. What were you feeling [fear] just then as you described his decision to go [wish]?"*

In analysis of conflict, we would infer her anger directly as it was manifested in a past conflict. In analysis of defense, we would focus on the level of anger that came up in this session: her report of his sudden decision. Just reporting his decision was enough for her to shift to describing herself. One might counter that this is simply an accurate historical report of what happened. However, from an analysis of defense perspective, we are interested in how her report of the past is shaped in the present. For example, how long can she describe her irritation with him? With what kind of detail? How does she shift from talking about him to talking about her response? How much elaboration of her feelings about him can occur before she shifts to herself? In other words, our reports of past events are shaped by our comfort or lack of comfort with those feelings when we tell the story. How she tells her story is as important as the story she tells.

☐ Case #1

This clinical hour is from Shave (1968). Underline where defenses occur, outline what the conflict appears to be, and write out what you might interpret, if anything.

Therapist: *I'm glad you made it.*

Patient: *This is a good day to sleep. It's so rainy and so gloomy. [pause] I don't ever know what to talk about with people. I always get anxious if I have to go somewhere and then have to stay. It makes me worry—I guess I'm just a worry wart. [She laughs anxiously] Well, what do you want me to talk about?*

Therapist: *Perhaps you can tell me how you've been feeling.*

Patient: *I just have a physical fear—a fear of being in this hospital. The tension builds up and keeps coming on, and the more I feel it, the worse I get depressed. I feel I've let so many people down by being here in the hospital. It's not right for me to be here when I should be at home taking care of the family and being a wife. It seems so sinful. I've let God down as well as everyone else.*

[She breaks down and cries.] *I've told it a thousand times to different people—religion is something from within a person and I just haven't been religious enough.*

Therapist: *I understand how you feel.*

Patient: *I haven't been strong enough to do my work at home. I guess I didn't try hard enough to get those awful thoughts out of my mind.*

Therapist: *Terrible thoughts?*

What are the defenses here? How would you interpret them?

Author's Analysis

Therapist: *I'm glad you made it.*

Patient: *This is a good day to sleep. It's so rainy and so gloomy.* [pause] *I don't ever know what to talk about with people. I always get anxious if I have to go somewhere and then have to stay. It makes me worry—I guess I'm just a worry wart. [#1]* [She laughs anxiously] *Well, what do you want me to talk about?*

Therapist: *Perhaps you can tell me how you've been feeling.*

Patient: *I just have a physical fear—a fear of being in this hospital. The tension builds up and keeps coming on and the more I feel it, the worse I get depressed. [#2] I feel I've let so many people down by being here in the hospital. It's not right for me to be here when I should be at home taking care of the family and being a wife. It seems so sinful. I've let God down as well as everyone else.* [She breaks down and cries.] *I've told it a thousand times to different people—religion is something from within a person and I just haven't been religious enough.*

Therapist: *I understand how you feel.*

Patient: *I haven't been strong enough to do my work at home. I guess I didn't try hard enough to get those awful thoughts out of my mind.*

Therapist: *Terrible thoughts?*

Defense #1:

Patient: *This is a good day to sleep. It's so rainy and so gloomy.* [pause] *I don't ever know what to talk about with people. I always get anxious if I have to go somewhere and then have to stay. It makes me worry—I guess I'm just a worry wart. [#1]* [She laughs anxiously] *Well, what do you want me to talk about?*

Here she shifts from describing herself to asking the therapist tell her what to describe.

Possible defense interpretation: *"You're inviting me to tell you what to talk about [defense] just after you said you were afraid that if you go somewhere [wish], you might have to stay there [fear]. Was there some discomfort just then as you shifted from your thoughts to me?"*

Notice the difference between this and **a possible transference interpretation:** *"Perhaps you're afraid that whatever you talk about here might lead you to a place or feeling you would have to stay in."*

Defense #2:

Patient: *I just have a physical fear—a fear of being in this hospital. The tension builds up and keeps coming on and the more I feel it, the worse I get depressed. [#2] I feel I've let so many people down be being here in the hospital. It's not right for me to be here when I should be at home taking care of the family and being a wife. It seems so sinful. I've let God down as well as everyone else.* [She breaks down and cries.]

Here she shifts from describing a building tension within herself to letting others down, from internal feeling to external obligations, from self to other. This shift is so subtle, however, and the defense probably so ego-syntonic that it is unlikely that any interpretation would be useful.

The hour continues:

Patient: *Thoughts like I was losing my mind and that I might do something terrible, like stabbing my children with a kitchen knife. I've read where that has happened before. Those thoughts are so weird, but I couldn't get them out of my mind. I couldn't even turn on the gas stove without thinking about turning all the jets on and blowing up the home. I couldn't even read the paper if there were any mention of accidents, murders, or war pictures.*

Therapist: *I know that you've been very uncomfortable.*

Patient: *You couldn't possibly know!* [Pause.] *I got so afraid that I couldn't sleep with my husband for fear that I might wake up at night and kill him when he was asleep. I couldn't touch any sharp objects and gave up trying to use knives in the kitchen. I'd go into such panic states when the children were around me that I couldn't even look at knives or scissors. Once, just after I frosted a cake and was cleaning the sink out with Drano, I had the weird thought of sprinkling some on the top of the frosting. I wanted to kill myself, but I was afraid of dying, but even more afraid of living. I just felt so trapped.*

Therapist: *I know it's been difficult for you.*

Patient: *And there's nothing that I hate more than to get sick. I'm sick and tired of being told too that I am sick.* [She looks down into her lap and snaps her fingernails one after the other.] *I'm just not comfortable with anyone and feel at times as though I have to just get away from it all. If I could go somewhere, everyone would be through with me. The family would be better off without me—I've been a burden to them as I've failed as a mother and a wife—I have no feelings at all. I'm just numb all over.*

Therapist: *I know how you feel.*

Patient: *No, you don't! How can you possibly know? You've never been through something like this.*

Therapist: [Gestures.]

Patient: *It seems as though I can't get along with anyone. It says in the Bible to "love thy neighbor as thyself"—but I hate myself. Do you understand?*

Therapist: [Gestures.]

What are the defenses here? How would you interpret them?

Author's Analysis

Therapist: *I know that you've been very uncomfortable.*

Patient: *You couldn't possibly know! [#3]* [Pause] I got so afraid that I couldn't sleep with my husband for fear that I might wake up at night and kill him when he was asleep. *I couldn't touch any sharp objects and gave up trying to use knives in the kitchen. I'd go into such panic states when the children were around me that I couldn't even look at knives or scissors. Once just after I frosted a cake and was cleaning the sink out with Drano, I had the weird thought of sprinkling some on the top of the frosting. I wanted to kill myself, [#4]* but I was afraid of dying, but even more afraid of living. *I just felt so trapped.*

Therapist: *I know it's been difficult for you.*

Patient: *And there's nothing that I hate more than to get sick. I'm sick and tired of being told too that I am sick. [#5]* [She looks down into her lap and snaps her fingernails one after the other.] *I'm just not comfortable with anyone and feel at times as though I have to just get away from it all. If I could go somewhere, everyone would be through with me. The family would be better off without me—I've been a burden to them as I've failed as a mother and a wife. I have no feelings at all. I'm just numb all over.*

Therapist: *I know how you feel.*

Patient: *No, you don't! How can you possibly know? You've never been through something like this.*

Therapist: [Gestures.]

Patient: *[#6] It seems as though I can't get along with anyone. It says in the Bible to "love thy neighbor as thyself"—but I hate myself.* Do you understand?

Therapist: [Gestures.]

Defense #3:

Therapist: *I know that you've been very uncomfortable.*

Patient: You couldn't possibly know! [Pause.] *I got so afraid that I couldn't sleep with my husband for fear that I might wake up at night and kill him when he was asleep.*

Here she restrains herself after criticizing the therapist by describing herself. A shift from a perception of the therapist to a perception of herself, from criticism of him to criticism of herself, from anger at him to the dangers of her being angry. During the pause the therapist might intervene.

Possible defense interpretation: *"You're talking about fear with your husband [defense] just after you mentioned something you felt about the therapy [wish]: that I couldn't know what you feel. It's true I couldn't possibly know exactly what you feel. Yet I sense you felt you had to restrain yourself as soon as you said that."*

Defense #4:

Patient: *I wanted to kill myself, but I was afraid of dying, but even more afraid of living.*

Here she shifts from describing her wish to kill herself to describing her fear. Talking about her fear, although quite understandable, helps her restrain herself at the very moment she begins to talk about wanting to kill herself.

Possible defense interpretation: *"You know, this may sound odd, but I wonder if this feeling of fear you're talking about now is putting on the brakes [defense] just when you said you had wanted to kill yourself [wish: to put these thoughts into words]. Is it scary to say that out loud here [fear]?"*

Defense #5:

Patient: I'm sick and tired of being told too that I am sick. [She looks down into her lap and snaps her fingernails one after the other.] *I'm just not comfortable with anyone and feel at times as though I have to just get away from it all. If I could go somewhere, everyone would be through with me. The family would be better off without me—I've been a burden to them as I've failed as a mother and a wife. I have no feelings at all. I'm just numb all over.*

Here she turns the anger she feels toward people who label her back onto herself.

Possible defense interpretation: *"You mention feeling like a burden to others* [defense] *just after you said you feel a bit burdened by people who tell you you are* sick [wish: to express anger towards others]. *Was there some discomfort you felt* [fear] *about that that led you to shift gears?"* Or, *"I wonder if this thought that you are a burden is blocking you from describing more fully how burdened you feel when people call you sick."*

Defense #6:

Therapist: *I know what you feel.*

Patient: *No, you don't! How can you possibly know? You've never been through something like this.*

Therapist: [Gestures.]

Patient: It seems as though I can't get along with anyone. It says in the Bible to "love thy neighbor as thyself"—but I hate myself. Do you understand?

Again, we see a turning of aggression upon the self when she turns her criticism towards the therapist against herself. It might seem obvious to point out to the patient that she hates herself to ward off her criticism of the therapist. However, the patient may be unable to respond to such an interpretation because 1) it is incomplete, addressing the wish and the defense but not the anxiety that leads to the defense, and 2) it refers to the wish in such a way that it stimulates the id. In other words, if it "pushes the patient's buttons" to say *"You've never been through something like this,"* anything as strong or stronger will push her buttons too, leading to another defense. That is why it is often useful to understate the wish portion of the conflict so that the defense is not stirred up by the interpretation and the patient is then freed up to look at what was dangerous. Rather than repeat what she said, you might refer in abstract language to her perceptions, descriptions, or thoughts. This allows you to refer to dangerous material without provoking defenses and then enable her to look at what may have felt risky about free associating to your failure to understand. Freud (1923) pointed out that the ego is responsible both for self-observation and for creating defenses. Hence, if we stimulate defensiveness, we decrease the patient's ability to engage in self-observation at that moment.

Possible defense interpretation: *"You are describing yourself now* [defense] *just after you were describing how you perceived me* [wish: to criticize therapist]. *Did you notice that shift?"* If she can see it, then proceed with something like, *"Do you remember what you were feeling* [fear] *that interfered with describing how you saw me?"*

The hour continues. The patient sits twisting her fingers in her lap.

Patient: *I have a dreadful fear of hurting someone, of hurting their feelings, and of losing my mind and doing something horrible. I have to hold back the feelings. You have to control them and you can't let them out. And I don't see how talking about this is going to help at all. [Pause.] Maybe I need shock treatment again.*

Therapist: *We'll handle it together.*

Patient: *My husband doesn't understand it at all! He thinks all I have to do is just snap out of it and I'll be all right. He can't possibly know how sick I really am down deep, but what good is staying here when it makes me so upset? Can you tell me that?*

Therapist: *We'll work it through.*

Patient: *What do you mean by that?*

Therapist: [Gestures.]

Patient: *You don't do any talking, either. Why don't you say something? It's the same thing all over again.* [She breaks down and cries.] *I just feel like screaming.* [She sits sobbing for a few minutes and then looks up.] *Well, will you excuse me now?*

Therapist: *I know you're anxious, but it's okay to stay.*

Patient: *But I haven't a hanky—my nose is running.* [She wipes her nose with the sleeve of her sweater.]

Therapist: *I have plenty of Kleenex.* [He lays a box of tissues out on his desk and she reaches over to take one.]

Patient: *Thank you.* [She audibly blows her nose, gives some deep sighs, smiles very briefly, and sits rather quietly.] *I've been awfully hard on my family and I'm putting my husband through an awful lot. It isn't right for me to be here and I'm just a burden to them all.* [She begins to cry softly.] *It must be time for me to go now.*

Therapist: *It's all right to stay longer.*

Patient: *Thank you for your time.* [Patient leaves ten minutes early.]

What are the defenses here? How would you interpret them? Using the last eight lines of this excerpt, try to formulate a possible transference interpretation.

Author's Analysis

The patient sits twisting her fingers in her lap.

Patient: *[#7] I have a dreadful fear of hurting someone, of hurting their feelings, and of losing my mind and doing something horrible. I have to do* *something to hold back the feelings. You have to control them and you can't let them out. And I don't see how talking about this is going to help at all. [#8]* [Pause] *Maybe I need shock treatment again.*

Therapist: *We'll handle it together.*

Patient: *My husband doesn't understand it at all! He thinks all I have to do is just snap out of it and I'll be all right. He can't possibly know how sick I really am down deep, [#9] but what good is staying here when it makes me so upset? Can you tell me that?*

Therapist: *We'll work it through.*

Patient: *What do you mean by that?*

Therapist: [Gestures.]

Patient: *You don't do any talking, either. Why don't you say something? [#10] It's the same thing all over again.* [She breaks down and cries.] *I just feel like screaming. [#11]* [She sits sobbing for a few minutes and then looks up.] Well, will you excuse me now?

Defense #7:
Patient: *I have a dreadful fear of hurting someone, of hurting their feelings and of losing my mind and doing something horrible. I have to hold back the feelings. You have to control them and you can't let them out.*

Here she shifts from images of action to an image of restraint, from what she wants to do to what she must hold back. Now one might argue that she should hold back feelings and actions so she won't hurt others. That is true in the world of action. What we are focusing on here though is somewhat different. From the perspective of process, we want to understand why talking about her thoughts of action became so dangerous just now in the room with the therapist that she suddenly shifted and said, "I have to hold back the feelings." That statement shows that it feels dangerous to her to let go of certain feelings in therapy at this moment, to free associate.

In this situation it may be helpful to reassure her about the need for self control in the real world so that she can be helped to understand her fears of loss of control in the therapy.

Possible defense interpretation: *"Obviously, you don't want to hurt your family, but I wonder if we might look at this in another way. I notice that you brought up the wish to hold back feelings [defense] just as you were talking about a fear of hurting someone [wish to explore this feeling]. Was there something that felt risky even just having those thoughts in the room here [fear]?"*

Defense #8:
Patient: *And I don't see how talking about this is going to help at all.* [Pause.] *Maybe I need shock treatment again.*

Here she shifts from describing her opinion about the therapy to her opinion about herself, again a turning of the focus back onto herself. This subtle kind of defense might not be interpreted at all early in treatment, since it would be very difficult for the patient to observe. However, later in therapy when the patient has an increased ability to observe herself, you might address the defense.

Now, you might counter that the statement that therapy won't help is itself a resistance. That is true. From a process point of view, however, we are more concerned with whatever inhibits the patient's free association, even if it is something that inhibits her from freely giving vent to her resistance!

Possible defense interpretation: *"I wonder if your thoughts about shock therapy* [defense] *are blocking you right now from expressing more fully your doubts about whether talking will help here* [wish]. *Was there some risk* [fear] *in letting me know about your doubts that led you to put on the brakes?"*

Defense #9:
Patient: *My husband doesn't understand it at all! He thinks all I have to do is just snap out of it and I'll be all right. He can't possibly know how sick I really am down deep, but what good is staying here when it makes me so upset. Can you tell me that?*

Here she shifts from criticizing her husband to criticizing the therapy and herself.

Possible defense interpretations: *"I wonder if your doubts about staying here* [defense] *help you slow down just when you had the idea that your husband may not understand that you really can't just snap out of it. Was there something risky about entertaining that thought* [fear]?"

Defense #10:
Patient: *You don't do any talking, either. Why don't you say something? It's the same thing all over again.* [She breaks down and cries.]

Here she shifts from criticizing the therapist to crying. Given the pattern and context, we could hypothesize that expressing criticism and anger is so terrifying for her that she must quickly turn it against herself.

Possible defense interpretation: *"It obviously makes you sad when I don't talk enough here. I notice though that your sadness* [defense] *came in here just after you asked me to say something* [wish to ask for more]. *I wonder if it feels dangerous* [fear] *for you to tell me what you want* [to express the wish], *and if the sadness is a way to deal with that risk."* Or, *"I wonder if your sadness prevents you from letting your request stand there— that I should say something."*

Defense #11:
Patient: *I just feel like screaming.* [She sits sobbing for a few minutes and then looks up.] *Well, will you excuse me now?*

Again we see the pattern of criticism of the therapist followed by crying. Here, the therapist must interpret because the patient is threatening to leave the therapy. When there is a threat of acting out, the therapist must interpret the anxiety and wish that are leading to the defense of acting out (Glover 1958).

Possible defense interpretation based on the process: *"You're asking to leave now* [defense] *just after you noted a powerful feeling you are struggling with* [wish]. *Rather than tell me about that feeling* [supporting the defense], *can you say what you are afraid would happen if you put it into words* [fear]?*"

Possible conflict interpretation based on the content: *"You know I have a hunch there are a lot of things you want to say here* [wish], *but that you are afraid of what will happen if you keep letting these thoughts out* [fear]. *And maybe that's why you are thinking of leaving, so you can put the brakes on and stop saying these uncomfortable thoughts* [defense]."* Or a more direct and stimulating interpretation: *"I have a hunch you are afraid that if you say you feel like screaming* [wish], *that you will start screaming* [fear] *unless you leave here as soon as possible* [defense]. *It sounds like you are trying to figure out how to talk about your thoughts without them turning into actions."*

Some might feel tempted to pursue her wish to scream, what she would want to scream and at whom. Generally, however, it is best to pursue the resistance before the content; that is, find out what she is afraid would happen if she revealed her thoughts (the anxiety and resistance), then explore the thoughts and fantasies about screaming. Often, if we explore the resistance and anxiety thoroughly, the content will emerge on its own.

Possible interpretation of defense: *"Rather than tell me about your wish to scream, let's put that off to the side for the moment. Instead, can you tell me what you're afraid would happen if you talked about that wish?"*

Possible transference interpretation: *"You mention how frustrating it is when people don't understand you. When they don't understand you can't just snap out of it. When you are frightened of these powerful feelings that don't go away. Maybe you're feeling frustrated with me too, fearing I don't understand how terrifying these feelings are. So that you wonder how our talking could possibly help, since it sounds like today, talking didn't help. It may be that you are tempted to scream here too, to let these feelings out, but are afraid you might hurt me in the process, and so to protect me, you wonder if you should leave the room before your feelings come out."*

☐ Case #2

This hour involves the same patient in her twentieth session (Shave 1968). Again, mark where defenses occur, describe the nature of the defenses, and propose possible interpretations.

Patient: *I've had a very pleasant week. My father is staying with me and it's nice having him around. Having him close makes me feel so much better. I feel safe around him and there's a sense of security I get, which I don't have when I'm alone. But I don't want to be so dependent—that bothers me so—I should be able to do things on my own and not depend on Dad, but I realize I can't. In spite of my feeling that way, it is nice to have him around and to know he's close, but I know he can't be with me very long.*

Therapist: *He'll be there.*

Patient: *I think my fears of being alone stem from a few past memories I have that I try not to think of, but so many things remind me of them that I can't forget them. They bother me and then I get frightened that I might have one of those "spells" I used to have—everything would become blurred and I'd begin to feel so weak, as though I might faint. I'd get a funny feeling. Just a funny feeling—I can't explain it, but just to think of those spells upsets me. The memories are still there, even though I try so hard to forget. What if I were alone—[She breaks off and sniffs as though she were on the verge of crying.] Those wrong thoughts that I had—those evil thoughts. If I could only not remember, if I could only forget those spells.*

Therapist: *We'll continue.*

What are the defenses here? How would you interpret them?

Author's Analysis

Patient: *I've had a very pleasant week. My father is staying with me and it's nice having him around. Having him close makes me feel so much better. I feel safe around him and there's a sense of security I get, which I don't have when I'm alone.* [#1] <u>*But I don't want to be so dependent—that bothers me so—I should be able to do things on my own and not depend on Dad, but I realize I can't.*</u> *In spite of my feeling that way, it is nice to have him around and to know he's close,* [#2] <u>*but I know he can't be with me very long.*</u>

Therapist: *He'll be there.*

Patient: <u>*I think my fears of being alone stem from a few past memories I have that I try not to think of, but so many things remind of them that I can't forget them. They bother me and then I get frightened that I might have one of those*</u>

*"spells" I used to have—everything would become blurred and I'd begin to feel
so weak, as though I might faint. I'd get a funny feeling. Just a funny feeling—I can't explain it, but just to think of those spells upsets me. The memories are still there, even though I try so hard to forget. What if I were alone—*
[She breaks off and sniffs as though she were on the verge of crying.]
*Those wrong thoughts that I had—those evil thoughts. If I could only not
remember, if I could only forget those spells..*

Therapist: *We'll continue.*

Defense #1:

Here she shifts from describing her enjoyment of closeness with her
father to judging her wish for closeness. One might explore the anxiety she felt as she described the sense of security with him that led her
to judge her wish for that safety.

Possible defense interpretation: *"You are judging your wish to depend
on your father* [defense] *just after you said how much you enjoy the sense of
security he provides* [wish]. *Did you notice any discomfort* [fear] *when you
described that sense of security?"*

Defense #2:

Here she shifts from a focus on experience in the present to experience
in the future.

Possible defense interpretation: *"It's true that he can't be with you very
long in the future, but I wonder if that fact holds you back* [defense] *from
talking more about how nice it is to have him around now, in the present*
[wish]." This would be a preliminary interpretation to help her see the
shift. Only when she could see this shift would we then go further and
ask what feelings she may have had at the moment she shifted.

The hour continues (underline the defenses):

Patient: *It's like when I come here, some of my memories come back and I feel
upset.*

Therapist: *I know it's difficult for you.*

Patient: *It sounds silly, but I do feel safe with my family and I want to be
with them always. But at times I get discouraged and think, "Oh, what the
heck." At times I don't want to talk about it because it upsets me so. It bothers
me and it often seems too much for me.*

Therapist: *We'll take it slow.*

Patient: *I know that I don't understand it all. I do get upset and I don't know
why I do. I don't what to—I try not to.* [She sighs deeply, then stares out
the window.] *It's the same old things every time I come.*

Therapist: We can handle it together.

Patient: I want my family with me always, but I don't know what the future will bring. I don't know what will happen next hour, next week, month, or year.

Therapist: We'll continue.

Patient: I shouldn't worry, I know; my family realizes I love them—to have them close makes me feel good. I want to hold them close and somehow I know I just can't go on without them. I want to be with them every minute, but I know that's not right and it makes me feel bad. It hurts knowing I have to depend on them so. They can't be bothered with me all the time. I'm just a burden to them.

What are the defenses here? How would you interpret them?

Author's Analysis

Patient: It's like when I come here, some of my memories come back and I feel upset.

Therapist: I know it's difficult for you.

Patient: It sounds silly, but I do feel safe with my family and I want to be with them always. [#3] But at times I get discouraged and think, "Oh, what the heck." At times I don't want to talk about it because it upsets me so. It bothers me and it often seems too much for me.

Defense #3 involves a shift from a wish to describe her desire to be and feel safe with her family to a wish not to talk and a feeling of discouragement.

Possible defense interpretation: *"You are talking about a feeling of discouragement now* [defense], *but a moment ago you were talking about a feeling of safety with your family* [wish]. *Did you notice that shift?"* If so, then, *"I wonder what you were feeling* [fear] *as you talked about feeling safe with them* [wish]?"*

Therapist: We'll take it slow.

Patient: I know that I don't understand it all. I do get upset [#4] and I don't know why I do. I don't want to—I try not to. [She sighs deeply, then stares out the window.] It's the same old things every time I come.

Therapist: We can handle it together.

Defense #4 involves a shift from saying she feels upset to wondering why she feels that and not wanting to feel that.

Possible defense interpretation: *"As soon as you mentioned that you get upset [wish], you switched gears and said you didn't know why you get upset [defense]. Perhaps wondering <u>why</u> you get upset blocks you from describing <u>what</u> that upset feeling is."*

Patient: *I want my family with me always, [#5] <u>but I don't know what the future will bring. I don't know what will happen next hour, next week, month, or year</u>.*
Therapist: *We'll continue.*

Defense #5 involves a shift from expressing her desire to have her family with her to not knowing what will be possible, from her desire in the future to the unknowability of the future. Interestingly, the mood itself would be viewed as a defense, something that blocks her from expanding on her wish to be with her family. One might note that her feeling of discouragement came up just after saying she always wants to be with her family. Then we might wonder with her if she were aware of any feeling of risk while saying she always wanted to be with them.

It is important to remember that the patient genuinely feels discouraged and is not aware of its defensive function. Hence, we should not question the reality of her mood but instead draw her attention to what she was feeling just before that mood so that we can hopefully investigate together why her mood shifted.

Possible defense interpretation: *"It's true that we don't know what will happen in the future. But I wonder if that fact [defense] coming in right now interferes with you describing another fact: that you would like your family always to be with you [wish]. Was there some feeling you had when you expressed that wish [fear]?"* Or, *"It's certainly true we don't know what the future will bring, but I wonder if this emphasis on the future [defense] puts the lid on your desire to be with your family always [wish]. I sense that something [fear] makes you put on the brakes as soon as you voice that desire."*

Patient: *I shouldn't worry, I know; my family realizes I love them—to have them close makes me feel good. I want to hold them close [#6] <u>and somehow I know I just can't go on without them</u>.*

Defense #6 involves a shift from expressing her pleasure when holding her family close to a fantasy involving displeasure being without her family.

Since this defense is so brief and the wish emerges fully again in the next sentence, it wouldn't need to be addressed. This is a good example of a defense making a brief appearance but not blocking the expression of the wish entirely. Usually, interpretations are best reserved for defenses that bring the expression of wish to a stop. For example, notice the difference in the next example.

Patient: *I want to be with them every minute, [#7]* <u>*but I know that's not*</u> <u>*right and it makes me feel bad. It hurts knowing I have to depend on them so.*</u> <u>*They can't be bothered with me all the time. I'm just a burden to them.*</u>

Defense #7:

This time the wish is totally blocked by a shift to a judgmental stance. She shifts from describing her wish to criticizing it, from her internal desire to external reality. The expression of the wish is now completely blocked and severe criticism of the wish ensues.

   Possible defense interpretation: *"You seem to be judging your wish to be close to your family* [defense]. *Just a moment ago though you were simply describing this wish* [wish]. *Did you notice that shift?"* If she cannot see it, then you would need to help her see the defense first before interpreting. For instance, *"Let me explain. You see this painting on the wall? We could describe the painting, the colors, the trees, the clouds, how they are portrayed, and so on. That would be a description, just saying what is there. Criticism would be saying that those are bad colors, or there shouldn't be a tree in the painting. Can you see that difference?"* If she understood, you could proceed: *"So when you said you want to be close to your family, that's a picture of you, a description of what you feel like today. When you said it's not right to have that feeling, you were no longer describing your feelings but criticizing them. See, what I'm curious about is that this criticism seemed to cut you short just when you were trying to describe your wish to be close to them."*

   If she has some experience observing her defenses one could make a simpler interpretation: *"You are judging your wish to be close to your family now* [defense], *but a moment ago you seemed freer to feel that wish and accept it* [wish]. *Was there some risk you felt* [fear] *about having that wish?"*

The hour continues:

Therapist: *They enjoy being with you.*

Patient: *I just feel as though I'm overdoing it—that I'm relying on them too much. I don't know how to explain it, but it's a fear—a fear of depending on them too much and a fear that I'll lose them, and both ways it hurts.* [She grimaces, breaks down, cries for several minutes, and then slowly recovers.] *I don't feel that fear all the time, but when I do it won't leave me.*

Therapist: *I understand.*

Patient: *You want to live right, you try so hard to do your best, but inside you realize how weak you are and how you need someone else. I remember too how I was before, so frightened and my thoughts all mixed up. I did things I didn't want to do and said things I didn't want to say.* [She begins to cry again.]

From a content point of view her conflict becomes clearer: a wish to depend, a fear of depending too much and of losing them, and a defense of trying not to depend. From a process point of view, this passage continues the patient's expression of defense. There is no re-emergence of her wish to be close.

From a defense analysis point of view, the therapist's intervention ["They enjoy being with you"] would be considered stimulating to the id. He is encouraging her to express the wish to be close to her family at the very moment she experiences it as dangerous. As a result, she works even harder to repress the wish through harsher self-criticism ("I'm relying on them too much") and images of self-punishment ("I'll lose them . . . it hurts"). Her defenses become harsher in response to his implicit invitation to express her wish to be close to them.

The hour continues:

Therapist: *It's all right to express yourself.*

Patient: *I'm so afraid when I go to the store. I almost dread having to do the shopping and when I go I fight so hard not to get upset, but I always do. I just can't seem to help it. I know I have to get the groceries for the week.*

Therapist: *It's okay to have feelings.*

Patient: *After I go there, and the shopping is done, it doesn't really seem so bad after all. But maybe it's because I know that Bill isn't so far away and is waiting for me.*

Therapist: *Bill cares.*

Patient: *Like coming here—I've seen and heard the things that happen here. All the fighting and smashing of windows and all the other violence. I'm so afraid it might happen to me. Afraid of what I might do. I went over to a neighbor lady's house to see their new baby. I held him in my arms and then I had those thoughts that I might squeeze him too tight—crush him or choke him to death.* [She breaks down and cries.] *That hurts me.* [She continues to cry.] *I don't want to hurt anyone. I don't ever want to hurt anyone.*

Therapist: *I understand.*

Patient: *But I'm afraid of my thoughts and no one can help me except God.* [she continues to cry.] *I know He forgives me, but I can't forgive myself.*

What are the defenses here? How would you interpret them?

Author's Analysis

Patient: *[#8] Like coming here—I've seen and heard the things that happen here. All the fighting and smashing of windows and all the other violence. I'm so afraid it might happen to me. Afraid of what I might do. I went over to a neighbor lady's house to see their new baby.*

Defense #8 involves a shift from describing a sense of comfort knowing Bill is waiting for her to images of violence. The same defense occurs later when she shifts from an image of holding a baby to images of violence again. Often, images of violence are viewed automatically as id material to be explored first. However, from a process orientation in defense analysis, we are interested in the function of these images of violence. Do they amplify what the patient is expressing or, as in this case, do they block the expression of other feelings and thoughts?

Possible defense interpretation: *"Yes, it's clear how afraid you are. But I'm wondering. This feeling of fear* [defense] *came up after you said how relieved you felt knowing Bill was waiting for you* [wish]. *Was there some feeling* [fear] *as you described that thought?"*

Patient: *I held him in my arms [#8a] and then I had those thoughts that I might squeeze him too tight—crush him or choke him to death. [She breaks down and cries.] That hurts me. [She continues to cry.] I don't want to hurt anyone. I don't ever want to hurt anyone.*

Therapist: *I understand.*

Patient: *But I'm afraid of my thoughts and no one can help me except God. [she continues to cry.] I know He forgives me, but I can't forgive myself.*

Defense #8a. The thought she would squeeze the baby too tight may have blocked her from describing her feelings while holding the baby.

Possible defense interpretation: *"You mentioned these fears of what you might do then, but I'm wondering, what did you feel just now when you were describing yourself holding the baby in your arms?"* What was the risk in the room with the therapist that occurred when she described herself holding a baby?

One might argue that the patient has murderous impulses. From a process point of view, however, her murderous impulses serve a defensive function. There is no need to deny the possibility that she has murderous impulses and that this content needs to be explored in treatment. The question is not whether to explore murderous impulses, but how to explore them when they function as expression of a wish or a defense.

The hour continues:

Therapist: *It's not your fault.*

Patient: *I guess I'm afraid I'll go to pieces. That feeling still comes. I have to face life without upsets. I know that everyone gets upset now and then, but not as much as I do. I feel so guilty, and yet I think it's also fear. Bill says that I use that fear for an excuse all the time. But it's not an excuse for me—it's real.*

Therapist: *Bill should be able to understand that.*

Patient: *I want to get rid of those bad thoughts. but so many things will remind me of them. It's only natural to have things remind you of other things. I wish they didn't, but they do. I can do things and go places now, but not like I want to. And that's what I want. I don't want to feel that every time I do anything or go anywhere, like for a long walk, that I have to hurry just so I can get home again with the family. I hurry through the shopping and it's difficult for me. I hurry through it and at times I feel it will never end.*

Therapist: *I know it's difficult for you.*

Patient: *Like Bill—I hold him close but I feel so guilty, and it's the same with the children. I don't want to need them. I don't want to be so dependent on them, but then without them life is nothing. And I always think, what if I should choke them—what if I should kill them?* [She breaks down and cries.] *I'll never forget my thoughts about my mother, how I wanted to reach out and shake her as she was lying in the coffin. Shake her to pieces for leaving me. I'm afraid there's evil inside of me and I'm afraid to let it out. I just can't figure out my thoughts and feelings I have, but God can.*

What are the defenses here? How would you interpret them?

Author's Analysis

Therapist: *It's not your fault.*

Patient: *I guess I'm afraid I'll go to pieces. That feeling still comes. I have to face life without upsets. I know that everyone gets upset now and then, but not as much as I do. I feel so guilty, and yet I think it's also fear. [#9] Bill says that I use that fear for an excuse all the time. But it's not an excuse for me—it's real.*

Therapist: *Bill should be able to understand that.*

Patient: *I want to get rid of those bad thoughts. But so many things will remind me of them. It's only natural to have things remind you of other things. I wish they didn't, but they do. I can do things and go places now, but not like I want to. And that's what I want. I don't want to feel that every time*

I do anything or go anywhere, like for a long walk, that I have to hurry just so I can get home again with the family. I hurry through the shopping and it's difficult for me. I hurry through it and at times I feel it will never end.
Therapist: *I know it's difficult for you.*

Defense #9 involves a shift from what she perceives to what Bill perceives. But in the next sentence she resumes describing her own perception so there is no need to interpret.

Patient: *Like Bill—I hold him close, [#10] but I feel so guilty and it's the same with the children. I don't want to need them. I don't want to be so dependent on them, but then without them life is nothing. And I always think, what if I should choke them—what if I should kill them? [She breaks down and cries.] I'll never forget my thoughts about my mother, how I wanted to reach out and shake her as she was lying in the coffin. Shake her to pieces for leaving me. [#11] I'm afraid there's evil inside of me and I'm afraid to let it out. [#12] I just can't figure out my thoughts and feelings I have; but God can.*

Defense #10 involves a shift from a feeling of closeness to one of guilt and self criticism. We also see here how important it is to interpret a defense quickly. Her defensive maneuvers begin with guilt, then move to a defense against need and dependence, then the wish for closeness emerges slightly: *"but then without them life is nothing."* Then this wish is crushed with the image that she could kill her family.

Possible defense interpretation: *"It sounds like the guilt [defense] restrains you from talking even here about how much you like to hold people close to you [wish]. I wonder what is hard [fear] about holding onto that thought, that you like to hold people close to you?"*

Defense #11 involves a shift from describing her thoughts about her mother to thoughts about herself.

Possible defense interpretation: *"I sense that you want to tell me your thoughts about your mother [wish] but you're afraid to let those thoughts out here [fear]. Maybe that's what has led you to start talking about you [defense] instead of her. Rather than tell me your thoughts about her just yet, could you maybe tell me what you are afraid would happen if you did?"* Or, *"Could you tell what you felt just now when were talking about her?"*

Defense #12 involves a shift from having thoughts about herself to not being able to figure out her thoughts, from thinking to an inability to think. This is an interesting example because the thought, "I'm afraid there's evil inside of me and I'm afraid to let it out," functions as a defense against the previous thought. But then the statement, "I just can't figure out my thoughts and feelings I have, but God can," functions as a defense against that defense. It's as if the patient says, "I am expressing my anger. I am evil to think this thought. I don't know what I think."

Possible defense interpretation: *"You became unable to figure out your thoughts* [defense: a regression in her ability to think—an ego function] *just after you were thinking about what is inside you* [wish]. *In fact, you were thinking very well until just then. I wonder if there is something frightening* [fear] *about thinking about what is inside you that leads your mind to get kind of gummed up."*

The hour continues:

Therapist: *He knows how you really feel and can accept you as you are.*

Patient: *But I feel as though it's all my fault.* [She cries.]

Therapist: *He knows it's not your fault.*

Patient: *I don't want any of my thoughts to happen.*

Therapist: *He understands.*

Patient: *It's like you want to do things, but you can't because you're afraid.*

Therapist: *It's okay to let yourself go.*

Patient: *You don't understand! I don't know what to let go. Don't you understand, I'm afraid! I feel so tense and stiff inside. I don't understand why. It's like you want to say you're sorry for the way you feel to your family, but you don't know how you really feel. I just can't figure it out, I just can't.*

Therapist: *I understand.*

Patient: *You want to tell your family you're sorry for the way you feel, but they don't understand how you really feel. They can't possibly know what I hide within.*

Therapist: *But they can accept all your feelings, no matter what they are.*

Patient: *I want to enjoy life without fear—without being afraid.*

Therapist: *You're not asking too much at all.*

Patient: *It's the same old things that bother me. I talk with Bill about them over and over again, so that I think he must get sick of hearing it.*

Therapist: *Not a bit so! It's important to him.*

Patient: *I went to a church the other day, a new one. We went down in the basement and it had a tunnel that reminded me of here and I got a little afraid.* [She laughs.] *It's kind of silly. It ran so deep!*

Therapist: *It's okay.*

Patient: *A lot of the time, I'm afraid when I really don't have to be. Like going to the store: I go very frightened, and after I get there and have all the groceries, it doesn't seem so bad after all. It all seems so silly—yet so important at the same time.*

Therapist: *I understand.*

Patient: *But I still don't like being so dependent on Bill. I really don't! I always have to have him waiting. And that makes me mad, but I guess it's better that way than not at all.*

Therapist: *It's okay.*

Patient: *Sometimes I get the uncomfortable feeling I'm saying more than I intend to—like I'm talking about one thing that seems so insignificant and yet somehow seems so important.*

Therapist: *Let's continue next Monday.*

Patient: *Okay.*

What are the defenses here? How would you interpret them?

Author's Analysis

Therapist: *He knows how you really feel and can accept you as you are.*

Patient: *But I feel as though it's all my fault.* [She cries.]

Therapist: *He knows it's not your fault.*

Patient: *I don't want any of my thoughts to happen.*

Therapist: *He understands.*

Patient: *It's like you want to do things, [#13] <u>but you can't because you're afraid.</u>*

Defense #13 involves a shift from describing her desire to her fear, from a desire for action expressed in the hour to an image of paralysis brought in from the past. In the hour, she says she wants to do things. When she says *"but you can't because you're afraid,"* she is bringing in a memory of a past episode of paralysis to block the current expression of her desire. One would not interpret this defense because it is too smooth for the patient to observe.

Another example of the therapist stimulating the id and the patient's increased defensiveness in response:

Therapist: *It's okay to let yourself go.*

Patient: *You don't understand! I don't know what to let go. Don't you understand, I'm afraid! I feel so tense and stiff inside.*

This illustrates one of the reasons that reassurance often does not help. If the patient doesn't feel comfortable expressing a thought or feeling, telling her it's okay is an empathic lapse, a failure to be attuned to her conflict. An empathic interpretation of conflict involves empathy with each of the parts of the patient's conflict: her wish, her fear, and her defense. To empathize only with her wish is to ignore her fear and her desire to keep the expression of her wish at a tolerable level.

This is why Anna Freud urged us to adopt an equidistant approach: address the wish, fear, and defense, supporting and understanding each but without siding with any part to the exclusion of the others. For example, *"It sounds like you want very much to say what you are feeling* [wish], *but are afraid of what will happen when you do* [fear]. *So you are feeling tense* [defense], *tempted to talk, but also afraid of what will happen if you do."*

Therapist: *It's okay to let yourself go.*

Patient: *You don't understand! I don't know what to let go. Don't you understand, I'm afraid! I feel so tense and stiff inside. [#14] I don't understand why. It's like you want to say you're sorry for the way you feel to your family, but you don't know how you really feel. I just can't figure it out, I just can't.*

Defense #14 involves a shift from describing the therapist as not understanding to describing herself that way: she identifies with the object of her criticism.

Possible defense interpretation: *"You are describing yourself now* [defense] *just after you were describing how you perceived me* [wish]. *Was there something that inhibited you from saying how I was off track?* [fear]*"*

Therapist: *I understand.*

Patient: *You want to tell your family you're sorry for the way you feel, [#15] but they don't understand how you really feel. They can't possibly know what I hide within.*

Defense #15 is another subtle defense like #13, where a memory was enlisted to block expression of a wish. This is so subtle that it would not ordinarily be interpreted, but we will continue anyway for heuristic purposes. Here, a belief that her family cannot understand blocks her from expressing the wish to tell them she is sorry. Keep in mind that the belief blocks her not from telling her family, but from telling her therapist more about that wish in the therapy hour. Even if the family is critical, we would still be curious about why that fact is enlisted in the therapy hour to block her from expressing a wish. The issue is not whether or not the family understands her, whether it is a "fact." The issue is what function does that "fact" serve at this moment: to facilitate or block expression of a wish in the therapy hour?

Possible defense interpretation: If there was a great deal of evidence about her family being critical, one might say, *"From what you have said* *it sounds like they wouldn't understand if you put that wish into action. But my question is different. I'm wondering if that fact helps you stop yourself right now from putting your wish into words here, the wish to tell them you're sorry."*

Or one might approach the defense in another way by focusing on it as a shift in perception from herself to her family:

Possible defense interpretation: *"In mentioning what they understand [defense], I realize we have moved away from what you understand: that you want to tell them you're sorry [wish]. Do you sense a hesitation [fear] in describing that wish here?"*

Therapist: *But they can accept all your feelings no matter what they are.*

Patient: *I want to enjoy life without fear—without being afraid.*

Therapist: *You're not asking too much at all.*

Patient: *It's the same old things that bother me. I talk with Bill about them over and over again, so that I think he must get sick of hearing it.*

Therapist: *Not a bit so! It's important to him.*

Patient: *I went to a church the other day, a new one. We went down in the basement and it had a tunnel that reminded me of here and I got a little afraid.* [She laughs.] *[#16] It's kind of silly. It ran so deep!*

Defense #16 involves a shift from describing her fear in the past to her judgement of her self now as silly. Since she is able to get back on track, no interpretation would be necessary.

Therapist: *It's okay.*

Patient: *A lot of the time, I'm afraid when I really don't have to be. Like going to the store: I go very frightened, and after I get there and have all the groceries, it doesn't seem so bad after all. It all seems so silly—yet so important at the same time.*

Therapist: *I understand.*

Patient: *But I still don't like being so dependent on Bill. I really don't! I always have to have him waiting. And that makes me mad, [#17] but I guess it's better that way than not at all.*

Therapist: *It's okay.*

Patient: *Sometimes I get the uncomfortable feeling I'm saying more than I intend to—like I'm talking about one thing that seems so insignificant and yet somehow seems so important.*

Therapist: *Let's continue next Monday.*

Patient: *Okay.*

Defense #17 involves a shift from the feeling she has to a feeling she imagines, from present experience to a future fantasy. Her following comments illustrate her conflict clearly: "Sometimes I get the uncomfortable feeling I'm saying more than I intend to—like I'm talking about one thing that seems so insignificant and yet somehow seems so important." And when those feelings suddenly seem so important, a defense becomes necessary.

Studies in Flexibility
of Listening

As you have learned the different approaches in this book, you have begun to think about these theories, to compare them, to be able to use them as tools rather than identify yourself with them. An astronomer does not refer to himself as a "telescopist." A telescope is a merely a tool he uses to discover and create worlds of meaning. Different tools allow him to discover and create different worlds. To say one is a self psychologist or a Freudian, from this perspective, is as absurd as an astronomer referring to himself as a telescopist. The astronomer uses many instruments to develop data he will think about. He will use findings from telescopes, radiation measures, satellite research, and geological studies of moon rocks and meteorites. Then, using findings from a variety of tools, he thinks about the data.

Imagine how limited he would be if he relied on only one of those tools. Now you can see how limited we are when we use only one approach to listening. Likewise, astronomers don't sit around arguing about which tool is best because each tool is valuable, allowing them to see something different, and that difference is valued. Each theory allows us to see something different, to intervene differently, and to create different interactions.

Ironically, the major disadvantage of the skills we learn with theories is that they really do work. The fact that they work in a given situation leads us to the mistaken assumption that they work in all situations or, worse, that they work best in every situation (Debono 1976). Our comfort with working from a particular approach leads to a kind of therapeutic prejudice. We become so skilled at a particular approach, capable of instant judgment and quick reaction, that we become convinced of the approach's unique value. Only as we work with more patients do we see its limitations. At that point, adherence to a given approach blocks us from developing further listening skills.

We also block ourselves from developing our listening skills by assuming that they occur naturally, as if we don't need to think about how we listen. Yet many of our skills are unnatural and are learned in artificial ways. When learning to ski, we have to learn to lean downhill when going down a slope. When learning a language, we have to memorize conjugations, cases, and idioms that feel unnatural until we develop a fluency in language that makes all the preparatory work pull together. When learning each of these skills, which eventually feel natural, we pass through a phase which feels extremely awkward. But since our listening style feels natural to us, we assume it is good enough. We are reluctant to go through an awkward stage that is necessary if we are to learn new ways of directing our attention.

Skill in psychotherapeutic listening involves broadening what we can perceive through being able to direct our attention. This allows us to explore the patient's and our own experience. Hence, this book has helped you broaden what you can perceive through learning to direct your attention in four different directions in addition to the direction that feels most natural to you. We mistakenly assume that we need to know more when we need to be able to perceive more.

> It may seem that what is called perceptual inadequacy is really ignorance or lack of knowledge. It may be said that no one should be blamed for the deficiency of an argument that has to be based on currently available knowledge rather than on absolute knowledge. This is true. But perception is not the same as knowledge. Perception is the way we look at available knowledge and the way we direct attention over available knowledge. The faults lie not so much in the inadequacy of knowledge but in the inadequacy of the way we look at it. If we look at a situation only in an egocentric manner that is because we choose to do so. If we arrogantly assume that a plausible explanation excludes all others that is because we choose to do so. (DeBono 1976:76).

The way we listen can seem so natural and comfortable to us that we get "captured" by it, unable to shift to another approach to listening. In this chapter, we will look at one session from three different approaches. These exercises will develop your flexibility of listening. Each section will be followed by questions designed to help you listen to the hour from the perspectives of conflict, defense analysis, and transference.

As you will see, each approach focuses on a different surface, resulting in different content and timing of interpretations.

And yet we are not listening flexibly only for the sake of flexibility. Only by understanding that the creative process involved in saying what comes to mind is "deep and complicated, that it may manifest itself in many different ways, and that it is primarily a process of search for meanings and exploration of meanings—only by understanding all this, can we understand how ideas, themes, meanings" (Brooks and Warren 1938:xxii–xxiii) get into the patient's words. Through listening flexibly, we arrive at an ever richer understanding of the patient, and we begin to glimpse that there is no end to what we could come to know.

☐ Flexibility Exercises

We will study an hour (Silverman 1987) from the perspectives of analysis of conflict, transference, and defense.

Patient: *The rain woke me up early this morning. It was beating down on my air conditioner so loudly it woke me up. I looked at the clock. It was 5:30. I thought in an hour I have to get up to come here. I didn't want to come today. I've been mad at you all week. It's not that I'm mad at you. I wanted to stay away from all this stuff I think I feel here.*

Reader's Notes

Analysis of Conflict and Transference

What is the conflict about therapy that the patient is describing? Offer a possible interpretation of the conflict and a translation of the transference.

Analysis of Defense

Make a note of the defense, describe the nature of the defense, and propose a possible interpretation.

Patient: *The rain woke me up early this morning. It was beating down on my air conditioner so loudly it woke me up. I looked at the clock. It was 5:30. I thought in an hour I have to get up to come here. I didn't want to come today. I've been mad at you all week. It's not that I'm mad at you. I wanted to stay away from all this stuff I think I feel here.*

Author's Notes

Analysis of Conflict

The conflict appears to be a wish to discuss her anger at the therapist, a fear of what would happen if she did, and a defense of wanting not to come and thereby avoid her feelings of anger. At this point her fear is still unknown.

Possible interpretation of conflict: *Perhaps you didn't want to come in today* [defense] *not just because you were mad* [wish], *but also because something about being mad made you uncomfortable* [fear].

Analysis of Transference

She says she is mad at the therapist but then moves away from saying that. This suggests that she is not only mad at the therapist but is afraid to say so. The transference involving anger is conscious (the transference of impulse) and, at least at this point in the hour, is not depicted in the displacement. However, we would be interested in what feelings may be making it dangerous to describe her anger at the therapist (the transference of defense).

Analysis of Defense

Patient: *The rain woke me up early this morning. It was beating down on my air conditioner so loudly it woke me up. I looked at the clock. It was 5:30. I thought in an hour I have to get up to come here. I didn't want to come today. I've been mad at you all week. [#1] It's not that I'm mad at you. I wanted to stay away from all this stuff I think I feel here.*

Defense #1 involves a shift from describing her anger to denying it, from focusing on the therapist to focusing on herself. Her analysis of a defense, "I wanted to stay away from all this stuff," serves as a defense: it blocks her from describing her anger at the therapist.

Possible defense interpretation: *"You say you aren't mad at me now* [defense], *yet a moment ago you seemed freer to entertain that possibility* [wish]. *Did you sense some reluctance* [fear] *there?"*

Each of these listening approaches focuses on a different aspect of the material: conflict depicted in the content; conflict in the therapy relationship depicted in the manifest and latent content; and conflict manifested in the process by which the content is revealed. Each approach generates different types of interpretations and the rules of timing are different as well. From the perspective of analysis of conflict, as soon as the patient has outlined her wish and defense in the content, we could make an interpretation that invites the patient to describe her fear.

From the perspective of analysis of transference we would not interpret at this point. One aspect of the transference is conscious and needs no interpretation: the fact that she is mad at the therapist. We don't understand yet why she is afraid to say that, nor do we understand what defensive purposes that transference might serve. Hence, we would not yet make a transference interpretation.

From the perspective of analysis of defense, we would interpret as soon as a defense has occurred in order to invite the patient to reflect on her experience just before the shift. In this example, we would interpret at the same time as we would from the perspective of analysis of conflict. However, the reasons for timing and the focus of the interpretation would be different. Analysis of conflict would be asking: "why are you afraid to tell me of your anger at me?" Analysis of defense would be asking: "what was the anxiety in this past moment that led you to reverse yourself?" Analysis of conflict would be asking a larger, more global question. Analysis of defense would be asking a question based only on a specific moment.

The hour continues:

Patient: *I also got angry at R.* [her roommate] *yesterday. In the bathroom, she takes two towel bars and a hook. And I just have one towel bar. I didn't say anything for a long time. I finally got up the courage and told her we have to change the arrangements in the bathroom. It sounds so silly. I get so worked up over such little things. I get so angry. She was talking about being all worked up because someone called her for a date. She hardly listened to what I was saying. She's so self-centered. Her boyfriend came, and he was there two minutes and he asked about my cousin. She never asks about my cousin. She only thinks about herself. I thought of saying "thanks for asking" to him because I was so grateful he'd asked, but I decided not to say it. Because I'd have been calling attention to her never asking. I get so mad at her.*

Reader's Notes

Analysis of Conflict

Mark passages to indicate where wishes, fears, and defenses are depicted in the content. What is the conflict which the patient is describing?

Analysis of Transference

Offer a translation of the transference and a possible interpretation of transference.

Analysis of Defense

Underline the defenses in the passage above and describe and interpret them.

Author's Notes

Analysis of Conflict

Patient: *I also got angry at R.* [her roommate] *yesterday* [wish]. *In the bathroom, she takes two towel bars and a hook. And I just have one towel bar. I didn't say anything for a long time* [defense]. *I finally got up the courage and told her we have to change the arrangements in the bathroom* [wish]. *It sounds so silly* [defense]. *I get so worked up over such little things* [defense]. *I get so angry* [defense]. *She was talking about being all worked up because someone called her for a date. She hardly listened to what I was saying. She's so self-centered* [culmination of increasingly strong expressions of the wish in the past two sentences]. *Her boyfriend came, and he was there two minutes and he asked about my cousin. She never asks about my cousin. She only thinks about herself. I thought of saying "thanks for asking" to him because I was so grateful he'd asked* [wish], *but I decided not to say it* [defense]. *Because I'd have been calling attention to her never asking* [fear]. *I get so mad at her* [wish].

The patient shifts from describing her conflict with the therapist to her conflict with the roommate. The conflict involves a wish to tell her roommate about her anger, a fear that she would be calling attention to her roommate's lack of interest in her, and a defense of remaining silent while her anger builds.

Possible interpretation of conflict: *"Although you wanted to express your irritation with her* [wish], *you were afraid you would be calling attention to her self-centeredness* [fear], *so you held back* [defense]. *What were you afraid would happen if you had called attention to her never asking* [fear]?"

Translation of the Transference

Patient: *I also got angry at R* [you] [her roommate] *yesterday. In the bathroom* [therapy], *she* [you] *takes two towel bars and a hook* [too much space]. *And I just have one towel bar. I didn't say anything for a long time* [to you]. *I finally got up the courage and told her* [you] *we have to change the arrangements in the bathroom* [therapy]. *It sounds so silly. I get so worked up over such little things. I get so angry* [at you]. *She was* [You were] *talking about being all worked up because someone* [the patient?]

called her [you] *for a date* [an appointment?]. *She* [You] *hardly listened to what I was saying. She's* [You're] *so self-centered. Her boyfriend came, and he was there two minutes* [Some interruption occurred in the session: a phone call, a different topic?] *and he asked about my cousin. She* [You] *never asks about my cousin* [things that concern me]. *She* [You] *only thinks about herself* [yourself]. *I thought of saying "thanks for asking" to him because I was so grateful he'd asked, but I decided not to say it. Because I'd have been calling attention to her* [your] *never asking. I get so mad at her* [you].

There has been no bridge statement made yet linking the latent content to the therapy so we would continue to listen.

Silent interpretation of transference: *"It sounds like it makes you angry that she takes up so much space and is so self-centered that she doesn't think to ask about what you feel. You're tempted to say something but are afraid of drawing too much attention to her self-centeredness so you hold back. I wonder if that same conflict may be at work here, because a moment ago you mentioned feeling mad at me during the week. I wonder if you were afraid of drawing attention to what I did that made you angry."*

Analysis of Defense

Patient: *I also got angry at R.* [her roommate] *yesterday. In the bathroom, she takes two towel bars and a hook. And I just have one towel bar.* [#2] I didn't say anything for a long time. *I finally got up the courage and told her we have to change the arrangements in the bathroom.* [#3] It sounds so silly. I get so worked up over such little things. I get so angry. *She was talking about being all worked up because someone called her for a date. She hardly listened to what I was saying. She's so self-centered. Her boyfriend came, and he was there two minutes and he asked about my cousin. She never asks about my cousin. She only thinks about herself. I thought of saying "thanks for asking" to him because I was so grateful he'd asked* [Notice in the previous five sentences the gradually emerging id derivative: the wish to express her anger at the roommate.]*,* [#4] but I decided not to say it. Because I'd have been calling attention to her never asking. *I get so mad at her.*

Defense #2 involves a shift from what she is saying in the present in the therapy room to what she did not say in the past in her home. Since she gets back on track right away, there would be no need to interpret.

Defense #3 involves a shift from saying what she told her roommate to what she is now telling herself. She turns her aggression against the self: "I told her, then I tell myself I sound so silly."

Possible defense interpretations: *"Right now you're judging yourself* [defense], *but a moment ago you seemed freer to describe how you asserted* *yourself* [wish to describe herself this way]. *Did you notice that shift from describing your assertiveness to judging it?"* If so, *"What were you feeling* [fear] *when you told me what you had told her?"* Or for a patient more familiar with her defenses: *"I wonder if judging yourself* [defense] *is helping you put on the brakes just now after you were describing your assertiveness* [wish]." Yet, since she does get back on track pretty quickly we might let this defense go by without comment.

Defense #4: she expresses the wish to respond to him, then shifts to describing how she decided not to respond.

This example illustrates the difference between a content and process oriented approach to defense analysis. From a content point of view, we would note that when she was with the boy she had a wish to respond, there was some unspecified anxiety, and a defense of deciding not to respond.

A content oriented interpretation: *"It sounds like you wanted to respond to his show of interest* [wish], *but it sounds like you were afraid of what would happen if you did* [fear], *so you decided to hold back* [defense]. *What do you think you were afraid of?"* The interpretation would explore the conflict in a current relationship.

From a process point of view we would note that when she was describing to you her wish to respond to the boy, she became anxious, and, to restrain herself from describing that wish any further with you, she brought in her memory of deciding not to respond to him.

Process oriented interpretation: *"This image of not saying something* [defense] *came up just when you were about to tell me what you wanted to say to him* [wish]. *Was there some discomfort* [fear] *when you described wanting to thank him?"*

As an aside, the reader may be thinking that the patient was simply reporting a memory: she wanted to say something to the boy and decided not to do it. That is true. From a process point of view we are not questioning that she decided not to say something. We can take for granted that is a truth. Instead, we are interested in the function that truth is having to serve at this moment. Why did this memory come up now? What impact did the memory have on her freely associating to a wish? The patient could have chosen a different memory to amplify her description of the wish to say thank you, but the memory she chose blocked her expression instead. Hence, from a process point of view we are interested in the functions of memories, thoughts, and feelings: do they promote or inhibit free association?

In this section of the hour, an interpretation of conflict would have occurred because the patient's reference to her fear gives us an opening to explore this area further. No interpretation of transference would have occurred due to the lack of a bridge statement. From the perspective of analysis of defense, more interpretive possibilities occur in this section. Of the three defenses in the process, probably Defense #3 would be the easiest for the patient to observe and analyze. Defenses #2 and #4 fit so easily into the narrative that their defensive function would not be observable to a patient until later stages of therapy, when her capacity for self-observation would be more advanced.

The hour continues:

Patient: *I thought about something else in the car on the way here. I went to have my hair cut and it was to be cut at seven o'clock. But I had to wait and wait till nine o'clock. I got angrier and angrier. I told the girl when I paid* (Therapist's notation: she'll get a bill from me in a few days, and it's the end of the week and she has to wait two days to see me again on Monday—like the two hours for the hairdresser—and in two weeks I leave for vacation, and she'll have to wait a month for me) *that I was angry. I told her that I can go to someone else to get my hair cut—or I can wait for him. I don't like either alternative. I don't even know why I go there. I don't fit in. They're mostly older women. But I didn't say anything to him. I'm intimidated by him the way I'm intimidated by M. [the tennis pro]. I don't know why. He's not big and tall like M. He's good-looking, but he's not my type. He's married and has children. He has their pictures up. With M., I think it has something to do with my knowing nothing about tennis and his knowing so much about it. And I couldn't understand when he was telling me what to do. "Hold it this way" and "turn that way," and I couldn't understand anything he said. It was just like with my father all my life. He thinks he gives such good directions and clear explanations, as I said yesterday, but he doesn't. I get intimidated with men. I always feel that they know they have the knowledge. They have the brains, and I'm dumb. And I always feel like I don't know anything and I can't understand and I get intimidated.*

Reader's Notes

Analysis of Conflict

Mark passages to indicate where wishes, fears, and defenses are depicted in the content. What is the conflict that the patient is describing? Offer a possible interpretation of the conflict in the displacement.

Analysis of Transference

Provide a translation and possible interpretation of the transference.

Analysis of Defense

Underline the defenses in the passage above, analyze them and offer possible interpretations.

Author's Notes

Analysis of Conflict

Patient: *I thought about something else in the car on the way here. I went to have my hair cut and it was to be cut at seven o'clock. But I had to wait and wait till nine o'clock. I got angrier and angrier. I told the girl when I paid* (Therapist's notation: she'll get a bill from me in a few days, and it's the end of the week and she has to wait two days to see me again on Monday—like the two hours for the hairdresser—and in two weeks I leave for vacation, and she'll have to wait a month for me) *that I was angry* [wish]. *I told her that I can go to someone else to get my hair cut* [wish]—*or I can wait for him* [defense]. *I don't like either alternative. I don't even know why I go there. I don't fit in. They're mostly older women. But I didn't say anything to* him [defense]. *I'm intimidated by him the way I'm intimidated by M.* [the tennis pro] [fear]. *I don't know why. He's not big and tall like M. He's good-looking, but he's not my type. He's married and has children. He has their pictures up. With M., I think it has something to do with my knowing nothing about tennis and his knowing so much about it. And I couldn't understand when he was telling me what to do. "Hold it this way" and "turn that way," and I couldn't understand anything he said. It was just like with my father all my life. He thinks he gives such good directions and clear explanations, as I said yesterday, but he doesn't. I get intimidated with men* [fear]. *I always feel that they know they have the knowledge. They have the brains, and I'm dumb. And I always feel like I don't know anything and I can't understand and I get intimidated.*

The wish is to express anger and criticism towards the hairdresser; her fear is that if she expresses herself she will be intimidated, perhaps attacked as not knowing anything, being dumb, unable to understand anything; and her defense is not to say anything. She elaborates on the fear which was not clear in the previous material.

Possible interpretation of conflict: *"When you wanted to tell the hairdresser that you were upset* [wish], *you were intimidated* [fear]. *I wonder if you were afraid that he might criticize you as if you didn't know what you were talking about* [fear], *and if it was your fear of his criticism that led you not to say anything to him* [defense]."

Translation of Transference

Patient: *I thought about something else in the car on the way here. I went to have my hair cut and it was to be cut at seven o'clock. But I had to wait and wait till nine o'clock.* [Did the therapist keep her waiting for her appointment recently or is this a reference to her having to wait until he returns from his vacation?] *I got* [am getting] *angrier and angrier* [with you]. *I told the girl* [you] *when I paid* (Therapist's notation: she'll get a bill from me in a few days, and it's the end of the week and she has to wait two days to see me again on Monday—like the two hours for the hairdresser—and in two weeks I leave for vacation, and she'll have to wait a month for me) *that I was angry. I told her* [you] *that I can go to someone else to get my hair cut* [therapy]—*or I can wait for him* [you]. *I don't like either alternative. I don't even know why I go there* [here]. *I don't fit in. They're mostly older women. But I didn't say anything to* him [you]. *I'm intimidated by him* [you] *the way I'm intimidated by M.* [the tennis pro]. *I don't know why. He's* [You're] *not big and tall like M. He's* [You're] *good-looking, but he's* [you're] *not my type. He's* [You're] *married and has children. He has* [You have] *their pictures up. With M.* [you], *I think it has something to do with my knowing nothing about tennis* [therapy] *and his* [your] *knowing so much about it. And I couldn't* [can't] *understand when he was* [you are] *telling me what to do. "Hold it this way" and "turn that way," and I couldn't* [can't] *understand anything he* [you] *said. It was just like with my father all my life. He* [You] *thinks he* [you] *gives such good directions and clear explanations* [interpretations], *as I said yesterday, but he doesn't* [you don't]. *I get intimidated with men* [you]. *I always feel that they* [you] *know they* [you] *have the knowledge. They* [You] *have the brains, and I'm dumb. And I always feel like I don't know anything and I can't understand and I get intimidated.*

The theme of "directions and clear explanations" provides a bridge statement, linking the latent content to the therapy.

Possible interpretation of transference: *"When you wanted to tell the hairdresser that you were upset, you felt intimidated, fearing he might criticize you as if you didn't know what you were talking about. So you decided not to say anything to him. I wonder if that may be linked here too. You mentioned earlier that you felt mad at me this week and then you shifted to talking about your roommate. I wonder if you felt intimidated letting me know you were angry with me and were afraid I would criticize you for having critical feelings about the therapy."*

Analysis of Defense

Patient: *[#5] I thought about something else in the car on the way here. I went to have my hair cut and it was to be cut at seven o'clock. But I had to* *wait and wait till nine o'clock. I got angrier and angrier. I told the girl when I paid that I was angry. I told her that I can go to someone else to get my hair cut [#6]—or I can wait for him. I don't like either alternative. I don't even know why I go there. I don't fit in. They're mostly older women. [#7] But I didn't say anything to him. I'm intimidated by him the way I'm intimidated by M. [the tennis pro]. [#8] I don't know why. He's not big and tall like M. He's good-looking, [#9] but he's not my type. He's married and has children. He has their pictures up. With M., I think it has something to do with my knowing nothing about tennis and his knowing so much about it. And I couldn't understand when he was telling me what to do. "Hold it this way" and "turn that way," and I couldn't understand anything he said. It was just like with my father all my life. He thinks he gives such good directions and clear explanations, as I said yesterday, but he doesn't. [#10] I get intimidated by men. I always feel that they know they have the knowledge. They have the brains, and I'm dumb. And I always feel like I don't know anything and I can't understand and I get intimidated.*

Defense #5 is a shift on many levels: from anger towards the room-mate being expressed here and now to a thought about someone else which occurred in the past somewhere else. A shift from feeling to thought, from one person to another, from here to there, from now to then: shifts in mode of experience, person, place, time.

Possible defense interpretation: *"Your thoughts about this person* [defense] *came up just after you said your roommate makes you really miffed** [wish to express her anger]. *What would happen* [fear] *if you let that statement stand now without moving to the other girl?"* [* The word "miffed" understates her anger to avoid stimulating more defensiveness, and make self observation more possible.]

Defense #6 involves a shift from wanting to leave to deciding to stay, turning active to passive.

Possible defense interpretation: *"Gosh, you know, it sounds almost like you made a U-turn just now. In your mind you were heading out the door* [wish], *and now you are talking about waiting* [defense]. *What were you feeling* [fear] *just a moment ago before you did that U-turn?"* Since she returns to the theme of her anger so quickly we probably would not interpret.

Defense #7 involves a number of shifts: from what she is saying now to you, to what she did not say then to him: shifts of negation, time, and person.

Possible defense interpretation: *"Yes it does sound like you didn't say anything to him then* [defense], *but I notice you mention that after saying to me here that you have some reservations* [wish to express this]. *Is there something risky* [fear] *about describing those reservations now?"*

Defense #8 involves a shift from what she knows to what she does not know. This example illustrates how curiosity can shift from an exploratory to a defensive function. She has shifted the focus of her curiosity from *what* she feels to *why* she feels intimidated.

Possible defense interpretation: *"The question "why" is a good one, but I'm wondering if asking "why" you felt that may be interrupting you just as you were describing what you felt."* This defense is so smooth and subtle that an interpretation would probably not be possible until later phases of therapy when she could observe these shifts with ease.

Defense #9 involves a shift of attention from what his traits are to what her desires are not, a shift of perception from him to her. The idea that he is not her type blocks her from simply describing him. Although one could infer romantic feelings here, it would not be necessary to bring them up since merely describing him evoked a defense.

Possible defense interpretation: *"I notice you are describing yourself* [defense] *just after you were describing him* [wish]. *It was as if you shifted the focus of the camera back onto you. Was there something* [fear] *that interfered with your ability to describe him?"* Yet given how brief this defense is and her shift to other material, it might be best to wait for a defense that more obviously blocks her and would be easier for her to see.

Defense #10 involves a shift from critical perceptions of others to a perception of herself as intimidated, a turning of aggression back onto the self.

Possible defense interpretation: *"I sense you did a bit of reversal just now. You are describing how you see yourself now* [defense], *but a moment ago you were describing how you see your father, as someone who can be a bit unclear* [wish to describe father]. *What were you feeling* [fear] *when you had the camera focused on his unclear directions?"*

When comparing the possible interpretations in this segment of the hour, we find that the transference and conflict interpretations would have occurred at the same time because the anxiety is more elaborated, allowing a fuller interpretation. From the perspective of defense analysis, there a number of possible interpretations. However Defenses #6 and #10 are probably the ones that are most observable to the patient and, hence, can be analyzed *with* her. The other defenses would be too subtle for her to analyze. Although we might offer our thoughts, she might be unable to observe the defenses in order to think about them. This would defeat the purpose of defense analysis because we would not be strengthening her capacity for self analysis and observation (Gray 1995).

The hour continues:

Patient: *It's the same thing here. I keep feeling like asking you, "What does it mean?" I always feel like you know. I feel like asking you now. I know you've* *told me you don't know anything until I've told it to you, but I don't feel that way. I feel you're always a step ahead of me. You know, because you're smarter than I am and all the training and experience you have.*

Reader's Notes

Analysis of Conflict

Mark passages to indicate where wishes, fears, and defenses are depicted in the content. What is the conflict which the patient is describing? Offer a possible interpretation of conflict in the displacement.

Analysis of Transference

Provide a translation of the transference.

Analysis of Defense

Underline the defenses in the passage above and describe the nature of the defenses and their possible interpretations.

Author's Comments

Analysis of Conflict

Patient: *It's the same thing here. I keep feeling like asking you, "What does it mean?"* [wish] *I always feel like you know. I feel like asking you now* [wish]. *I know you've told me you don't know anything until I've told it to you* [defense], *but I don't feel that way. I feel you're always a step ahead of me. You* know, *because you're smarter than I am and all the training and experience you have.*

Now she has shifted to describing the conflict within the therapy relationship. She wants to say what things mean to her [wish], but fears something if she does, and so she asks the therapist to tell her the meaning of events, treating him as if he is smarter, more knowledgeable [defense]. However, at this moment she has a new conflict: a wish to ask him what something means, an unspecified fear about how he would respond, and a defense of not exactly asking. Viewing him as smarter allows her to talk around her wish to ask but without actually asking him.

Possible interpretation of conflict: *"Well, it's true I do have training and experience, so it's understandable you would want to ask me what things mean* [wish]. *I sensed though that you moved away from asking the question* [defense]. *Was there some risk* [fear] *about letting that question stand here?"*

This, of course, is not strictly speaking an interpretation of content but of process. Conflict is not being portrayed in the content now; it is being enacted.

Translation of the Transference

Patient: *It's the same thing here. I keep feeling like asking you, "What does it mean?" I always feel like you know. I feel like asking you now. I know you've told me you don't know anything until I've told it to you, but I don't feel that way. I feel you're always a step ahead of me. You know, because you're smarter than I am and all the training and experience you have.*

In contrast to the previous material, the transference is now expressed directly rather than symbolized in the displacement. Ordinarily, if the transference is depicted only in the displacement, our interpretations focus on helping the patient become aware of the transference. Now that the patient is aware of the transference, the focus of our interpretations would shift to the function of the transference (Gill and Hoffman 1982).

We might infer that she now views the therapist as an intimidating, all-knowing figure at this moment to help restrain herself from expressing what she knows: her anger at him. In other words, her view of him as smarter is a transference of defense that wards off her anger, which is a transference of impulse. Although one might interpret that process, I suspect that it would be too far from the patient's awareness for her to work with usefully, and the dosage of impulse would be unmanageable for her. Instead, we would help her elaborate on this conscious fantasy, waiting to find out what its defensive function might be and waiting for an opening where we might be able to help her analyze it.

Analysis of Defense

Patient: *It's the same thing here. I keep feeling like asking you, "What does it mean?"* [#11] *I always feel like you know. I feel like asking you now.* [#12] *I know you've told me you don't know anything until I've told it to you, but I don't feel that way. I feel you're always a step ahead of me. You* know, *because you're smarter than I am and all the training and experience you have.*

Defense #11 involves a shift from demanding something from the therapist to describing him.

Possible defense interpretation: *"By thinking about what I know [defense], you interrupted yourself just when you feel tempted to ask me a question [wish]. What were you afraid you might feel [fear] if you could let your question hang there in the air between us?"*

Defense #12 involves a shift from expressing a wish to ask a question to imagining what he might answer, from her wish to his thoughts, from her voice to his.

Possible defense interpretation: *"It's as if you are trying to answer your question [defense] so I won't have to respond to you. Was there some risk [fear] there in wanting to ask me a question [wish]?"*

The wish to ask the question and the question itself are in her awareness. Although they are at a smaller dosage than the anger that is expressed at the hairdresser in the transference, they still stimulate defenses in the hour. These examples show how the issue of warding off aggressive impulses can be addressed in smaller dosages. The timing of interpretations for analysis of conflict and analysis of defense was the same. In this case, analysis of conflict would focus on the process since there is no conflict depicted at this point in the content. Since she is aware of her fantasy that the therapist is smarter, we would listen and help her elaborate it until its defensive function becomes apparent.

The hour continues:

Therapist: *I don't think that's what it is. I think you feel I know because I'm a man, that as a woman you don't have the brains.*

Patient: *I get intimidated by men.* [anxiously] *Do you think I signal it to them and that drives them away? So they think, "Who wants her!" I think it started in a way when my father said to me, "Every man is going to want the same thing from you." I got so angry. Why? Why would he expect that of me? What right does he have? I heard R. and her boyfriend kissing just outside the door. She likes it! When my father said what he did, first I was mad at them for wanting sex eventually, and then I got mad if I thought they wanted to kiss on the first date. Then I started getting mad that they'd ever want to kiss. I got so angry. I'm such an angry person.* [Possible interpretation of conflict #1? Possible transference interpretation #1?]

Therapist: *As you've said, you get mad to push away other feelings.*

Patient: *With A.* [A. is a young man she had met on a singles weekend trip, at which she had relaxed her usual guarded stiffness and had danced and smiled and joked. A. had become interested in her and arranged to come in from out of town to spend two days with her, only to stand her up when she went to meet him.], *I told him when he* *said he would come down here that he could stay at my apartment. And he got all excited about it and eager to come. And then I got frightened about what I'd said to him, and I said, "Wait a minute," and I made it clear to him I meant he could sleep over at my apartment—on the couch—not with me.* [with emotion] *Do you think that's why he didn't show up? Did I chase him away? Men intimidate me. It's like with my father. It's a mixture of excitement and pain and hurt and fear.*

[Possible interpretation of transference #2?]

Reader's Notes

Analysis of Conflict

Mark passages to indicate where wishes, fears, and defenses are depicted in the content. What is the conflict which the patient is describing? Provide an alternative interpretation of conflict and a possible interpretation of conflict in the displacement.

Analysis of Transference

Offer a translation of the transference and possible interpretations of transferences #1 and #2.

Analysis of Defense

Underline the defenses in the passage above and describe the defenses and possible interpretations.

Author's Notes

Analysis of Conflict

Therapist: *I don't think that's what it is. I think you feel I know because I'm a man, that as a woman you don't have the brains.* [The therapist interprets the unconscious fantasy underlying her transference to him, but not the defensive function of this transference or the anxiety it is helping the patient cope with.]

Patient: *I get intimidated by men* [fear]. [anxiously] *Do you think I signal it to them and that drives them away? So they think, "Who wants her!" I think it started in a way when my father said to me, "Every man is going to want the same thing from you* [wish]." *I got so angry* [defense]. *Why? Why would he expect that of me* [defense]? *What right does he have* [defense]? *I* *heard R. and her boyfriend kissing just outside the door* [wish]. *She* likes *it* [wish]*! When my father said what he did, first I was mad at them for wanting sex eventually* [wish], *and then I got mad* [defense] *if I thought they wanted to kiss on the first date* [wish]. *Then I started getting mad* [defense] *that they'd ever want to kiss. I got so angry. I'm such an angry person.*

Therapist: *As you've said, you get mad to push away* [defense] *other feelings* [wish]. [Therapist addresses the defensive function of her anger but not the fear or wish.]

Alternative interpretation of conflict: *"I don't know that I would say you are such an angry person. [This comment is designed to help her think about herself and her feelings. In other words, "You are not an angry person. You are a person who becomes angry at different times for different reasons and purposes. Let's see what those reasons and purposes might be in this case."] I would say that you are a person who gets angry* [defense] *as soon as you think about the idea of men wanting to kiss you* [wish]. *I wonder if there is something about the thought of men kissing you that is uncomfortable* [fear] *and leads you to become angry* [defense]."

Patient: *With A.* [A. is a young man she had met on a singles weekend trip, at which she had relaxed her usual guarded stiffness and had danced and smiled and joked. A. had become interested in her and arranged to come in from out of town to spend two days with her, only to stand her up when she went to meet him.], *I told him when he said he would come down here that he could stay at my apartment* [wish]. *And he got all excited about it and eager to come* [wish]. *And then I got frightened about what I'd said to him* [fear], *and I said, "Wait a minute," and I made it clear to him I meant he could sleep over at my apartment—on the couch—not with me* [defense]. [with emotion] *Do you think that's why he didn't show up? Did I chase him away?* [defense] *Men intimidate me* [fear]. *It's like with my father. It's a mixture of excitement and pain and hurt and fear* [wish, fear, and defense].

The wish is to be close to a man [invitation of the boyfriend to the apartment], a fear of what sexual experience might occur, and a defense of pushing the man away. Having described this, she then invites the therapist to judge her for her defense and wish. The focus shifts from the story in the displacement to an enactment between the patient and therapist.

Possible interpretation of conflict: *"And it's that mixture that makes it so complicated when you want to get close to a man. With A. you were excited about inviting him to stay with you* [wish], *but you got frightened* [fear] *and then told him he'd have to sleep on the couch* [defense]. *I wonder if you were afraid that not only he would get excited but that you would too. That you* *might really like it. So perhaps it wasn't just him you wanted to push away but your excitement as well."*

Translation of the Transference

Therapist: *I don't think that's what it is. I think you feel I know because I'm a man, that as a woman you don't have the brains.* [The therapist confronts her defense, but not the anxiety that leads the patient to deny her intelligence nor the patient's wish to acknowledge her brains.]

Patient: *I get intimidated by men* [you]. [I found your comment intimidating and bullying.] [anxiously] *Do you think I signal it to them* [you] *and that drives them* [you] *away? So they* [you] *think, "Who wants her!"* [Her response suggests that she experienced his comment as a refusal to be empathic and she fears that there is something about her that makes the therapist not want to know her experience.] *I think it started in a way when my father* [you] *said to me, "Every man is going to want the same thing from you." I got so angry. Why? Why would he* [you] *expect that of me? What right does he* [you] *have? I heard R. and her boyfriend kissing just outside the door. She likes it! When my father* [you] *said what he* [you] *did, first I was mad at them* [you] *for wanting sex* [and emotional intimacy in therapy] *eventually, and then I got mad if I thought they* [you] *wanted to kiss* [be intimate] *on the first date* [therapy session]. *Then I started getting mad that they'd* [you'd] *ever want to kiss. I got so angry. I'm such an angry person.*

> **Possible interpretation of transference #1:** *"You get angry when men expect sex with you and want to get intimate right away. They seem intimidating in terms of what they want and how they push for it. I wonder if you are experiencing the therapy in that way. Perhaps my questions and probing make you feel as if I am another man who is pushing you to be intimate more quickly than you feel comfortable with."*

Therapist: *As you've said, you get mad to push away other feelings.*
[The therapist addresses her defense but not her fear or wish to give voice to her feelings.]

Patient: *With A.* [you] [A. is a young man she had met on a singles weekend trip, at which she had relaxed her usual guarded stiffness and had danced and smiled and joked. A. had become interested in her and arranged to come in from out of town to spend two days with her, only to stand her up when she went to meet him.], *I told him* [you] *when he* [you] *said he* [you] *would come down here that he* [you] *could stay at my apartment* [visit my mind and my heart]. *And he* [you] *got all excited about it and eager to come. And then I got frightened about what I'd* *said to him [you], and I said, "Wait a minute," and I made it clear to him [you] I meant he [you] could sleep over at my apartment—on the couch—not with me. [with emotion] Do you think that's why he [you] didn't show up [were just unempathic in your last two comments]? Did I chase him [you] away? Men [You] intimidate me. It's like with my father. It's [Your interpretation elicited] a mixture of excitement and pain and hurt and fear.*

Possible interpretation of transference #2: *"And it's that mixture that makes it so complicated when you want to get close to a man. With A. you were excited about inviting him to stay with you, but you got frightened and then told him he'd have to sleep on the couch. And here, I suspect, you have felt excited about the possibility of my getting to know you better too. But when I am excited, when I push to find out more about your feelings, I wonder if that makes you feel intimidated and want a little more distance."*

Analysis of Defense

Therapist: *I don't think that's what it is. I think you feel I know because I'm a man, that as a woman you don't have the brains.*

Patient: *I get intimidated by men.* [anxiously] *[#13]* <u>*Do you think I signal it to them and that drives them away?*</u> *So they think, "Who wants her!" I think it started in a way when my father said to me, "Every man is going to want the same thing from you." I got so angry. [#14]* <u>*Why?*</u> *Why would he expect that of me? What right does he have? I heard R. and her boyfriend kissing just outside the door. She* likes *it! [#15]* <u>*When my father said what he did,*</u> *first I was mad at them for wanting sex eventually, and then I got mad if I thought they wanted to kiss on the first date. Then I started getting mad that they'd ever want to kiss. I got so* angry. *[#16]* <u>*I'm such an angry person.*</u>

Therapist: *As you've said, you get mad to push away other feelings.*

Patient: *With A. I told him when he said he would come down here that he could stay at my apartment. And he got all excited about it and eager to come. [#17]* <u>*And then I got frightened about what I'd said to him,*</u> *and I said, "Wait a minute," and I made it clear to him I meant he could sleep over at my apartment—on the couch—not with me.* [with emotion] *[#18]* <u>*Do you think that's why he didn't show up?*</u> *Did I chase him away? Men intimidate me. It's like with my father.*

Defense #13 involves several shifts, from expressing her own opinion to inviting his instead, from feeling intimidated to fearing she is intimidating.

This is a good example of a question that serves a defensive function. By asking for his thoughts, she blocks herself from further expressing her own. The therapist would neither answer the question nor remain silent, but would instead analyze the question's function.

Possible defense interpretation: *"You're inviting my voice in here* [defense] *just after you gave expression to your own* [wish]. *Was there something risky* [fear] *about letting me know that you do feel intimidated?"*

Defense #14 involves a shift from describing what she feels to what men feel, from her voice to the therapist's voice (the question).

Possible defense interpretation: *"It's as if you turned the car off onto another road. You are wondering what men want* [defense] *just after you were beginning to describe how you feel about your father's comment* [wish to describe her feelings]. *Did you sense some hesitancy* [fear] *about describing your opinion of his comment?"*

Defense #15 involves a shift from her perceptions of an amorous couple to her memory of what her father said, a shift from images of love to feelings of anger, from a couple to a person.

Possible defense interpretation: *"This memory of your father comes up* [defense] *just after you were describing the couple outside your door. I sensed you were a bit jarred* [fear] *when you mentioned how your roommate felt* about kissing* [wish]. *What happened inside you just then?"* [*An understatement of "liking" the kissing which spurred the defense.]

Defense #16 involves a shift from expressing her anger to criticizing it, from perception to evaluation, the point of view shifts from inside ("I was so angry.") to outside ("Looking at myself from the outside, I see 'such an angry person.'").

Possible defense interpretation: *"You are evaluating your feelings now* [defense], *but a moment ago you seemed freer simply to express them* [wish], *without evaluating them. Do you see that change?"* If so, continue: *"I wonder what you might have felt* [fear] *while expressing yourself that would have made you less free?"*

Defense #17 involves a shift from describing his excitement to her fear. Again, this defense raises the question of historical fact. One might argue, "She did get frightened, that's a fact." We are also interested though in how the facts are told to us. The boyfriend's excitement is also a fact. The question for us is this: how long can she talk about that fact with us before needing to shift to another fact that provokes less anxiety? Does the telling of one fact get cut short because of the anxiety it arouses?

Possible defense interpretation: *"It sounds like you did get frightened. But I notice that you have turned the camera back onto yourself* [defense] *just after were focusing on his excitement* [wish]. *Is there something scary for you* [fear] *even now when you remember his excitement then?"*

Defense #18 involves a shift from expressing her voice to inviting her therapist's voice, from expressing her assertiveness to turning it against herself in the form of self-criticism. This is another example of a question functioning as a defense, in this case, against expressing her assertiveness.

Possible defense interpretation: *"It's as if you're handing me the micro-phone* [defense] *just after you described how you asserted yourself with him* [wish]. *Is there some kind of stage fright* [fear] *here when you describe your assertiveness?"*

Let's pause for a moment and compare the possible interpretation of conflict with defense interpretation #17.

Possible interpretation of conflict: *"And it's that mixture that makes it so complicated when you want to get close to a man. With A., you were excited about inviting him to stay with you* [wish], *but you got frightened* [fear] *and then told him he'd have to sleep on the couch* [defense]. *I wonder if you were afraid that not only he would get excited but that you would too. That you might really like it. So perhaps it wasn't just him you wanted to push away, but your sexual feelings that were so frightening."*

Possible defense interpretation: *"It sounds like you did get frightened. But I notice that you have turned the camera back onto yourself just after were focusing in on his excitement. Is there something scary for you even now in remembering his excitement then?"*

The interpretation of conflict addresses conflict as it occurred in the past, in the content of the associations. Timing was determined by getting a full *portrayal* of the entire conflict. The defense interpretation addresses the conflict as it occurs in the present, in the process of the associations. Timing was determined by the *enactment* of the conflict. The interpretation of conflict addresses a large-scale pattern of behavior that occurs throughout her life. The interpretation of defense focuses on the microscopic piece of behavior as it occurs at this moment. The interpretation of conflict addresses what she does and has done elsewhere. The interpretation of defense addresses what she is doing at this moment.

The alternative interpretation of conflict occurred because the wish and defense were exhibited so clearly that it was possible to invite the patient to wonder about the fear in the conflict. The transference interpretation #1 occurred at the same time since there was enough material to come up with a theme that could be linked to the therapy. However, this interpretation might be difficult for the patient to experience as plausible. Instead, the therapist might just summarize the theme in the displacement and wait for the patient to associate to the theme in terms that more closely symbolized the therapy. From the perspective of defense analysis, several openings already occurred. However, a defense interpretation could have been made at this same place as the other two interpretations we've discussed. What is interesting is the difference in focus. In terms of conflict, we would be analyzing her anger as a defense against exploring the idea that men want to kiss her. In terms of transference analysis, we would be analyzing her anger as a defense against the intimacy the therapist is seeking. In defense analysis, we would analyze her phrase, "I get so angry," as a defense, a criticism of her anger, which was in turn a defense against sexual thoughts.

The hour continues:

Patient: *But wait a minute. It's not only men who intimidate me, I get intimidated about money. Paying and tipping intimidates me. I avoid it if I can. Until lately, when I've been thinking about it here and trying not to avoid the things I tend to avoid. When I left the hairdresser's, I looked for the girl who'd shampooed my hair to give her a dollar. But I'd have avoided it if I could. If they had a can with tips in it I would've put it in there. I was too intimidated about tipping the girl who shampooed my hair. Why?* [slight pause] *I can't figure it out. There's no rhyme or reason. I don't understand it.*

Reader's Notes

Analysis of Conflict

Mark passages to indicate where wishes, fears, and defenses are depicted in the content. What is the conflict which the patient is describing? Provide a possible interpretation of conflict in the displacement.

Analysis of Transference

Translate the transference.

Analysis of Defense

Make a note of the defenses in the passage above and describe the defenses and offer possible interpretations.

Author's Notes

Analysis of Conflict

Patient: *But wait a minute. It's not only men who intimidate me, I get intimidated about money* [fear]. *Paying and tipping intimidates me. I avoid it if I can* [defense]. *Until lately, when I've been thinking about it here and trying not to avoid the things I tend to avoid. When I left the hairdresser's I looked for the girl who'd shampooed my hair to give her a dollar* [wish]. *But I'd have avoided it if I could. If they had a can with tips in it I would've put it in there* [defense]. *I was too intimidated about tipping the girl who sham-*

pooed my hair [fear]. *Why?* [slight pause] *I can't figure it out. There's no rhyme or reason. I don't understand it.*

She wanted to pay the girl who shampooed her hair, but fears something that is intimidating, so she avoids paying or does so anonymously in a can for tips. This is a parallel to her conflict about sexuality: a wish for contact, an unspecified fear, and a defense of distancing and avoiding contact.

Possible interpretation of conflict: *"When you wanted to pay her* [wish] *there, was something intimidating about the idea of paying her* [fear], *and so you wanted to avoid it* [defense]? *How is the idea of money and payment intimidating* [fear]?"

Translation of the Transference

Patient: *But wait a minute. It's not only men* [you] *who intimidate me, I get intimidated about money. Paying* [the therapy bill] *and tipping intimidates me. I avoid it if I can. Until lately, when I've been thinking about it here and trying not to avoid the things I tend to avoid. When I left the hairdresser's* [the therapy office], *I looked for the girl who'd shampooed my hair* [you who gave me the therapy] *to give her* [you your fee] *a dollar. But I'd have avoided it if I could. If they had a can with tips in it I would've put it in there.* [If I could pay you without having to face it, I would.] *I was too intimidated about tipping the girl who shampooed my hair* [paying you]. *Why?* [slight pause] *I can't figure it out. There's no rhyme or reason. I don't understand it.*

"Paying the therapy bill intimidates me and I would like to avoid it if I could. If I could pay you anonymously I'd do that. I don't understand it." Although we can hear the transference reference to the fee and billing, we still should wait for a bridge statement. Further, we don't understand yet what is intimidating about the idea of payment. By listening further, we would be able to infer more accurately the nature of her conflict and then interpret it. Addressing the conflict in the displacement would allow us to gain information about her anxiety which we could then link to the transference.

Analysis of Defense

Patient: *It's a mixture of excitement and pain and hurt and fear.* [#19] But wait a minute. *It's not only men who intimidate me, I get intimidated about money. Paying and tipping intimidates me. I avoid it if I can.* [#20] Until lately, when I've been thinking about it here and trying not to avoid the things I tend to avoid. *When I left the hairdresser's, I looked for the girl who'd* *shampooed my hair to give her a dollar. But I'd have avoided it if I could. If they had a can with tips in it I would've put it in there. I was too intimidated about tipping the girl who shampooed my hair. [#21] Why? [slight pause] I can't figure it out. There's no rhyme or reason. I don't understand it.*

Defense #19 involves a shift from feelings toward her father to feelings toward others. In comparison to other defenses in this session, this is the least smooth in transition.

Possible defense interpretation: *"It's true that men intimidate you too* [defense]. *I wonder though if that fact is steering you away from another thought you had: that there's a mixture of feelings about your father* [wish to describe these feelings]. *Rather than expand on those feelings right now, can you say what you were afraid would happen if you let yourself describe those feelings with him?"*

Defense #20 involves a shift from expressing her wish to avoid to denying that wish. It's as if she is reassuring the therapist not to worry, she won't be too resistant. Yet from a process oriented point of view, we are concerned about any inhibitions of thinking and feeling, even inhibitions of resistance. If she wants to talk about being a "bad" patient, we want to interpret any shifts that inhibit her from exploring those thoughts and feelings.

Possible defense interpretation: *"Obviously, you are here in part because you want to overcome problems and obstacles. But I find myself wondering if that fact* [functioning as a defense] *coming up now also blocks you from saying you'd prefer to avoid intimidating situations* [wish to say this]. *Is there some hesitancy about voicing that wish out loud here?"*

Defense #21 involves a shift from describing her feelings of intimidation to asking the therapist his thoughts, from her voice to his, from what she knew to what the therapist knew.

Possible defense interpretation: *"Right now you're describing what you don't know* [defense]. *But a moment ago you were describing what you do know: that you feel uncomfortable about tipping* [wish to say this]. *I wonder if wondering _why_ you feel intimidated blocks you from saying _what_ you feel."*

In this passage, we might interpret the conflict since all three aspects are depicted—wish, fear, and defense—and the patient by her question, "why?" invites us to help her understand her conflict. No transference interpretation would be made at this point since the material is not well enough organized around a coherent theme that could be presented to the patient in an easily understandable form. From the perspective of defense analysis, only Defense #21 would probably be interpretable. The other defenses would probably be too subtle for the patient to be able to observe during the initial phase of therapy. Defense #21, with its pause and complete change of direction from knowing to not knowing, offers the best opening of the three defenses.

Although the interpretation of conflict and the interpretation of defense appear to be close together, there is a difference in timing that, though small, is important. The interpretation of conflict would wait until the patient finishes her sentences at the end of the section. The interpretation of defense might enter after the first or second sentence after "why?" As soon as there is a shift in her ability to know, we would enter. If we wait longer, she will be less able to observe the shift.

The hour continues:

Therapist: *So long as you take that attitude, so long as you don't think it out and find out the rhyme and reason. . . .*

Patient: *Well,* he *cut my hair. He* cut *me. But she just put her fingers into my hair. I don't understand.*

Therapist: *He stuck scissors into your hair and she stuck fingers into your hair. You were talking before that about avoiding sexual excitement. Scissors and fingers into your hair* sounds *sexual. You turn away and avoid the excitement, pain, and hurt with men, and when you turn away from men altogether and turn toward a woman you get scared all over again.*

Patient: *Yes. But there's something that doesn't fit. I had no problem about tipping the woman who gave me a manicure. And she massaged my fingers. And that didn't get me anxious. I like it. It's relaxing. I thought of something. I told you about it a long time ago and then I dropped it and avoided it. It's a masturbation fantasy.* [Now her voice changes, becomes more hollow, tending toward a chilled monotone, drained of all emotion. She speaks this way for much of the remainder of the session, constantly pausing between words. I found her slow, start-and-stop delivery agonizing, and have tried to convey it on the page by the use of dashes to indicate her briefer pauses, reserving the word pause, in brackets, for the longer ones.] *There's—a doctor—a mad scientist—and his nurse and—he ties me down to—do things to me. I don't know what this has to do with being intimidated by the hairdresser and feeling inhibited tipping the girl who washes my hair but not the manicurist. It makes no sense* [pause].

Reader's Notes

Analysis of Conflict

Mark passages to indicate where wishes, fears, and defenses are depicted in the content. What is the conflict which the patient is describing? Provide a possible interpretation of conflict in the displacement.

Analysis of Transference

Provide a translation and possible interpretation of transference.

Analysis of Defense

Make a note of the defenses in the passage above, describe their nature, and offer possible interpretations.

Author's Notes

Analysis of Conflict

Therapist: *So long as you take that attitude, so long as you don't think it out and find out the rhyme and reason . . .* [The therapist points out the price she pays for her defense, but not the fear that makes the defense necessary, nor the wish that arouses so much fear.]

Patient: *Well,* he cut my hair. He cut me. *But she just put her fingers into my hair. I don't understand.*

Therapist: *He stuck scissors into your hair and she stuck fingers into your hair. You were talking before that about avoiding sexual excitement. Scissors and fingers into your hair sounds sexual. You turn away and avoid the excitement, pain, and hurt with men, and when you turn away from men altogether and turn toward a woman you get scared all over again.* [The therapist is focusing on conflict the patient has about unconscious phantasies which are symbolized by the associations. He is trying to interpret unconscious material directly and bypass the defense of displacement and the fear that makes that defense necessary.]

Patient: *Yes. But there's something that doesn't fit. I had no problem about tipping the woman who gave me a manicure. And she massaged my fingers. And that didn't get me anxious. I like it. It's relaxing.* [Now she shifts from disagreeing with the therapist to discussing a masturbation fantasy.] *I thought of something. I told you about it a long time ago and then I dropped it and avoided it. It's a masturbation fantasy.* [Now her voice changes, becomes more hollow, tending toward a chilled monotone, drained of all emotion. She speaks this way for much of the remainder of the session, constantly pausing between words. I found her slow, start-and-stop delivery agonizing, and have tried to convey it on the page by the use of dashes to indicate her briefer pauses, reserving the word pause, in brackets, for the longer ones.] *There's—a doctor—a mad scientist—and his nurse and—he ties me down to—do things to me.* [The function of this fantasy is defensive, to move away from disagreeing with the therapist.] *I don't know what this has to do with being intimidated by the hairdresser and feeling inhibited tipping the girl who washes my hair but not the manicurist. It makes no sense* [pause].

A wish to criticize the therapist, an unspecified fear, and a defense of discussing a masturbation fantasy instead. The content of the fantasy probably also involves a conflict, but we don't know its components yet. However, rather than focus on this alone, we might gain from using several perspectives at once. From a transference point of view, she is criticizing the therapist for trying to tie her down with his last interpretation, which she found intimidating. If we combine these points of view, a new picture emerges: a wish to disagree with the therapist but she is intimidated because she fears he wants to tie her down with his interpretations and inhibit her. So her defense is to offer him a topic he can't resist. The fantasy then is a compromise formation: as a defense, it moves away from disagreeing with the therapist directly and portrays her as being punished, but as an expression of the wish to describe the therapist, it describes her view of the therapist's interpretation as a sado-masochistic interaction, thus allowing her to express her criticism through the displacement.

Possible interpretation of conflict and transference: *"Well, maybe it makes sense in a different context. Perhaps you are feeling intimidated by me like by the hairdresser* [fear]. *I realize my last comment here tried to tie you down, as if to say: 'this is what you feel!' So you tried to disagree with me to show me that I was off target* [wish]. *But I think you got scared of describing how I was off* [fear] *and shifted to describing this fantasy instead* [defense].*"

Translation of the Transference

Therapist: *So long as you take that attitude, so long as you don't think it out and find out the rhyme and reason. . . .*

Patient: *Well,* he [you] *cut my hair. He* [You] *cut* me [with that cutting comment you just made. You were judging me for being reluctant.] *But she just put her fingers into my hair. I don't understand.*

Therapist: *He stuck scissors into your hair and she stuck fingers into your hair. You were talking before that about avoiding sexual excitement. Scissors and fingers into your hair sounds sexual. You turn away and avoid the excitement, pain, and hurt with men, and when you turn away from men altogether and turn toward a woman you get scared all over again.* [The therapist notes a possible sexual wish and the patient's defense against it, but does so in a way that could feel critical to the patient.]

Patient: *Yes. But there's something that doesn't fit. I had no problem about tipping the woman* [you] *who gave me a manicure. And she* [you] *massaged* *my fingers* [touched me emotionally]. *And that didn't get me anxious. I like it. It's relaxing. I thought of something. I told you about it a long time ago and then I dropped it and avoided it. It's a masturbation fantasy.* [Now her voice changes, becomes more hollow, tending toward a chilled monotone, drained of all emotion. She speaks this way for much of the remainder of the session, constantly pausing between words. I found her slow, start-and-stop delivery agonizing, and have tried to convey it on the page by the use of dashes to indicate her briefer pauses, reserving the word pause, in brackets, for the longer ones.] *There's—a doctor* [therapist]—*a mad scientist—and his nurse and—he* [you] *ties me down to—do things to me. I don't know what this has to do with being intimidated by the hairdresser* [you] *and feeling inhibited tipping the girl who washes my hair* [paying you] *but not the manicurist. It makes no sense* [pause].

It may be that the therapist's interpretive style feels intimidating to the patient as if he is trying to tie her down to uncomfortable meanings. For instance, "So long as you take that attitude . . .", and "you turn away and avoid," are phrases which push the patient to experience something. So although the patient may be masochistic, the therapist's interaction could be plausibly experienced as dominating. Both may be contributing to this sado-masochistic transference perception. Hence, a transference interpretation made at this point might usefully allude to the therapist's contribution.

Possible transference interpretation that includes the therapist's role in creating the transference: *"Well, maybe it makes sense in another way. There is a theme here about how hard it is to tell the hairdresser when something upsets you; that he's intimidating. I have a hunch that my last comment upset you. And you naturally disagreed with me. But I sense that you got scared of letting me know that so you started to talk about your fantasy instead. And yet even the fantasy suggests that my comments are tying you down, as if to say: 'this is what you feel and nothing else.'"*

Possible transference interpretation that excludes the therapist's role in creating the transference: *"Well, maybe it makes sense in another way. You mentioned that it is hard to tell the hairdresser when something upsets you because he is intimidating. I have a hunch that you were upset by my last comment too but were scared to disagree with me. And yet the fantasy may symbolize why you are afraid: that if you tell me things I will use them to tie you down and control you, as if to say: 'this is what you feel and nothing else.'"*

Analysis of Defense

Therapist: *So long as you take that attitude, so long as you don't think it out and find out the rhyme and reason. . . .*

Patient: *Well,* he *cut my hair. He* cut *me. But she just put her fingers into my hair. [#22] I don't understand.*

Therapist: *He stuck scissors into your hair and she stuck fingers into your hair. You were talking before that about avoiding sexual excitement. Scissors and fingers into your hair* sounds *sexual. You turn away and avoid the excitement, pain, and hurt with men, and when you turn away from men altogether and turn toward a woman you get scared all over again.*

Patient: *Yes. But there's something that doesn't fit. I had no problem about tipping the woman who gave me a manicure. And she massaged my fingers. And that didn't get me anxious. I like it. It's relaxing. [#23] I thought of something. I told you about it a long time ago and then I dropped it and avoided it. It's a masturbation fantasy. There's—a doctor—a mad scientist— and his nurse and—he ties me down to—do things to me. [#24] I don't know what this has to do with being intimidated by the hairdresser and feeling inhibited tipping the girl who washes my hair but not the manicurist. It makes no sense* [pause].

Defense #22 involves a shift from describing what she does understand to what she does not understand, suggesting that she becomes anxious when she disagrees with the therapist. An interpretation along the lines of the one offered for Defense #21 might be useful.

Defense #23 involves a shift from describing how she disagrees with the therapist to reporting a sado-masochistic fantasy. This is particularly interesting because our understanding of the fantasy is completely different depending on whether we approach it from the perspective of unconscious content or defensive process. The therapist in this hour tries to interpret the fantasy as a symbol of the patient's transference feelings towards him. By focusing on the content of the fantasy, he infers what he believes her feelings are towards him. Hence, his interpretation of unconscious content tries to address her character: her enduring long-term style of handling conflict.

From a process oriented point of view, however, this fantasy would be seen as serving a defensive function. At the moment it came up, it blocked the patient from expressing her disagreement with the therapist any further.

Possible defense interpretations: *"As important as this fantasy is, it seemed to interfere with your freedom to describe how you liked being with the manicurist."* Or for a patient more tolerant of her aggressive impulses: *"I wonder if this fantasy is interfering with your freedom to disagree with me."* Or, even more tolerant of aggressive impulses: *"This theme of being subject to someone else's will comes up just after you expressed your own will here: that you disagree with me. What might be the risk for you in letting me know I'm off target?"* Hence, from a process point of view, the therapist would try to address not large-scale character, per se, but small-scale defensive processes occurring at the moment in the session.

Defense #24 involves a shift from what she knows to what she does not know. Again, from a process point of view the therapist would focus neither on the content of what she knows or does not know, but on the shift in state from knowing to not knowing. This shift would be considered a regression in ego functioning, serving defensive purposes.

Possible defense interpretation: *"Although you are telling me what you do not know* [defense], *a moment ago you seemed freer to tell me what you do know* [wish]. *Do you have any sense what* [fear] *might have restricted your freedom to tell me what you do know—that you felt comfortable tipping the manicurist"*

The interpretation of conflict and transference flow out of the elaboration of the content. What may be missed is the importance of Defense #22. She dares to disagree with the therapist, then suddenly says she doesn't understand. This abrupt and important defense would have been a critical one to address from the perspective of defense analysis. Defenses #23 and 24 are more subtle and would be more difficult for the patient to observe.

The hour continues:

Therapist: *You've blocked yourself from hearing the answer you gave: the hairdresser sticking scissors in your hair and cutting you; the young woman preparing you for the haircut; they're the mad scientist doctor and his nurse.*

Patient: *The fantasy had to do with—something—it had to do with getting bigger breasts. It's foolish—I feel sheepish* [pause]. *It's so silly* [pause].

Therapist: *There's nothing silly about it; you mobilize those feelings to push away and avoid looking into the fantasy and the feelings.*

Provide an alternative interpretation of conflict and transference.

Patient: *I'd try not to think the fantasy. I didn't want to dig into it. You're right. I feel sheepish to push it away.*

Therapist: *And what happens to sheep?*

Patient: *They get sheared, their hair cut off.*

Therapist: *And so do "fallen women."*

Patient: *In old times, they did. I know about that. The hairdresser was cutting my hair off. Maybe it was my "crowning glory." And sheep certainly get their hair cut off. When I was in New Zealand, I saw the sheep getting sheared. There was one brown one I remember. They held it and sheared it, and piled the wool, and all that.* [The emotion's gone from her voice.]

Therapist: *You're getting away to avoid uncomfortable feelings.*

Provide an alternative transference interpretation.

Patient: *You're right. That fantasy makes me very uncomfortable. The mad scientist would do something to give me bigger breasts. I wanted bigger breasts very much* [pause].

Therapist: *Notice you're interrupting yourself, stopping yourself?*

Patient: *I don't want to talk about it, think about it; I'm afraid you'll think I'm foolish. I had to submit to the mad scientist, like I was his slave and he was my master. When I'm intimidated by men, it's like I have to put up with anything, like I'm a slave and he's a master and it makes me angry* [pause]. *That slave and master theme in relations between women and men gets me mad.* [Her voice changed again.]

Provide a possible transference interpretation.

Reader's Notes

Analysis of Conflict

What is her conflict in this passage about revealing her masturbation fantasy? How might the fantasy itself symbolize a conflict?

Analysis of Transference

Offer a translation of the transference and possible transference interpretations.

Analysis of Defense

Make a note of the defenses in the passage above, describe them, and offer possible interpretations.

Author's Notes

Analysis of Conflict

Therapist: *You've blocked yourself from hearing the answer you gave: the hairdresser sticking scissors in your hair and cutting you, the young woman preparing you for the haircut—they're the mad scientist doctor and his nurse.* [The therapist addresses her defense: that she displaces her inferred sexual conflict regarding the hairdresser onto the mad doctor. This involves a leap of faith for the patient. First of all, she is not aware of any sexual feelings towards the hairdresser; that was inferred by the therapist. Secondly, the defense of displacement, if true, is also outside her awareness. She is asked to believe that without knowing it, she warded off a feeling which she is not aware of feeling. The interpretation confronts the defense and infers a wish.]

Patient: *The fantasy had to do with—something—it had to do with getting bigger breasts. It's foolish—I feel sheepish* [pause]. *It's so silly* [pause]. [The patient feels guilty for having used a defense.]

Therapist: *There's nothing silly about it; you mobilize those feelings to push away and avoid looking into the fantasy and the feelings.* [The therapist identifies the patient's defense, but not her wish or anxiety.]

Patient: *I'd try not to think the fantasy. I didn't want to dig into it. You're right. I feel sheepish to push it away.* [She agrees that she used a defense and feels guilty for doing so, but she is unable to analyze the conflict further.]

Therapist: *And what happens to sheep?*

Patient: *They get sheared, their hair cut off.*

Therapist: *And so do "fallen women."*

Patient: *In old times, they did. I know about that. The hairdresser was cutting my hair off. Maybe it was my "crowning glory." And sheep certainly get their hair cut off. When I was in New Zealand, I saw the sheep getting sheared. There was one brown one I remember. They held it and sheared it, and piled the wool, and all that.* [The emotion's gone from her voice.] [She tries to describe the fantasy and gets blocked.]

Therapist: *You're getting away to avoid uncomfortable feelings.* [Therapist addresses her defense in a critical way.]

Patient: *You're right. That fantasy makes me very uncomfortable. The mad scientist would do something to give me bigger breasts. I wanted bigger breasts very much* [pause]. [She agrees that she is uncomfortable about her wish but can not describe the nature of that discomfort.]

Therapist: *Notice you're interrupting yourself, stopping yourself?* [The therapist focuses only on the defense, not her wish or anxiety.]

Patient: *I don't want to talk about it, think about it* [defense]; *I'm afraid you'll think I'm foolish* [fear]. *I had to submit to the mad scientist, like I was his slave and he was my master. When I'm intimidated by men, it's like I have to put up with anything, like I'm a slave and he's a master* [fear] *and it makes me angry* [wish] [pause]. *That slave and master theme in relations between women and men gets me mad.* [Her voice changed again.]

A wish to describe her fantasy of receiving larger breasts from a scientist to whom she would submit, a fear the therapist would think her foolish, and a defense of not wanting to talk about it. This conflict is also alive in the transference as we will see in the next section. However, the therapist addresses conflict in a one-sided manner, addressing the patient's defenses but not the the wish and anxiety that make her defenses necessary. She is in conflict: she wards off uncomfortable feelings but she is also trying to describe them. In this sense, we can see that a one-sided approach to analysis of conflict yields static comments.

The therapist's interpretations in this passage were static, failing to capture the dynamic tensions between her feelings and motivations. As we will see in the following comments, his therapeutic approach is an enactment of the sado-masochistic transference. Before we leap to judge the therapist, however, we should remind ourselves that many regard this as an inevitable occurrence (Levenson 1972, 1996). Our way of working is very much influenced by unconscious forces in the room—so much so that the way we interpret, in the heat of the moment, is almost always shaped unconsciously by the transference feelings in the room.

Translation of the Transference

Therapist: *You've blocked yourself from hearing the answer you gave: the hairdresser sticking scissors in your hair and cutting you; the young woman preparing you for the haircut; they're the mad scientist doctor and his nurse.* [The therapist confronts her defense against acknowledging the transference but not the anxiety that makes her defend against these feelings.]

Patient: *The fantasy had to do with—something—it had to do with getting bigger breasts.* [Perhaps you would think] *It's foolish—I feel sheepish* [pause]. *It's so silly* [pause].

Therapist: *There's nothing silly about it; you mobilize those feelings to push away and avoid looking into the fantasy and the feelings.* [The therapist addresses the defense and the wish but not the anxiety. This kind of interpretation makes her feeling that he is trying to tie her down more and is more plausible.]

Alternative interpretation of conflict and transference: *"As you tell me this fantasy* [wish], *I sense you're afraid I would judge you as foolish and silly* [fear]. *Is that what's making you hesitate* [defense]?*" Or more simply, *"Or maybe that's what you're afraid I am thinking."*

Patient: *I'd try not to think the fantasy. I didn't want to dig into it. You're right. I feel sheepish to push it away.* [Having felt criticized, she agrees that she did the wrong thing by using a defense.]

Therapist: *And what happens to sheep?*

Patient: *They get sheared, their hair cut off.*

Therapist: *And so do "fallen women."*

Patient: *In old times, they did. I know about that* [because I feel you are shearing me right now]. *The hairdresser was* [You are] *cutting my hair off. Maybe it was my "crowning glory." And sheep certainly get their hair cut off. When I was in New Zealand, I saw the sheep getting sheared. There was one brown one I remember. They held it and sheared it* [You are holding me and shearing me, piling up the defenses you have sheared off.], *and piled the wool, and all that.* [The emotion's gone from her voice.]

Therapist: *You're getting away to avoid uncomfortable feelings.* [The therapist addresses the defense, but not the anxiety or wish.]

Alternative transference interpretation: *"I imagine those sheep must feel helpless, being held, sheared against their will, and then left shivering without their wool coats. I wonder if you are feeling like a sheep here with me because I realize as I look back now that I have been trying to cut away your defenses, leaving you defenseless. But perhaps you're afraid if you say that I will shear you again."*

Patient: *You're right. That fantasy makes me very uncomfortable. The mad scientist* [You] *would do something to give me bigger breasts* [an interpretation]. *I wanted bigger breasts very much* [pause]. [I wanted help from you very much.]

Therapist: *Notice you're interrupting yourself, stopping yourself?* [The therapist addresses only the defense.]

Patient: *I don't want to talk about it, think about it; I'm afraid you'll think I'm foolish.* [The patient's fear re-emerges in the associations.] *I had to submit to the mad scientist* [you], *like I was his* [am your] *slave and he was* [you are] *my master. When I'm intimidated by men* [you], *it's like I have to put up with anything, like I'm a slave and he's* [you're] *a master and it makes me angry* [pause]. *That slave and master theme in relations between women and men* [us] *gets me mad.* [Her voice changed again.]

The therapist's phrase, "You're getting away to avoid uncomfortable feelings," illustrates the plausibility of the patient's transference. His comment says, in effect, "Submit to therapy and face your uncomfortable feelings. Even if you fear I will think you are foolish, submit to my request, be my slave."

Possible transference interpretation: *"I wonder if this master-slave theme may be related to us. You may be feeling that you are supposed to submit to me as if you are a subordinate and I'm the one in charge. And when you feel intimidated by me, you have to put up with anything I do or say. That gets you mad but you submit to me to keep your anger hidden."*

Analysis of Defense

Therapist: *You've blocked yourself from hearing the answer you gave: the hairdresser sticking scissors in your hair and cutting you, the young woman preparing you for the haircut—they're the mad scientist doctor and his nurse.*

Patient: *The fantasy had to do with [#25]—something—it had to do with getting bigger breasts. [#26] It's foolish—I feel sheepish [pause]. It's so silly [pause].*

Therapist: *There's nothing silly about it; you mobilize those feelings to push away and avoid looking into the fantasy and the feelings.*

Patient: *I'd try not to think the fantasy. I didn't want to dig into it. [#27] You're right. I feel sheepish to push it away.*

Therapist: *And what happens to sheep?*

Patient: *They get sheared, their hair cut off.*

Therapist: *And so do "fallen women."*

Patient: *In old times, they did. I know about that. The hairdresser was cutting my hair off. Maybe it was my "crowning glory."[#28] And sheep certainly get their hair cut off. When I was in New Zealand, I saw the sheep getting sheared. There was one brown one I remember. They held it and sheared it, and piled the wool, and all that.* [The emotion's gone from her voice.]

Therapist: *You're getting away to avoid uncomfortable feelings.*

Patient: *You're right. That fantasy makes me very uncomfortable. The mad scientist would do something to give me bigger breasts. I wanted bigger breasts very much [#29] [pause].*

Therapist: *Notice you're interrupting yourself, stopping yourself?*

Patient: *I don't want to talk about it, think about it; [#30] I'm afraid you'll think I'm foolish. I had to submit to the mad scientist, like I was his slave and he was my master. When I'm intimidated by men, it's like I have to put up with anything, like I'm a slave and he's a master and it makes me angry [#31] [pause]. That slave and master theme in relations between women and men gets me mad.* [Her voice changed again.]

Defense #25 involves a temporary shift in her ability to describe her fantasy. The pauses and the vagueness implied by "something" indicate an inhibition in her ability to tell the therapist what she is thinking.

Possible defense interpretation: *"Just when you were about to tell me your fantasy [wish] something inhibited you from going further. Did you sense that?"* We might let this defense go by without comment because the patient is able to resume talking about the fantasy after Defense #25, whereas she cannot after Defense #26, where an interpretation would be necessary.

Defense #26 involves a shift from describing her fantasy to judging it and herself.

Possible defense interpretation: *"As you try to tell me about this fantasy* [wish] *it sounds like you're afraid of how you might look* [fear] *which makes you hesitate for a moment* [defense]. *If we leave the fantasy to the side for a moment, can you tell me more about your fear that you would look foolish?"* Rather than interpret the id-transference [the wish that he give her larger breasts], you might explore the transference of defense [the fear you would judge her wish as foolish.]

Defense #27 involves a shift from expressing her point of view (a wish not to talk about her fantasy) to voicing the therapist's point of view ("You're right.") and judging herself, perhaps to ward off her feared judgement by him.

We might miss this defense because it is a defense against expressing her wish to resist, to refuse to talk, to avoid issues. Her seeming compliant could be easily mistaken for a good working alliance, when it may represent a quick submission to the therapist out of fear of revealing her wish to resist.

Possible defense interpretation: *"I wonder if your feeling sheepish* [defense] *about pushing the fantasy away interferes with your freedom to tell me more about your wish to push it away* [wish]."

Defense #28 involves a shift from describing her experience in that city to the experience of a sheep in New Zealand.

Possible defense interpretation: *"It's almost as if the train jumped tracks. Here we are headed to a New Zealand sheep farm when just a moment ago we were hearing about the haircutter. You seemed to shift tracks just after you mentioned that maybe your hair was your crowning glory* [wish to describe her feelings]. *Do you have any sense what you were feeling when you said that?"* Of course, the following material symbolically expresses her feelings. From a process point of view, however, we are interested in what anxiety led her to shift from a direct expression of her feelings to a more symbolic form.

Defense #29 involves a shift from talking to silence.

Possible defense interpretation: *"You seemed freer a moment ago to tell me your thoughts* [wish]. *Do you notice a change in that freedom just now* [defense]?"

Defense #30 involves a shift from her desire to resist to her fear the therapist would judge her fantasy about breasts. This is the clearest indication yet that she is aware of her fear that the therapist would judge her revelations.

Possible defense interpretation: *"Although you brought up the fantasy and wanted to talk about it* [wish], *it sounds like you were afraid I would judge you* [fear], *so you naturally want to avoid discussing it* [defense]. *Could you say more about this fear I would think of you as foolish?"*

Defense #31 involves a shift from describing her anger over having to submit. She pauses, unable to speak.

Possible defense interpretation: *"You seemed freer a moment ago to describe your thoughts about master-slave relationships. Do you have a sense of what might be holding you back just now?"*

The timing of the interpretation of conflict and transference was made possible by her statement, "it's so silly." This provided an opening to discuss the anxiety in the conflict and the transference of judgment that created the anxiety.

The content of the later material about the sheep does not lend itself to an interpretation of conflict. However, the latent content clearly relates to her experience of his "cutting" comments and provides us with an opportunity to make the alternative interpretation of transference. The last paragraph portrays the transference openly, which allows for its interpretation. Hence, the conflict can be explored directly in the room rather than in the displacement, as might otherwise be done in analysis of conflict. As usual, there are many defenses to choose from. However, Defenses #26, 29, and 30 are the ones most likely to be accessible to the patient. Let's review for a moment the three different interpretations offered for Defense #26 to illustrate differences in focus.

Comparison of Three Interpretations.

Patient: *The fantasy had to do with—something—it had to do with getting bigger breasts. It's foolish—I feel sheepish* [pause]. *It's so silly* [pause].

Therapist: *There's nothing silly about it; you mobilize those feelings to push away and avoid looking into the fantasy and the feelings.*

The therapist contradicts the patient's anxiety: "there's nothing silly about it." He interprets that she mobilizes the anxiety to defend against revealing a wish. He infers that the fantasy of the mad doctor represents a wish.

Interpretation of conflict and transference: *"As you tell me this fantasy* [wish], *I sense you're afraid I would judge you as foolish and silly* [fear]. *Is that what's making you hesitate* [defense]?" Or more simply, *"Or maybe that's what you're afraid I am thinking."*

This interpretation differs from the previous interpretation by addressing her wish to speak, which was not addressed in the previous interpretation. It infers that her anxiety is due to a fear of his judgment and that the defense functions to help her cope with that anxiety, but no other inferences of unconscious wishes are made.

Defense interpretation: *"As you try to tell me about this fantasy* [wish] *it sounds like you're afraid of how you might look* [fear] *which makes you* *hesitate for a moment* [defense]. *If we leave the fantasy to the side for a moment can you tell me more about your fear that you would look foolish?"*

This interpretation is very similar to the previous one. Her wish to speak is acknowledged, the role of her fear is highlighted, and her defense is touched upon only lightly. This interpretation differs, however, in that the patient is encouraged not to explore the wish for the moment, and instead to focus on the fear. There is no inference that the fear is related to the therapist yet. This is the least inferential interpretation, leaving it up to the patient to describe and analyze her anxiety. Also, this interpretation focuses much more on the fear, whereas the first interpretation we analyzed focused almost exclusively on the defense.

The hour continues:

Therapist: *Notice you switched from uncomfortable thinking about the wish for the mad scientist to give you bigger breasts to the slave and master theme?*
Patient: [Back to working voice.] *There's something about—it's not called S & M—something and bondage—in porno—people waiting to be tied up and things done to them* [pause].
Therapist: *I notice you keep interrupting yourself and stopping yourself.*

Offer an alternative transference interpretation.

Patient: *You've told me several times that you couldn't promise that this would always be easy—I'd be uncomfortable at times—If I could be comfortable, I could talk about these things—I could look into them—and understand—but—it's—too—hard—if I could find a way to do this without feeling so uncomfortable* [pause].
Therapist: *You want me to make you do it. You're having all that trouble talking about, thinking all those thoughts about pain and hurt, S & M, bondage, because of a wish to enact the fantasy with me rather than think and feel it out and understand it. You want me to be the mad scientist doctor, forcing and hurting you and making changes in you.*

Offer an alternative interpretation of conflict.

Patient: *I want you to use your knowledge and your understanding to change me. Instead of working at this myself and making changes, I want you to do it. But you say it's because I want you to be the mad scientist of my fantasy, that if you force me and hurt me, it's exciting. I have to reject that. I can't agree with you on that. That would mean I don't really want to change. But I do want to change. I have to think about it. Maybe I'm undecided and that's why it's so difficult and uncomfortable. I'll have to think about it.*

Reader's Notes

Analysis of Conflict

What is her conflict about her wish to change as expressed in the material here?

Analysis of Transference

Provide a translation of the transference.

Analysis of Defense

Underline the defenses in the passage above, describe the defenses, and offer possible interpretations.

Author's Notes

Analysis of Conflict

Therapist: *Notice you switched from uncomfortable thinking about the wish for the mad scientist to give you bigger breasts to the slave and master theme?* [The therapist points out the defense, but not why she used it.]

Patient: [Back to working voice.] *There's something about—it's not called S & M—something and bondage—in porno—people waiting to be tied up and things done to them* [pause]. [The patient complies and describes the fantasy about the mad scientist further.]

Therapist: *I notice you keep interrupting yourself and stopping yourself.* [The therapist points out the defense again, but not her attempt to describe the wish, and the fear which led her to pause.]

Patient: *You've told me several times that you couldn't promise that this would always be easy—I'd be uncomfortable at times—If I could be comfortable, I could talk about these things—I could look into them* [wish]—*and understand —but—it's—too—hard—if I could find a way to do this without feeling so uncomfortable* [fear] [pause]. [The patient chastises the therapist for having forgotten that her anxiety is the factor for him to focus on.]

Therapist: *You want me to make you do it. You're having all that trouble talking about, thinking all those thoughts about pain and hurt, S & M, bondage, because of a wish to enact the fantasy with me rather than think and feel it out and understand it. You want me to be the mad scientist doctor, forcing and hurting you and making changes in you.*

From a conflict point of view, an interpretation would address a wish to talk about a fantasy, a fear of what would happen, and a defense of acting it out instead. However, the therapist's interpretation does not address the patient's wish to talk about her fantasy and the fear it arouses.

Alternative interpretation of conflict: *"Well, maybe we need to focus on that discomfort for a moment [fear]. You've been trying to describe this fantasy and think about it [wish]. But there is some discomfort that comes up [fear] that leads you to pause [defense]. Rather than tell me more about your fantasy right now, let's leave it to the side for the moment. Instead, can you tell me what you're afraid you would feel [fear] if you talked about it [wish]?"*

Patient: *I want you to use your knowledge and your understanding to change me. Instead of working at this myself and making changes. I want you to do it. But you say it's because I want you to be the mad scientist of my fantasy, that if you force me and hurt me it's exciting. I have to reject that. I can't agree with you on that. That would mean I don't really want to change. But I do want to change. I have to think about it. Maybe I'm undecided and that's why it's so difficult and uncomfortable. I'll have to think about it.*

Translation of the Transference

Therapist: *Notice you switched from uncomfortable thinking about the wish for the mad scientist to give you bigger breasts to the slave and master theme?* [The therapist addresses the wish and defense but not the anxiety.]

Patient: [Back to working voice.] *There's something about—it's not called S & M—something and bondage—in porno—people [I'm] waiting to be tied up [by you] and things done to them [me] [pause].* [The patient is trying to offer the therapist unconscious supervision: his interpretations try to tie her down and make her face uncomfortable feelings. (Hoffman 1983)]

Therapist: *I notice you keep interrupting yourself and stopping yourself.* [The therapist does not address the latent content but focuses on her defenses instead.]

Alternative transference interpretation: *"Well, this makes me think we need to shift gears for a moment. You've been talking about a theme of a woman having to submit to a scientist, put up with whatever he does. And then there's the idea of people being tied up and things being done to them. I'm wondering if these themes may be related to us. Maybe you are feeling you have to submit to me and put up with whatever I say. You may be feeling tied down by my comments rather than being set free."*

Patient: *You've told me several times that you couldn't promise that this would always be easy—I'd be uncomfortable at times—If I could be comfortable, I could talk about these things—I could look into them—and under-*

stand—but—it's—too—hard—if I could find a way to do this without feeling so uncomfortable [pause]. [Now she tries to supervise him consciously. She points out that she could handle her wishes better if it weren't for the discomfort, her anxiety. She is inviting him to address this transference of defense: her fear that he might think she is foolish. The critical focus of his interpretations have made her fear plausible. By criticizing her for her defenses he has implied that she is foolish not to express her wishes more directly.]

Therapist: *You want me to make you do it. You're having all that trouble talking about, thinking all those thoughts about pain and hurt, S & M, bondage, because of a wish to enact the fantasy with me rather than think and feel it out and understand it. You want me to be the mad scientist doctor forcing and hurting you and making changes in you.* [The therapist focuses on the wish in a critical manner, suggesting she wants him to hurt her. From an interpersonal perspective, the therapist is acting out the very transference he is trying to interpret. By interpreting so much that is out of her awareness, he is forcing interpretations on her that hurt. As mentioned earlier, from an interpersonal perspective, this would be viewed as an inevitable occurrence in the therapeutic process.]

Patient: *I want you to use your knowledge and your understanding to change me. Instead of working at this myself and making changes. I want you to do it.* [I want you to start working as a therapist and make some changes in how you do this.] *But you say it's because I want you to be the mad scientist of my fantasy, that if you force me and hurt me, it's exciting. I have to reject that. I can't agree with you on that. That would mean I don't really want to change. But I do want to change. I have to think about it. Maybe I'm undecided and that's why it's so difficult and uncomfortable. I'll have to think about it.* [She openly questions him, inviting him to reconsider the problem.]

The therapist's focus on the patient's defenses has not addressed the patient's conflict between her wish to change and her fear of the feelings involved when she does. Now the patient highlights this part of the conflict: "I do want to change."

This hour illustrates the challenges involved when the patient's transference is plausible because it is a response to the therapist's interpretive style. It also illustrates how at all times our interpretations are shaped by transference feelings outside our awareness.

Analysis of Defense

Therapist: *Notice you switched from uncomfortable thinking about the wish for the mad scientist to give you bigger breasts to the slave and master theme?*

Patient: [Back to working voice.] *There's something about [#32]—it's not* *called S & M*—*something and bondage*—*in porno*—*people waiting to be tied up and things done to them [#33]* [pause].

Therapist: *I notice you keep interrupting yourself and stopping yourself.*

Patient: *You've told me several times that you couldn't promise that this would always be easy*—*I'd be uncomfortable at times*—*If I could be comfortable, I could talk about these things*—*I could look into them*—*and understand*—*but*—*it's*—*too*—*hard*—*if I could find a way to do this without feeling so uncomfortable [#34]* [pause].

Therapist: *You want me to make you do it. You're having all that trouble talking about, thinking all those thoughts about pain and hurt, S & M, bondage, because of a wish to enact the fantasy with me rather than think and feel it out and understand it. You want me to be the mad scientist doctor, forcing and hurting you and making changes in you.*

Patient: *I want you to use your knowledge and your understanding to change me. Instead of working at this myself and making changes. I want you to do it. [#35] But you say it's because I want you to be the mad scientist of my fantasy, that if you force me and hurt me it's exciting.* I have to reject that. I can't agree with you on that. That would mean I don't really want to change. But I do want to change. [#36] I have to think about it. Maybe I'm undecided and that's why it's so difficult and uncomfortable. I'll have to think about it.*

Defense #32 involves a number of defenses in the form of pauses and a shift. However, since the patient seems able to continue speaking about the theme of domination and submission, one might not interpret these shifts early in treatment. Instead, one would wait until she becomes blocked at Defense #34.

Defense #33 involves a shift from describing people being tied up to a pause, a complete block in her ability to tell the therapist her thoughts.

Possible defense interpretation: *"You seemed freer a moment ago to describe your thoughts. Do you have a sense of what might be holding you back just now?"*

Following this defense, the patient again engages in a series of defenses (pauses), but the material continues to unfold without changing direction dramatically. This continues until **Defense #34,** which brings her criticism to a stop.

Let's review three interpretive options for this point in the hour:

Therapist's interpretation: *"You want me to make you do it. You're having all that trouble talking about, thinking all those thoughts about pain and hurt, S & M, bondage, because of a wish to enact the fantasy with me rather than think and feel it out and understand it. You want me to be the mad scientist doctor forcing and hurting you and making changes in you."*

The therapist interprets the fantasy as a transference statement and infers that this transference represents a wish. This involves three levels of inferred unconscious material: 1)—that the patient can become aware that she feels this way toward the therapist, 2) that she wants to enact this fantasy with the therapist, and 3)—that this wish is in turn a defense against wanting to talk about and analyze the fantasy. From a conflict point of view, this interpretation supposes that there is a wish to talk about a fantasy, a fear of what would happen, and a defense of acting it out instead. However, the therapist's interpretation ignores the patient's wish to talk about her fantasy and the fear it arouses.

Alternative interpretation of conflict: *"Well, maybe we need to focus on that discomfort for a moment* [fear]. *You've been trying to describe this fantasy and think about it* [wish]. *But there is some discomfort that comes up* [fear] *that leads you to pause* [defense]. *Rather than tell me more about your fantasy right now, let's leave it to the side for the moment. Instead, can you tell me what you're afraid you would feel* [fear] *if you talked about it* [wish]?*"

This interpretation acknowledges her wish to talk, invites her to put the wish aside for the moment, and focuses on the fear.

Interpretation of defense: *"You seem to be having a harder time talking now* [defense], *but a moment ago you were more free in telling me that it would be easier to talk without discomfort* [wish]. *What were you feeling* [fear] *just before you paused?"*

Defense #35 involves a shift from what she thinks to what he thinks, from her voice to his voice. This holds her back from further disagreeing with the therapist.

Possible defense interpretation: *"You are giving voice to my opinion* [defense] *just after you gave voice to your own: that there is something I should do* [wish to say this]. *Let's see what might have felt risky* [fear] *to you just now to give voice to your opinion about what I should do."*

Defense #36 involves a shift from how she disagrees with the therapist to a sense of confusion, from knowing what she thinks to feeling undecided about what she thinks.

Possible defense interpretations: *"You seem less certain about what you think now* [defense], *whereas a moment ago you seemed quite clear about what you think* [wish]. *What were you feeling* [fear] *that reduced your sense of certainty?"* Or with a patient more tolerant of her aggression: *"You began to feel undecided here* [defense] *just when you felt free to say you really do want to change* [wish]. *I wonder if it felt risky* [fear] *to let me know you really do want to change."*

11

Harnessing Thinking and Intuition

Meaning is always richer than interpretation.
Hans Urs Von Balthasar (1995)

Although we talk about psychodynamic psychotherapy as if everyone is doing the same thing, this book reveals that therapists listen in many different ways. Psychodynamic therapists share a common assumption that there is conflict at work outside the patient's awareness, but they do not share a common listening approach. They use many approaches, some of which are not even addressed in this book. Having learned to use different listening approaches, you see how each approach leads us to listen for different material, to hear different meanings, to interpret different content at different moments. How we listen shapes the interaction.

These startling realizations can lead therapists into trouble. Seeking the one, right, true theory, they wonder how to choose. They start to ask the following questions: 1) Should I believe this theory, 2) Which theory is right, and 3) Why use this theory, since it obviously leaves out something important?

Should I believe this theory? No. A theory is not intended to be believed. You do not believe a map, nor do you believe in a screwdriver. They are useful insofar as they fit. For example, a map is useful insofar as its structure fits the structure you are looking at (Bateson 1972), such as a street in a city. A Phillips screwdriver is useful if it turns the screw that must be tightened.

"No," you counter, "I know not to believe in a theory, but what I mean is, is this theory true?" In a relative sense, yes. In an absolute sense, no. A theory is never true in an absolute sense. A theory is never what it describes. For example, a menu is not the food you hope to eat. A map of Paris is not Paris. A theory is a kind of map; it is never the absolute truth, only a description of it. A map is relatively true, however, in the sense that it has a structure similar to the territory it represents. Its similar structure accounts for its usefulness.

Which theory is right? No theory is right or true. Freud (1937a) himself noted this when he observed that "the first step toward the intellectual mastery of the world in which we live is the discovery of general principles, rules, and laws that bring order into chaos. By such mental operations we simplify the world of phenomena, *but we cannot avoid falsifying it in doing so, especially when we are dealing with processes of development and change* [my italics]." Insofar as any theory is a simplification and falsification of reality, it cannot be absolutely true.

However, theories can be *useful*. Questions of whether a theory is right or wrong misunderstand the nature of theories. To ask if a theory is right is to ask if the menu is the meal. The map of Paris is never Paris. Instead, we need to ask a different kind of question. Does this map help us find what we are looking for? For example, a street map of Paris may be very useful for a tourist, but be useless to an engineer who needs to find a buried gas line.

"But," you may counter, "clearly some theories leave so much out and don't address certain issues." That is true. Yet that is not a flaw in a theory, but its function. Since we cannot observe everything at once, we need to focus our attention in order to perceive things. All theories, in order to focus our attention on one thing, exclude other things from our attention. This training and refocusing of your listening attention was the function of the listening studies in this book. Theories might be thought of as instruments for attention focusing. Instead of raising this criticism, which is equivalent to criticizing a theory for being a theory, or for criticizing it for not having the focus you want, we should ask other questions. What does this theory allow us to see? How and when is that focus useful?

As an analogy, the telescope, microscope, electron-microscope, and MRI allow us to see different phenomena. No one of these instruments is intrinsically better than the others, but each is better than the others insofar as it is designed to focus on particular phenomena not visible with the other instruments. Likewise, psychological theories focus our attention on different phenomena: transference patterns encoded in associations, defensive shifts in process, relational patterns in the counter-transference, etc. Based on which patterns seem most salient in the hour, the therapist chooses a theory and approach.

But sometimes, yearning for certainty, therapists identify with a theory. For instance, "I am a Freudian," may be a way of saying, "I am the theory I use." This takes several forms: "I don't have to think about what I do since I do one thing"; or, "I don't have to think about what you do, since I equate it with a given theoretical approach and therefore don't have to try to understand it." Given our yearning for certainty, we long for one theory, one approach that explains everything.

People who think in terms of only one theory often have quick reactions according to a thought pattern. Their quickness is often mistaken for brilliance when it is simply a reflex pattern (Debono 1976). Minds inhabited by such ideas operate like computers infected with a virus.

Instead of practicing psychology, we begin to practice psychologism: we equate how we look at things with what is there to be seen. "An ideational tool may possess its possessor, turning all events into the shape and likeness of the tool, fixing us in its own literalism" (Hillman 1975:143). For instance, if we idolize any one listening approach, we forget that there are other valid modes of listening, that there are other experiences to be heard. We forget that a listening approach is a perspective, a tool.

Instead of thought we see mental tape loops. Statements like, "I am a Freudian" or "self psychologist" or "cognitive-behavioral therapist" attempt to reify flowing thought. Instead of being one who tries to think about patterns, we identify with a pattern of thinking. In our modern form of totemism, we identify ourselves with various object relations, self psychology, or cognitive-behavioral clans instead of bear clans.

But you may counter, "Ok. I don't identify with a theory. I think about them. But what is the relationship of a theory to truth?" All theories are relative truths that serve as channels to the absolute truth, which is beyond verbal categories. Kant (1881) reminded us that our ideas are concepts which arbitrarily divide up reality. Whitehead (1933: 185–186) referred to our belief that a theory is true as the dogmatic fallacy, the certainty that our ideas can adequately capture the complexity of living relationships in the real world: "Canst thou by searching describe the universe? . . . Our task is to understand how in fact the human mind can successfully set to work for the gradual definition of its habitual ideas. It is a step by step process, achieving no triumphs of finality." Whitehead observed, "the concordance of ideas within any one such system shows the scope and virility of the basic notions of that scheme of thought." In other words, if you approach a session from a given listening approach, what you listen for, what you hear, and what you say will have a degree of concordance. The fact that everything fits and makes sense leads us to believe that we have found *the* system for listening. When we compare different listening approaches, we discover that each yields a coherent picture, but these pictures, when compared, yield conflicting perceptions, meanings, and interpretations. Those differences warn us of the limitations of any listening model, any theory.

From a humanistic point of view, G. K. Chesterton advises us to be humble when imagining that any theory can be true. One who makes such an assumption "is assuming that a man has a word for ever reality in earth, or heaven, or hell. He knows that there are in the soul tints more bewildering, more numberless, and more nameless, than the colours of an autumn forest; he knows that there are abroad in the world and doing strange and terrible service in it, crimes that have never been condemned and virtues that have never been christened. Yet he seriously believes that these things can, every one of them, in all their tones and semitones, in all their blends and unions, be accurately represented by an arbitrary system of grunts and squeals. He believes that an ordinary, civilized stockbroker can really produce out of his own inside, noises which denote all the mysteries of memory and all the agonies of desire."

And yet how often we or our patients assert that we have the truth, or that something we have said is true. What Whitehead refers to as the dogmatic fallacy object relations theorists refer to as symbolic equation, the tendency to equate our feelings, thoughts, and fantasies with reality. For instance, the hysterical patient often believes that if she feels strongly something is true it must be true. The obsessional holds that if he thinks something is true, it must be true. These feelings and thoughts (all kinds of maps) are equated with reality. The patient unable to see the difference between the map and reality feels trapped in a world of torment without an exit. The patient is unable to see that the map is not the territory, the truth.

We therapists do not have the truth, nor are our theories the truth. *Rather, we try to develop an ability to think about ideas, feelings, fantasies, and theories as relative truths, and understand these relative truths as channels to an absolute truth, the ineffable experience of relating that is beyond words.* The difference is not that the patient sees fantasy and the therapist sees reality. Rather, both the patient and therapist strive to know and bear the impossibility of knowing absolute truth through words and theories and to bear the uncertainty of all our knowing.

"A scientific hypothesis does not say the world is so and so. A scientific hypothesis says the world behaves *as if* it were so and so" (Chisholm

1994:19). Equating a theory with truth is a refusal to play *as if* it were true. Thinking about theories and listening from different perspectives to see how they inform us about our perspectives is a form of play. Winnicott (1971) referred to this as the location of cultural experience. The potential space between a therapist and a patient is a space for play where we say, in effect, "I will play as if this theory is correct about you while knowing of course that no theory will ever accurately describe you." Patients can trust us only when we can truly play with theory, when our thoughts are not equated with them, where they can exist as something connected to, but always separate from our ideas and images of them.

Understanding theories as maps, creations arising out of play, helps us differentiate problems in theories from problems in the ways we use theories. This book represents a plea that we learn to think about and play with theories rather than identify with them. Each theory has its own focus for listening and intervening. Each creates its own kind of process of interaction. And by learning to think within these different theories, you can see their respective strengths and limitations "within which our intuitions are hedged."

☐ Harnessing Intellect with Intuition

And with this mention of intuition, we return to a concern mentioned at the beginning of the book, that we speak so much about theory and technique within a field that is more art than science, that relies so much on intuition. Although the book has focused almost exclusively on thinking, I do not elevate thinking above intuition. Both have their functions and methods of expression, and neither is immune from error. We tend to assume our intuitions are correct and our thinking eventually limited, therefore wrong. Yet both are capable of their own forms of distortion and limitation (Jackson 1947). The best therapists harness their thinking and intuition together. And as we are now discovering, at no time is our responsiveness completely attributable only to conscious thinking. The unconscious elements of interpretation are far more active in our work than we ever imagined before (Hoffman 1992, 1994; Levenson 1996).

In therapy, as in all the arts, intuition is most expressive when linked with a certain kind of automatism in connection with technique. Siegried Sassoon (1939:7) observes, "The poets themselves admit that in their best lines they discover meanings and metaphors of which they knew nothing while composing them. There was more in it than they knew at the time. Technique had been instinctive; *thought* had been somehow uncensored. The brain-work was there, but it had been fundamentally mysterious!"

Through our experience, practice, and skill development, we become adept enough that we can abandon self-consciousness and, by doing so, allow our intuition to have free play. This applies to any skilled activity, since all art is dependent upon what Jackson (1947:261) refers to as "the auto-intoxication during which technique becomes automatic," when artists' "technical skill is so perfect that they can afford to forget it. . . . Paderewski . . . used to say that unless he practised for many hours a day his recitals suffered. The drudgery kept his technique in such perfect condition that he was able to forget it on the platform and so give his genius its head when he appeared before the public. Art is thus inspiration plus technique, but minus the consciousness of technique. . . . If a craftsman allows his technique to get in the way of his inspiration, he is a technician not an artist."

Theories and concepts are instruments, not tyrants. Whatever analyses, phrases, or interpretations best suit your own expressive purposes "can be turned to form—possibly just your own personal form, but form; and that . . . too might in time take its place in the hierarchy of poetic devices." (Shahn 1957:19) Yet it is not that the mind of the creative therapist expresses itself in words, images, feelings, and forms as its medium; on the contrary, *words, images, feelings and form express themselves through the medium of the creative mind. It is not that we try to push for or pull out a certain meaning, but that we give shape to the implicit, dynamic meaning that is unfolding within ourselves and the relationship.* The finer that medium, the better words, images, feelings, and form can express themselves. The greater the genius, the less it speaks *itself*, the more it lends its voice to the words, images, feelings, the forms. In this sense, then, interpretations create themselves through us. "The law of falling bodies is no invention of the genius of Galileo. The work of the genius consists in bringing his mind, through years of practice, so into harmony with things that things can express their laws through him. . . . This is as true of the scientific as of the artistic genius. Every great musical thought is, in its way, rather a discovery than an invention." (Zuckerkandl 1956:222–223)

And yet even if we can use these theories as tools for understanding, we must remember Balthasar's (1995) warning that meaning is always richer than the best interpretations we offer. First of all, each of us is changing; new meanings for our lives are always emerging. No understanding we discover is ever the final all-encompassing understanding of another person. The Russian linguist Bahktin (1984:166) refers to this as our unfinalizability. Paraphrasing Dostoevsky he says, "Nothing conclusive has yet taken place in the world, the ultimate word of the world and about the world has not yet been spoken, the world is open and free, everything is still in the future and will always be in the future." Our meaning as human beings is not located entirely in what we say or consciously intend. We grow in meaning over time, an impossibility if our meaning as persons was fixed. No matter how fully anyone describes us, that description is never exhaustive because we contain multiple potentials that could be realized in unforseeable ways. Who we are now is not the same as who we might become. Whatever understanding we arrive at will be changed in the next moment. Wilfred Bion (1970) referred to this as well when he noted that every insight becomes the defense against the next insight. We try to make our insights into others and ourselves final, as if we stopped evolving and changing.

Secondly, our rational understandings express only the knowability of a person possible through our words and concepts, not their subjective life and being. Our theories and concepts can grasp only the logical aspects of someone's being, a concept of them. But no theory can ever grasp a human being's immediate and subjective actuality. In that sense, every person is *unfathomable*. Each of us has our inner, subjective being, in which we are absolutely singular and unique, wholly inexpressible; from this point of view any person we encounter is always beyond our words, outside the bounds of what rationality can describe (Solovyov 1995:92).

We are infinitely deep. From this perspective, the result of psychoanalysis or psychodynamic psychotherapy is not just cure or even insight, but a renewed sense of humility. We begin to realize that however much we have learned about ourselves, there is more yet to know. We will never reach a point where we have discovered all there is to know about ourselves. Patients will always have more they can learn from their therapists, and, what is essential for us to remember, we therapists will always have more to learn from our patients.

REFERENCES

Bacon, F. (1625). *Essays*. Freeport, NY: Books for Libraries Press.

Bahktin, M. (1984). *Problems of Dostoevsky's Poetics*. Trans. Caryl Emerson. Minneapolis, MN: University of Minnesota Press.

Balthasar, H.U.V. (1995). *The Grain of Wheat*. Trans. E. Leiva-Merikakis. San Francisco: Ignatius Press.

Bateson, G. (1972). *Steps to an Ecology of Mind*. New York: Random House.

Bergson, H. (1946). *The Creative Mind*. Trans. M. Andison. New York: Philosophical Library, Inc.

Bion, W. (1970). Attention and interpretation. In *Seven Servants*. New York: Jason Aronson.

Bollas, C. (1989). *Forces of Destiny*. London: Free Association Press.

Brenner, C. (1976). *Psychoanalytic Technique and Psychic Conflict*. New York: International Universities Press.

Brenner, C. (1982). *The Mind in Conflict*. New York: International Universities Press.

Brooks, C., Warren, R. (1938). *Understanding Poetry*. New York: Henry Holt and Company.

Busch, R. (1996). *The Ego at the Center of Clinical Technique*. New York: Aronson Press.

Chisholm, F. (1994). *Introductory Lectures on General Semantics*. Lakeville, CT: Institute of General Semantics.

Dahl, H., Kachele, H., and Thoma, H. (eds.). (1988). The specimen hour. In *Psychoanalytic Process Research Strategies*, pp. 15–28. New York: Springer Verlag.

Davison, W., Bristol, C., and Pray, M. (1986). Turning aggression on the self: A study of psychoanalytic process. *Psychoanalytic Quarterly* 55:273–295.

Davison, W., Bristol, C., and Pray, M. (1990). Mutative interpretation and close process monitoring in a study of psychoanalytic process. *Psychoanalytic Quarterly* 59:599–628.

Debono, E. (1976). *Teaching Thinking*. New York: Penguin Books.

De Lubac, H. (1958). *Further Paradoxes*. Trans. E. Beaumont. London: Longmans, Green.

Fenichel, O. (1941). *Problems of Psychoanalytic Technique*. New York: Psychoanalytic Quarterly.

Fliess, R. (1942). The metapsychology of the analyst. *Psychoanalytic Quarterly* 11:211–227.

Freud, A. (1936). *The Ego and the Mechanisms of Defense*. New York: International Universities Press.

Freud, S. (1896). Further remarks on the neuropsychoses of defense. *Standard Edition* 3:43–68.

Freud, S. (1900). Interpretation of dreams. *Standard Edition* 4–5.

Freud, S. (1904). On psychotherapy. *Standard Edition* 7:257–268.

Freud, S. (1910a). Wild psychoanalysis. *Standard Edition* 11:221–227.

Freud, S. (1910b). Five lectures on psychoanalysis. *Standard Edition* 11:9–55.

Freud, S. (1912a). The dynamics of transference. *Standard Edition* 12:98–108.

Freud, S. (1912b). Recommendations on analytic technique. *Standard Edition* 12:111–120.

Freud, S. (1912c). A note on the unconscious in psychoanalysis. *Standard Edition* 12:255–267.

Freud, S. (1913). On beginning the treatment. *Standard Edition* 12:121–144.

Freud, S. (1914). Remembering, repeating, and working through. *Standard Edition* 12:147–156.

Freud, S. (1915a). The Unconscious. *Standard Edition* 14:159–215.

Freud, S. (1915b). Observations on transference love. *Standard Edition* 12:157–173.

Freud, S. (1917). Introductory lectures on psychoanalysis. *Standard Edition* 15–16.

Freud, S. (1917). Mourning and melancholia. *Standard Edition* 14:243–258.

Freud, S. (1923). The ego and the id. *Standard Edition* 20:75–176.

Freud, S. (1925). On negation. *Standard Edition* 19:235–239.

Freud, S. (1926). Inhibitions, symptoms and anxiety. *Standard Edition* 20:77–175.

Freud, S. (1937a). Constructions in analysis. *Standard Edition* 23:255–270.

Freud, S. (1937b). Analysis terminable and interminable. *Standard Edition* 23:216–253.

Gendlin, E. (1968). The Experiential Response. Chapter 26. In E. Hammer, ed. *Uses of Interpretation in Treatment*. New York: Grune and Stratton, Inc.

Gill, M., Hoffman, I. (1982). *The Analysis of Transference: Volumes I and II*. New York: International Universities Press.

Glover, E. (1958). *The Technique of Psychoanalysis*. New York: International Universities Press.

Goldberger, M. (ed.). (1996). *Danger and Defense*. New York: Jason Aronson Press.

Gray, P. (1995). *The Ego and the Analysis of Defense*. New York: Jason Aronson Press.

Greenson, R. (1967). *The Technique and Practice of Psychoanalysis*. New York: International Universities Press.

Havens, L. (1976). *Participant Observation*. New York: Jason Aronson.

Havens, L. (1986). *Making Contact: Uses of Language in Psychotherapy*. Cambridge, MA: Harvard University Press.

Hill, D., Grand, C. (eds). (1996). *The British Schools of Psychoanalysis*. New York: Jason Aronson.

Hillman, J. (1975). *Revisioning Psychology*. New York: Harper and Row, Publishers.

Hoffman, I. (1983). The patient as interpreter of the therapist's experience. *Contemporary Psychoanalysis* 19:389–422.

Hoffman, I. (1992). Expressive participation and psychoanalytic discipline. *Contemporary Psychoanalysis* 28:1–15.

Hoffman, I. (1994). Dialectical thinking and therapeutic action in the psychoanalytic process. *Psychoanalytic Quarterly* 63:187– 213.

Jackson, H. (1947). *The Reading of Books*. New York: Charles Scribner's Sons.

Kant, I. (1881). *Critique of Pure Reason*. Trans. F. Müller. London: Macmillan.

Kohut, H. (1959). Introspection, empathy, and psychoanalysis. An examination of the relationship between mode of observation and theory. *Journal of the American Psychoanalytic Association* 7:459–483.

Kohut, H. (1971). *The Analysis of the Self*. New York: International Universities Press.

Kris, A.O. (1990). Helping patients by analyzing self-criticism. *Journal of the American Psychoanalytic Association* 38:605–636.

Langs, R. (1973a). *The Technique of Psychoanalytic Psychotherapy. Volumes one and two*. New York: Jason Aronson.

Langs, R. (1973b). The patient's view of the therapist: Reality or fantasy? *International Journal of Psychoanalytic Psychotherapy* 2:411–431.

Langs, R. (1975). The patient's unconscious perception of the therapist's errors. In *Tactics and Techniques of Psychoanalytic Therapy, Volume 2: Countertransference*, P. Giovacchini (ed.), pp. 239–250. New York: Jason Aronson.

Langs, R. (1976). *The Bipersonal Field*. New York: Jason Aronson.

Langs, R. (1985). *Workbooks for Therapists Volume III*. Emerson, NJ: Newconcept Press, Inc.

Laplanche, J., Pontalis, J. (1973). *The Language of Psychoanalysis*. London: Karnac Books.

Levenson, E. (1972). *The Fallacy of Understanding*. New York: Basic Books.

Levenson, E. (1996). The politics of interpretation. *Contemporary Psychoanalysis* 32:631–648.

Levy, S., Inderbitzen, L. (1990). The analytic surface and the theory of technique. *Journal of the American Psychoanalytic Association* 38:371–392.

Malan, D. (1979). *Individual Psychotherapy and the Science of Psychodynamics*. London: Butterworths.

Nunberg, H. (1925). The will to recovery. *International Journal of Psychoanalysis* 7:64–78.

Pascal, B. (1966). *Pensees*. New York: Penguin Books.

Pottash, R. (1957). A psychoanalytic intervention with an adolescent. In H. Balser (ed.), *Psychotherapy of Adolescents*. New York: International University Press.

Pray, M. (1994). Personal communication.

Racker, H. (1968). *Transference and Countertransference*. New York: International Universities Press.

Raney, J. (ed.). (1984). *Listening and Interpreting: The Challenge of the Work of Robert Langs*. New York: Jason Aronson Press.

Reich, W. (1928). On character analysis. In *The Psychoanalytic Reader,* Volume 1, pp. 129–147. New York: International Universities Press.

Rogers, C. (1961). *On Becoming a Person*. Boston: Houghton Mifflin Company.

Rosenfeld, H. (1987). *Impasse and Interpretation*. Breakdown of Communication between Patient and Analyst. Chapter 3. London: Tavistock Publications.

Sassoon, S. (1939). On Poetry. In H. Jackson, *The Reading of Books*. New York: Charles Scribners Sons.

Schafer, R. (1976). *A New Language for Psychoanalysis*. New Haven: Yale University Press.

Searl, M. (1936). Some queries on principles of technique. *International Journal of Psychoanalysis* 17:471–493.

Searles, H. (1979). The function of the patient's realistic perceptions of the analyst in delusional transference. In *Countertransference and Related Subjects: Selected Papers.* pp. 196–227. New York: International Universities Press.

Shave, D. (1962). *The Language of the Transference*. Boston: Little, Brown, and Company.

Shahn, B. (1957). *The Shape of Content*. Cambridge, MA: Harvard University Press.

Silverman, M. (1987). Clinical material. *Psychoanalytic Inquiry* 7/2:147–165.

Solovyov, V. (1995). *Lectures on Divine Humanity*. Trans. Peter Zouboff. Hudson, NY: Lindesfarne Press.

Spotnitz, H. (1976). *Psychotherapy of Pre-Oedipal Conditions*. New York: Jason Aronson.

Spotnitz, H. (1985). *Modern Psychoanalysis of the Schizophrenic Patient*. 2nd Edition. New York: Human Sciences Press.

Sterba, R. (1934). The fate of the ego in psychoanalytic therapy. *International Journal of Psychoanalysis* 15:117–126.

Sterba, R. (1940). The dynamics of the dissolution of the transference resistance. *Psychoanalytic Quarterly* 9:363–379.

Sterba, R. (1941). The abuse of interpretation. *Psychiatry* 4:9–12.

Sterba, R. (1953). Clinical and therapeutic aspects of character resistance. *Psychoanalytic Quarterly* 221–220.

Strachey, J. (1934). The nature of the therapeutic action of psychoanalysis. *International Journal of Psychoanalysis* 50:275–292.

Strean, H. (1990). *Resolving Resistances in Psychotherapy*. New York: Bruner/Mazel.

Wachtel, P. (1987). *Action and Insight*. New York: Guilford Press.

Wachtel, P. (1993). *Therapeutic Communication: Principles and Effective Practice.* New York: Guilford Press.

Waelder, R. (1936). The principle of multiple function: Observations on over-determination. *Psychoanalytic Quarterly* 5:45–62.

Weil, S. (1952). *Gravity and Grace.* London: Routledge and Kegan Paul, 1987.

Whitehead, A. (1933). *Adventures of Ideas.* New York: The MacMillan Co.

Winnicott, D.W. (1971). *Playing and Reality.* London: Tavistock Publication.

Zuckerkandl, V. (1956). *Sound and Symbol: Music and the External World.* Princeton, NJ: Princeton University Press.

Zuckerkandl, V. (1972). *Man the Musician.* Princeton, NJ: Princeton University Press.

INDEX